# Storytime
## Around the Year

## Kimberly K. Faurot

UpstartBooks

Janesville, Wisconsin

## Permissions

All Folkmanis Puppet images are used with permission.

"The Mitten Song" from *A Pocketful of Poems* by Marie Louise Allen. Text copyright © 1957 by Marie Allen Howarth. Used by permission of HarperCollins Publishers.

"May" from *Dog Days: Rhymes Around the Year* by Jack Prelutsky, illustrated by Dyanna Wolcott, copyright ©1999 by Jack Prelutsky. Illustrations copyright ©1999 by Dyanna Wolcott. Used by permission of Alfred A. Knopf, an imprint of Random House Children's Books, a division of Random House, Inc.

"Inch-Worm" from *Hello Day* by Dorothy Aldis, copyright ©1959 by Dorothy Aldis. Used by permission of G.P. Putnam's Sons, A Division of Penguin Young Readers Group, A Member of Penguin Group (USA) Inc., 345 Hudson Street, New York, NY 10014. All rights reserved.

"Message from a Caterpillar" by Lilian Moore from *Little Raccoon and Poems From the Woods* copyright ©1975 Lilian Moore. All Rights Reserved. Used by permission of Marian Reiner.

Hymes Jr., *Oodles of Noodles*, p. 7 "Oodles of Noodles," © 1964 Lucia and James Hymes Jr. Reproduced by permission of Pearson Education, Inc. All rights reserved.

Published by UpstartBooks
401 S. Wright Road
Janesville, WI 53547

1-800-448-4887


© Kimberly K. Faurot, 2008
Cover design: Debra Neu

*Note: All efforts have been made to obtain permission for the fingerplays and songs in this book. If the author is not listed, the original author is unknown. We apologize for any omissions.*

# Contents

# Acknowledgments

Special thanks to the following individuals and institutions:

- Brad Kruse
- Lyle and JoAnne Faurot
- Rob Reid
- Dr. Shirley Fitzgibbons
- Cathy Norris
- Beth Murray
- Marcia Tyriver
- Children's Department staff, past and present, of the Hedberg Public Library, Janesville, Wisconsin
- Crosby Coghill
- Sara L. Waters
- Leah Langby
- Diane Findlay
- Saint Paul Public Library, Saint Paul, Minnesota
- The Red Balloon Bookshop, Saint Paul, Minnesota

All Upstart staff who worked on this project, including:

- Matt Mulder, Publisher
- Virginia Harrison, Editor
- Heidi Green, Graphic Design Manager
- April Van Etten, Graphic Designer
- Michelle McCardell, former Editor

# Preface

*We're fortunate, you know. Too many people in this world spend their lives doing work that doesn't really matter in the great scheme of things. But bringing children and books together does matter. And we get to do it.*

—Excerpted from "Back from IBBY" by Katherine Paterson in *The Horn Book Magazine*, January/February 1999; Vol. 75, No. 1.

## This Book Is for You

Lucky you—you get to share stories with children! Reading, telling, and singing stories; talking about stories and creatively acting them out—all of these activities are gifts that will last a lifetime. Sharing the delights of books, poetry, rhymes, and songs can help pave the way for a child's ultimate reading success. Modeling early literacy techniques for children's caregivers provides them with effective tools to use at home in their vital role as their child's "first teacher," helping the child establish a solid foundation of skills in preparation for reading later on as well as encouraging interactive opportunities for positive bonding.

As adults, many of us have read a story aloud to one or several children at some time or another; however, successfully leading an entire disparate group through an extended storytime experience is not necessarily something that we instinctively know how to do. Some of us have had the opportunity to attend formal classes on "Programming for Children" or "Library Services for Children and Young Adults," and many of us actively seek out storytime training opportunities whenever possible. To an extent, though, there are certain aspects of group programming that we all essentially "figure out as we go along." Being equipped with the knowledge of what books and materials should work well with a group of children and actually sharing those materials effectively in a storytime setting are related, but the second does not automatically follow from the first.

Many of my favorite resource titles were written by individuals who wished that particular type of book had been available when they were beginning their own careers. The motivation for this volume is the same: I wish I had something like it when I was a brand-new librarian "figuring it out." Although I was particularly fortunate and began my career in a library that had fabulous storytellers to guide and model best practices for me, getting to the point where my own programs could truly delight my audiences was still quite a learning process. Whether you are a new librarian, teacher, or storytime presenter, or an experienced storyteller looking for new ideas and inspiration to enhance your storytime programs, this book is my gift to you.

# Introduction

## What Is Included

Each chapter of *Storytime Around the Year* outlines a possible complete preschool/early elementary/family storytime program based on a particular seasonal theme. Books, segues, and action rhymes and songs are included, as well as an annotated list of additional books on the theme. Patterns and/or directions for one or more storytime props to use during the program (and which may subsequently be used in conjunction with other themes) are also explained, along with follow-up craft or extension ideas. Suggestions for weaving in early literacy components are incorporated.

Although the body of each storytime program outline encompasses approximately 45 minutes excluding any crafts or additional early literacy activities, it is imperative to time yourself before you present since different individuals naturally present at different rates of speed. You may also need to adjust the program content during your actual presentation if some activities engender a lot of participation or questions. Shorten or lengthen the programs as desired or as necessary. Many preschool storytime programs are scheduled for 30 minutes; if that is your program length, adjust the outlines suggested here to reflect your available time. A fairly standard guideline is that you will use approximately three books in a 30-minute program, or two books and one prop or flannel story, in conjunction with introductory/ closing and movement activities. If you find yourself with so much material that you want to linger over a particular topic, consider using the same theme and framework over several weeks—or even for an entire month!

A box at the beginning of each chapter summarizes suggestions for various routine and early literacy activities that you may wish to incorporate into your programs on a regular basis. See www.pla.org/ala/alsc/ecrr/ ecrrhomepage.htm for a comprehensive overview of "Every Child Ready to Read @ Your Library," the early literacy partnership project between the Public Library Association and the Association for Library Service to Children, divisions of the American Library Association, and the National Institute of Child Health and Human Development (NICHD) of the National Institutes of Health. A clear explanation of recommended focus areas as well as wonderful activity suggestions and language to convey these skills to parents/caregivers are included in the excellent resource *Early Literacy Storytimes @ Your Library* by Saroj Nadkarni Ghoting and Pamela Martin-Diaz (ALA Editions, 2006).

## Name Tags

Encouraging the children to practice writing their names, even if the initial result is merely scribbling, is an important early literacy activity. Support all efforts with enthusiastic comments. Use large-size, sticky-back mailing labels for the children to write on so there is plenty of room; many children are still developing the fine motor skills required for small-size writing, so having large tags accommodates larger motor movements. Display a note to parents and caregivers that reads, "Scribbling is an important precursor to reading and writing!" so they may be more inclined to allow their children to help make their own name tags. In addition to this early literacy practice, name tags will enable you to call the children by name and to begin to learn their names. Wear a name tag yourself as well, and point to your name when you introduce yourself. Encourage all attending adults to also wear name tags.

If possible, stamp or sticker a small image on the side of the tag that provides a "clue" to the theme of the program. For example, an umbrella image might be a clue that the stories will be about rain; a heart for Valentine's Day; and so forth. If you organize your stories around a particular letter of the alphabet, consider rubber-stamping that letter on the side of the tag. Place a sign on the name tag table that says: "Please make a name tag, then come and join us for storytime! Can you guess what our stories will be about today?"

## Clues

Incorporate additional visual storytime theme "clues" throughout your setup, and consider using a small emergent puppet to present a focal clue. The puppet might have a contained place to hide from which you call him/her, such as a box or bag, or some puppets are made to pop up from eggs, hats, or sleeping bags. The puppet does not need to talk; it can nod its head in response to yes/no questions, or it can "whisper" to you or make little gestures. You can conversationally interpret for the audience, such as "What? You think we should start?" and so forth. Explain that it is a puppet, and emphasize its small size to help avoid anxiety. Young children are still grappling with what is "real" and what is not, so it is important to be verbally clear that the character is a puppet. The children will enjoy it just as much, and indeed the puppet will still be "real" to them. Manipulate it creatively and lovingly, and you will have a "hit" on your hands!

Consider having the puppet "snore," and wake him/her up by collectively calling softly, "1-2-3, wake up, _____!" Call him in multiple languages if you have a multilingual group or simply to expose the children to other languages. It's nice to have the puppet start to awaken but then fall back asleep, requiring a second call. If the group gets too loud, remind them of how small the puppet is and advise that you don't want to frighten him. You could also sing a wake-up song to a well-known tune.

Ask the puppet if he brought a clue for the storytime theme, and have him retrieve it. For example, the puppet might bring a packet of seeds to introduce a "Growing Gardens" storytime (see May chapter) or several plastic bugs for "I Like Bugs" (see June chapter). Discussing these visual clues as a group will help the children with the process of interpreting clues in their daily lives and in the world around them.

When you are finished with your puppet's storytime introduction, have him wave farewell to the audience, possibly blow kisses, and

lead everyone in clapping. Rock the puppet in your arms until he "falls asleep" and begins to "snore" again, or sing a favorite lullaby to the puppet as a group.

## "Letter of the Day"

Highlighting a "Letter of the Day" helps to promote the early literacy skill of letter knowledge. Children learn to recognize and identify letters, knowing that they have different names and sounds and that the same letter can look different.

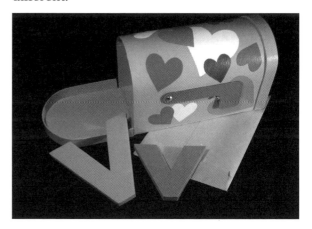

Your emergent puppet can bring the "Letter of the Day" along with the storytime clue. Or consider having a special mailbox for the "letter" of the day. Ahead of time, address a large-size envelope to your storytime group with the library or school address. The return address may be listed as "Letter of the Day Inc." or something similar. Put a sticker or old postage stamp in the upper right-hand corner of the envelope and "cancel" it with a rubber stamp. You will be able to use this same envelope each week for the "Letter of the Day."

Use large-size cutout or magnet-backed foam letters, both uppercase and lowercase (see Resources, page 215). Place both letters in the envelope, and hide the envelope/"letter" in the mailbox before storytime begins. When you reach that portion of your program each week, sing the following song together while clapping rhythmically and enthusiastically:

( *Tune: "Bluebird, Bluebird, Through My Window."* Listen to the sound recording *Mainly Mother Goose: Songs and Rhymes For Merry Young Souls.* Elephant Records, 1984; musical notation is in the songbook *Sharon, Lois & Bram's Mother Goose.* Little, Brown and Company, 1985.)

*Mailman, mailman, through my window*
*Mailman, mailman, through my window*
*Mailman, mailman, through my window*
*Oh, I hope he brought a letter!*
*Run outside and look inside the mailbox,*
*Run outside and look inside the mailbox,*
*Run outside and look inside the mailbox,*
*Look! The mailman brought a letter!*

Open the envelope and produce the capital "Letter of the Day." Say, "Here is the letter B—a big uppercase, or capital B." Draw the capital letter "B" in the air as a group. (Note: There are many different handwriting methods, and they vary in the specific way that some letters are taught. Familiarize yourself with the method used by your local school system, and feature handwriting cues from that particular method on any "Letter of the Day" handouts you provide.) Affix the letter to a magnet board or Velcro board so it is visible throughout the program. Produce the lowercase "b" and say, "Here is also the letter b—a small, lowercase b." Draw a lowercase "b" in the air as a group. Affix the letter to the board next to the capital letter. Make the /b/ sound while pointing to the letters and say, "B is for book; B is for bear; B is for bike; B is for baseball; B is for bunny." Encourage the audience to repeat each phrase after you. Include three or four examples.

Choose word examples that correspond to the letter sounds. For example, "S is for silly." Avoid word examples such as "S is for shoe," which begins with the "sh" sound rather than a hard "s."

Sing a song together each week about the sound(s) made by the "Letter of the Day":

"Letter of the Day Echo Song" *(Sung to the tune: "Where Is Thumbkin?")*

| Leader: | *What does M say?* |
|---|---|
| Audience: | *What does M say?* |
| Leader: | */M/, /m/, /m/!* |
| Audience: | */M/, /m/, /m/!* |
| Leader: | *Mouse and Moon and Milkshake.* (Or whatever words you choose.) |
| Audience: | *Mouse and Moon and Milkshake.* |
| Leader: | */M/, /m/, /m/!* |
| Audience: | */M/, /m/, /m/!* |

Introduce this group of letters first, one at a time, though not necessarily in this order:

B, M, D, T, W, P, N, Y, H

Introduce this group of letters next:

S, F, G, V, Z, K, C

Introduce this group of letters last:

L, R, J

## Mother Goose Rhyme Time

Incorporate nursery rhymes and poetry into your programs whenever possible. The rhythms and rhymes promote phonological awareness/ sensitivity, the ability to recognize that spoken words consist of sound segments; oral language abilities, including the internalization of characteristic speech rhythms and intonation patterns; and sensitivity to and ability to detect rhyme and alliteration. Share a new nursery rhyme each week, or incorporate a single rhyme in different ways over a series of weeks so the children become familiar with it. Act the rhyme out, share it with enthusiastic actions and clapping, and talk about the rhyme's characters and the sequence of events. *Mother Goose Rhyme Time* support materials, including large-size cutouts, posters, and activity suggestions, are available from UpstartBooks (see Resources, page 216).

## Rhyming Basket

Promote rhythm and rhyme with a rhyming basket! Make your own "little yellow [rhyming] basket," or purchase a teacher starter basket (see Resources) and expand it with additional rhyming items. If you have difficulty finding small three-dimensional pieces, print clip-art images to illustrate the words.

Explain to the children that rhyming words sound the same at the end.

"Rhyming Basket" Introduction *(Sung to the tune: "A Tisket, a Tasket.")*

*A tisket, a tasket,*
*A little yellow basket.*
*It's time to find*
*Some words that rhyme*
*Inside our yellow basket.*

Hold up your first item, such as a large plastic FLY and identify it together as a "fly." Hold up your next item, a small plastic PIE and identify it together as a "pie." Sing:

CHORUS* (*Sung to the tune:* "Skip to My Lou.")

_____, _____, *these words rhyme.*

_____, _____, *these words rhyme.*

_____, _____, *these words rhyme.*

*So rhyme along with me!*

(*This chorus is from *Early Literacy Storytimes @ Your Library* by Saroj Nadkarni Ghoting and Pamela Martin-Diaz, ALA Editions, 2006; it may also be sung and played as a game without visual support items. See page 25 of *Early Literacy Storytimes @ Your Library*.)

### Early Literacy Skill

If adults are in your audience, incorporate early literacy tips and explanations as recommended in "Every Child Ready to Read @ Your Library" (www.pla.org/ala/alsc/ecrr/ecrrhomepage.htm) and *Early Literacy Storytimes @ Your Library* by Saroj Nadkarni Ghoting and Pamela Martin-Diaz (ALA Editions, 2006).

### Storytime

Each storytime section begins with a brief program summary and ideas for creating a thematic environment or overall ambience. These small touches serve to enhance the storytime experience, and to provide visual clues and information for the children about the topic. When your programming space feels special, your audience tends to respond accordingly with increased attention and focus. Creating this type of ambience doesn't need to be time-consuming—it may simply constitute a beautiful piece of fabric draped over the storytime table where you have your books, and hanging a few stars or other representational items over the space. (Note: Affix the fabric firmly to the table so tiny wandering siblings can't pull the fabric off along with everything else on the table!)

Always prepare the props, puppets, and supporting materials ahead of time so you can use them throughout the program, and keep the storytime puppets and pieces hidden away until their scheduled appearance. Colored corrugated boxes with hinged lids work well for this purpose (see Resources, page 216).

### Sample Program

The sample program outline is exactly that—a sample. Utilize the recommendations that are best suited to you and your storytime group or classroom, and adapt the ideas as desired. Experiment with new ideas and techniques. Always practice the entire program ahead of time, both silently and out loud, so you feel comfortable with the material and can focus on your audience. Stay attuned to the needs of your audience, and be flexible.

### Music

Play thematic music as the audience is gathering in your storytime area. The songs can provide additional clues in another format about the day's storytime topic, and can serve as a welcoming and calming ritual to signal that the program will soon begin. Ideas for possible songs and sound recordings are included in each chapter, but for more suggestions on these or other themes please refer to Rob Reid's fabulous musical support books *Children's Jukebox: The Select Guide to Children's Musical Recordings,* second edition (ALA Editions, 2007); *Children's Jukebox: A Subject Guide to Musical Recordings and Programming Ideas for Songsters Ages One to Twelve* (ALA Editions, 1995); and *Something Musical Happened at the Library: Adding Song and Dance to Children's Story Programs* (ALA Editions, 2007).

### Set the Stage: Introduction

The possible introductions outlined can help you set the stage for the program and naturally introduce your first story. The introduction may be long and incorporate interesting facts to help the children understand upcoming content, or brief and catchy—whatever fits naturally to launch the storytime. Perhaps you will want to tie your introduction in to a weekly "Hello" or "Welcome" song, or to a regular visit by a puppet with "Clues" and "Letter of the Day" activities (see pages 8–9).

Before you begin speaking, gradually turn down the background theme music as a signal that it is time to begin. Take control of the group by practicing the attention-getting techniques outlined on pages 15–16. Always introduce yourself saying, "I know many of you, but if you don't know me or forgot my name, my name is _____." Let the audience know that you are excited to spend the upcoming time together.

## Read Alouds

Recommended read-aloud titles are carefully selected based on repeated, proven success with a group. Pictures are large enough to be seen from a distance, language is poetic and/or interesting, plots are appealing, and overall length is well suited to young children's group attention spans (approximately five minutes).

Book titles are included with brief summaries and age-level guidelines. Please note that recommended age levels are *age guidelines for large group sharing purposes*. Many titles may work beautifully one-on-one with younger or older children, but would likely be unsuccessful in a large group setting of children that age. It can be tempting to think that if your own two-year-old loves a particular book at home, surely a large group of two-year-olds will likewise love the book presented in a library toddler storytime setting. Although this may be true on occasion, it is not always the case.

Ideas for enhancing the book as a group read-aloud through participation or movements are included where applicable. You will undoubtedly come up with more possibilities as you practice ahead of time. Incorporate various techniques judiciously: you want to help maintain the children's attention through these involvements, but take care that they enhance rather than distract from the story!

## Segues

Suggested segues are not intended to be prescriptive or directive. They are included especially for new storytime presenters who may not have extensive experience or confidence in weaving a program together into a cohesive whole. Segues help children transition between books and activities, and from book to book as you help them make connections between the materials. The program should flow effortlessly and naturally. Segues should be thought through and practiced ahead of time, just like the stories and other components. Always be flexible and relaxed, however, and respond to your group's interests, suggestions, and questions as you go along.

## Fun Facts

Non-fiction facts and information are fascinating for young children, who are actively learning about the amazing world around them. Pair information with large, clear explanatory photographs or with touchable realia whenever possible.

## Action

Take full advantage of action rhymes. It is important to include several in each program. Be enthusiastic, and incorporate large-muscle, full-body movements whenever possible. Children love to move their bodies, not just their fingers! Younger audiences will need to move more throughout the program; older children can typically sit for longer periods of time. Be sensitive to the dynamics of your group, however, and add an extra stretch or two if needed.

Write out the words to the rhymes and songs on large pieces of grid board (available at office supply stores) whenever possible, and encourage parents and caregivers to say the rhymes and sing the songs along with you (as well as to do the motions). Clearly tell the audience "we get to stand up" or "we get to do this one sitting down." Always "practice" the movements that you will be doing together as you slowly and clearly say the words before you begin. Repeat short rhymes or songs several times, quickly and slowly, loudly and quietly. When the action rhyme/song is done, let the audience know that "we get to sit back down;" otherwise the children don't necessarily know that is what's expected.

It is fine if some children prefer not to stand up and participate in action rhymes and songs. Many young children have few opportunities to make choices for themselves, and they may just be exercising and asserting their freedom and independence. Just make sure they won't get stepped on or jumped on by the others who are participating!

## Props, Flannel Boards, Puppets, and Realia

Some chapters suggest a prop or flannel story to share as a program finale, or using props to illustrate a poem. Many of the programs weave realia throughout. Visual support materials can introduce a story; convey meaning, context and vocabulary; add variety; and provide a cohesive framework. For example, producing valentines sequentially from a mailbox and matching them to the next book or activity (February—"Be My Valentine") or following a "Storytime Vacation" map (August—"Taking A Trip") creates a sense of structure as well as expectation. This type of enhancement and engagement is key, as the developmental characteristics of preschool- and early-elementary-age children suggest that their learning processes are significantly enhanced by visual components. Variety is important, as individual children respond and engage in many different ways with alternative media and presentation methods.

## Conclusion

The possible conclusions outlined can help you wrap up the storytime. Thank the audience for coming, and tell them you hope you will see them again soon. Invite them to check out materials from the library's collection and to ask any questions.

You may wish to end the program with a regular weekly "goodbye song," and/or call your introductory puppet back again for final farewells. The puppet can point out the "Letter of the Day" once again and highlight the early literacy skill in the style of Sesame Street™: "Today's storytime was brought to you by the letter B ..." and so forth.

The puppet can kiss everyone's hand as he/she is leaving, and give hugs (try to avoid the children all kissing the puppet due to the spread of germs). Consider distributing "Letter of the Day" practice coloring sheets or other parent/caregiver early literacy support materials (see Resources, page 214 and 216).

## Special Handout Ideas

On occasion, I have included ideas for a "special handout" that ties in to the chapter's overall storytime theme. This type of handout is most appropriate for a special event program or for a particular treat.

## Craft Ideas (Story Crafts; Miscellaneous Craft or Extension Ideas)

"Story crafts" are crafts that relate to a story, poem, or song that you share together during storytime. Such crafts can extend the story experience and provide the children with tools to relive the activity again and again at home. Some story crafts, such as stick puppet characters, may be utilized within the context of the story itself; other crafts and extension ideas simply serve as a follow-up to the storytime theme or concepts.

Some libraries regularly include a storytime craft component, while others do so only on rare occasions. If you do choose to include craft activities in your programs, provide materials for adult attendees as well as children whenever possible. Encourage children and adults to talk together about what they are making, and to use the completed crafts to retell or act out rhymes or stories from the storytime program. Crafts should always promote individual creativity. If you have very young children in your group, also remember to avoid using craft materials that could be a choking hazard.

## Additional Books and Resources

Each chapter contains an annotated bibliography of additional titles (and sometimes rhymes and more extension ideas) to substitute for the books and activities included in the Sample Program outline. I purposely included only titles that I feel work well with groups of children. I am sure that I missed some favorites and even some classics in these lists! Please write additional ideas into your own copy of this book to make it as useful as possible.

As mentioned earlier, recommended age levels listed were assigned based on their suitability for large group presentations. Many titles could be shared effectively one-on-one or in very small groups with older or younger children.

See Resources (page 212) for a list of support resources for storytime program planning.

## Summary

I hope *Storytime Around the Year* will inspire you to try new techniques and material as you seek to engage and inspire the children of your community and their families with the transformative gift of stories.

# General Storytime Planning and Presentation Guidelines

## General Tips

- Plan ahead and prepare thoroughly. Practice the entire program out loud: read-alouds, segues, prop/flannel storytelling, and so forth. Work on rhythms, pacing, volume, and energy. Be familiar enough with your books and materials that you will be able to look away from them and make frequent eye contact with the children. Always be over-prepared, with back-up materials at a variety of levels.

- Make your programming space feel special through the use of firmly affixed fabric tablecloths, hanging thematic cutouts or realia, and so forth.

- Keep the props and puppets you will use in the actual storytime program out of sight until time for their appearance. Colored corrugated boxes with hinged lids work well for this purpose (see Resources, page 216).

- Greet children and their caregivers as they arrive, making them feel welcome. If families arrive late and you are in the middle of a story, smile and nod to them and/or make a small welcoming motion to integrate them into your group. Help the children find a place to sit if necessary.

- Encourage both children and adults to make name tags on large-size sticky-back mailing labels. This supports early literacy, enables you to learn participants' names, and helps attending adults learn each other's names and feel more connected to the group.

- Encourage adult caregivers to sit with their children and to participate with rhymes, songs, and actions.

- Sit on a low chair with the audience on the floor in front of you. You should be up high enough so the children can see you and the books and materials you are holding, but not so high that you feel far away from them. Encourage the group to move in closer so they can see better. If you do end up with people far to the sides, make sure to include them as you show illustrations and materials. (Note: If you end up with a tiny group where everyone can easily see, you may wish to join them on the floor for a more intimate storytime.)

- Introduce yourself at the beginning of the program, and share your excitement about the privilege of sharing stories with the group.

- Incorporate regular opening and closing routines, such as a weekly puppet greeter, song or rhyme, and so forth. The younger your audience, the more routines you typically should include. Toddlers especially love repetition.

- Include several large-muscle, full-body movement participation opportunities in the program to break up the stretches of sitting. Encourage everyone to participate, both children and adults, and make it fun and appealing to do so; however, never force participation. Tell the audience when to stand and when to sit. Always demonstrate and "practice" movements you will be doing before you begin so the children know what to expect and can more easily follow along.

- Write out words to rhymes and songs ahead of time on grid board whenever possible. Point out to the children that the words are up on the board, and encourage the adults and older children to help you chant and sing.

- Pay attention to the order in which you present materials. The longest or most difficult read-aloud should typically be shared first, followed by a shorter poem or an action rhyme or song.

- Be flexible and relaxed. Be willing and able to alter your storytime plan if needed!

- Have a few "emergency" favorite songs or rhymes that you can fall back on (such as "If You're Happy and You Know It"), and/or a special "gimmick" pop-up or flap book that's always a sure-fire hit.

- Be patient and gentle—remember that young children are still learning appropriate group behaviors.

- Integrate the six early literacy focus areas into your programs in a fun and engaging manner as a matter of course, and highlight one of them each week as the "Early Literacy Skill of the Day." Refer to *Early Literacy Storytimes @ Your Library* by Saroj Nadkarni Ghoting and Pamela Martin-Diaz (ALA Editions, 2006) for an in-depth discussion of practical early literacy storytime techniques.

- As part of your closing routine, thank the audience for coming. Tell them how much fun you had and how great they are, and thank the adults for supporting their children's education both by making the effort to bring them to storytime and by reading to their child regularly and talking together about letters and words at home during the week. Recap the "Letter of the Day" and highlighted early literacy skill.

## Presenting

- The most important thing to remember about presenting storytimes is this: **Have fun!** Enthusiasm is contagious. If you are having the time of your life, your audience will too. It is like you are the host or hostess of a celebration—a celebration of books, of reading, of children, of words, of stories, and of sharing these delights together.

- Always treat children (and everyone) with respect—never condescend.

- Slow down and take your time.

- Be careful not to turn your back to your audience. If you must turn away for a moment to reach for a prop or pick something up, don't try to talk or continue telling a story while your back is turned. Your voice will suddenly be projecting away from your audience rather than toward them, and it will likely be difficult for them to hear and understand what you are saying.

- If any children announce that they already know the story you are about to share or that they have it at home, tell them you're glad that they will know how it goes!

- Answer a child's brief questions about the book or story as you go along—it's fine to pause briefly and explain what is happening. If it's a more involved question, you may need to talk about it when the story is over. Sometimes the story itself will answer the questions, so play it by ear.

- If a child interjects an unrelated comment into the narrative, such as "I have an owie," or "We're going to the park," or "My grandma's dog died," acknowledge the child briefly with a quick nod or smile or "I'm sorry that happened." If you don't acknowledge them in some small way, they will often continue to repeat the comment incessantly until you do. If a child launches into a long commentary or other involved aside, gently interrupt and ask them to remember it so they can tell you all about it when storytime is done. Quickly redirect attention back to the story. It's important to help that child return to the topic at hand as well as to avoid the chaos of all the other children suddenly thinking about their own "owies" to show you and tell you about. Redirect everyone to the story in progress, speculating, "I wonder what (the storybook character) is going to do next?"

- When reading aloud to a group, hold the book approximately at your shoulder height to your left or your right. If you are right-eye dominant, hold the book out to your right; if you are left-eye dominant, hold the book out to your left. Hold the book at the top or the bottom along the book's center gutter (where it is stitched together) in a way that is comfortable for you and that covers up as little of the illustrations you are showing as possible. The heel of your hand and your thumb will typically be behind the book to stabilize it, while your fingers will hold the pages in place in front. Hold the book perpendicular, not tilted toward the floor or ceiling. Turn your head to the side so you can read the text. Turn the pages with your other hand. You may also use your other hand to help stabilize the book if needed and to point out details in the illustrations or to run your index finger under words for group participation.

If the group is small, they may all be able to see the pictures clearly with the book in the primary position next to your shoulder. If you have a larger group or if they are seated out to the sides, however, you will need to move the book back and forth slowly so everyone can see the illustrations. If there is a particular small detail that you want the children to see but it is not clear from a distance, get up and carry the book around the audience so they can all see it up close (this is only manageable with small- to medium-size groups). Although you don't want to do this often—if the illustrations aren't clear from a distance, it's probably not a good read-aloud choice—it can work when necessary in special situations. Be familiar with the text so you can possibly even say portions of it without looking at the words—this enables you to hold the book out closer to the audience.

- BIG Books can be a wonderful tool, since the pictures are much larger and easier for the audience to see clearly. Although some of the smaller-size BIG Books can be held in the manner described above, it is usually best to support the book on a BIG Book easel or an extra-wide, sturdy music stand. I have had the best luck with a "Fourscore Stand" or "Conductor's Stand." Approximately 32" wide and with a solid "desk," they can swivel in their base so you can stand behind or next to the book on the stand and swivel it slowly to the left and right so everyone in the audience can see. (See Resources, page 215.)

- Vary your voice as you read aloud with pauses, rhythms, singing, or character

voices when appropriate. Take care that you don't let voice variations overtake the story, but rather enhance it. Pauses can help build dramatic tension and give the children time to anticipate what might come next, and character voices can help them understand which storybook character is talking when. (You can also clarify this by pointing at the illustration of the character who is talking as you read.) The reading should flow naturally and effortlessly after a reasonable amount of practice.

- You need to clearly lead and guide the program for the audience to get the most from the experience. Take suggestions, encourage participation, and embrace input, but be in charge. This helps the audience to feel "safe" and to relax into the experience. If you have properly prepared for the program, you will have special things to share with the group, and you want to make sure that the children are able to enjoy them.

- Some people seem able to take charge of a group naturally, while others need to learn and practice techniques to do so more effectively. Have you noticed how some presenters try in vain to get an audience's attention and start talking, but much of the audience keeps talking as well, whereas other presenters take the stage and a hush falls over the crowd before the person even opens his/her mouth? A presenter's "stage presence" and choices define his/her expectations for the group. Be deliberate and expectant in your motions. Signal the audience that it is time to begin and time for them to be ready. Expect them to want to be quiet, and wait for them to be quiet and attentive before you begin. For example, turn the welcome background music briefly up and then gradually down as a signal that storytime is about to begin. Stand up and hold your palms up and outward toward your audience, pausing expectantly and smiling a welcome until everyone turns toward you and is quiet for your introduction to storytime. As you do this, seek to physically radiate your energy, joy, and excitement about the upcoming program, and to emotionally connect with and embrace your audience. Performers describe this as being "yourself, only larger."

If an audience is particularly unruly and does not calm down with these initial cues, try singing an introduction (even something simple like "Hey everybody, it's storytime, it's storytime!") or joyfully beating a rhythm to grab their attention. Another possibility is to call out the time and say, "It's storytime! Let's say yaaaayyy!!!?" and applaud together. This applause engenders a natural pause afterward in which you can begin your welcome and introduction. Some storytellers also use a special musical instrument with a distinctive sound, such as a train whistle, to call everyone to attention.

- If your audience becomes restless or has a hard time calming down again after an action interlude, try singing a few notes of an introduction (e.g., "This story goes like this") or singing part of the page you are reading. It will grab their attention and help them re-focus.

- Use rhythms as an introduction, to gain or regain attention, or to add a participatory element to a story. Clap, pat your lap, or drum on a cardboard or plastic box.

- If a child stands up or sits up on his/her knees or feet and is impeding the sight lines or attention of other children, gently whisper and motion to the child to "sit down so friends can see." You may have to remind him/her several times throughout the program, particularly if an organized group setting is new for the child. The children are not trying to make you crazy—they just honestly forget in the excitement of what is going on!

- Utilize segues to help the audience transition between stories and activities.

- Embrace your personal style while resisting the trap of indulging your own perceived inhibitions or shyness, or your ego. When you tell stories you are giving a gift, and it is important that you hold that gift out to your audience joyfully and without allowing your inhibitions or ego to get in the way. Remember and emulate the uninhibited

imaginative and creative play in which you engaged as a child. Your audience will love it if you embrace your stories and your characters wholeheartedly. The only way you will look stupid in front of an audience is if you act like you feel stupid or self-conscious.

- Experiment with new ideas and techniques. Practice ahead of time so you feel comfortable with the material and can focus on the audience.

- Be willing to learn from other people. You will see ideas and techniques that you want to emulate and possibly other practices that you want to avoid! Strive to be inspired by others rather than just copying them, and adapt ideas in new ways to fit your own personality and style.

- Keep an eye on the time, and be respectful of your audience. If a program is advertised as 30 minutes, you really shouldn't exceed that time length by more than five minutes or so. You may need to readjust your outline and skip some materials that you had planned to share, but you can do those things another time. Many families are on a schedule—en route to another engagement, close to naptime, possibly on a parking meter, maybe needing to catch a bus—and if you greatly exceed the storytime length the caregivers are expecting, they may become anxious or pull their children away early as well as think twice about coming again. It's always better to leave the audience "wanting more" at the end than to have them wishing it would have ended sooner!

## Choosing Materials

- Choose materials that you truly like. If you love it, your audience typically will, too.

- Presenting materials thematically can be helpful to the storyteller for planning purposes as well as to the children, but it is not essential. Whether or not you have chosen to use a theme, weave the stories and activities together with natural transitions.

- Choose quality materials with beautiful illustrations and lyrical, engaging language or rhythms. Quality materials and presentation are a manifestation of respect for children. You are also helping children understand and learn to appreciate quality.

- Reflect the diversity of your group and of your community as well as the wider world in the materials that you choose. All materials should reflect accurate, respectful images of the culture.

- Be aware of and sensitive to cultural diversity issues. For example, if families in your group are from a culture where pigs or dogs are considered "unclean" animals, don't do a "Plenty of Pigs" or "Dozens of Dogs" themed storytime, and be sensitive about including stories or activities that feature these animals.

- Avoid choosing controversial materials such as "Halloween" unless sharing stories at an event specifically marketed as a "Halloween Storytime" or "Scary/Spooky Stories" program. There are plenty of wonderful seasonal alternatives such as "Pumpkins," "Bats," or "Scarecrows," and it simply isn't necessary to include stories or content that makes part of your audience uncomfortable. Similarly, avoid stories or activities about religious holidays unless they are part of a "Holidays Around the World" type of special event program.

- Select materials that lend themselves well to group sharing, with clear visual images and short text (typically no more than one to five lines per page).

- Plan ahead with "Story Program Theme Folders."

When I was just starting out as a brand-new children's librarian, I came across a newsletter article by Rob Reid that revolutionized my programming future. Rob wrote:

*Collect your story program ideas by themes in a folder. An inexpensive pocket folder will do. Copy poems, fingerplays, songs, and activities that fit your theme. Make a list of good picture books. Include only those that work well with groups of children. Make sample copies of lesson plans. Throw everything into your theme folder. Soon you'll have more material than you know what to do with.*

("Story Program Theme Folders" Part 1 in the "Shortcuts" youth section of Indianhead Federated Library System's newsletter "Directions," November 1991, vol. 13, no. 5, p. 2.)

Perhaps I would have come across this idea elsewhere or thought it up myself eventually, but as it was I got a head start and have been happily organized ever since. If a possibility spans multiple themes such as Judith Viorst's poem "Mother Doesn't Want a Dog," I make multiple photocopies and put one in my "Pets" folder, one in "Dogs," and one in "Snakes." When I decide to do a storytime (or write a storytime article or book chapter) on a particular topic, I simply pull out my folder on that theme and inevitably find that I truly do "have more material than I know what do with."

## Variety

- Include a variety of books, a variety of formats, and a variety of activities in your programs. Individual children learn in different ways: some children are visual learners, some learn more through auditory input, and others are kinesthetic or tactile learners—learning by moving, touching, and doing. It is therefore important to share materials in a variety of ways to connect with different learning styles.

- Incorporate realia to introduce concepts and convey meaning, context, and vocabulary.

- Consider employing the element of surprise as you produce your next storytime book or representational object from an unexpected place (such as the giant mittens in January's "Many Mittens" and the "Story Soup" in November's "Fabulous Food").

- Learn simple "magic" tricks to delight and amaze your audience. For example, use a "magic change bag" (see Resources, page 216) to turn a tiny key into a library card, a caterpillar finger puppet into a butterfly, small cut-out letters spelling the word B-U-S into a miniature die-cast metal school bus, or whatever transformation you can imagine!

- Experiment with tell-and-draw and cut-and-tell stories and poems. Be discerning and creative in your selections. Try out new ideas of your own!

- Many poems and songs lend themselves to simple gathered props and realia. Use these to enhance your programs and to maintain interest.

- Use sound effect recordings to introduce stories, puppets, or topics.

- If you or other staff members don't have the time, inclination, or ability to make some of the storytime props and visual support pieces you would like, find volunteers who love to make things and who are good at it. Supply the materials and frequent "thank yous," and extend an invitation to storytime so they can see first-hand how you engage the children with the wonderful pieces they have made!

## Puppets

- Incorporate puppets into your presentations whenever possible. This can be achieved through a greeter/welcome puppet as described previously; with a simple introduction or puppet "interview" lead-in to a story; using a puppet as an "actor" in a prop story or poem; or as part of an elaborate puppet show. The possibilities are endless and do not have to be difficult or especially involved to be highly effective.

- When presenting with puppets, go ahead and say it's a puppet. Children are figuring out what is "real" and what is not, and can become distracted or anxious if this reality is not clear to them. They will enjoy the puppet just as much knowing that it is a puppet, and it will indeed still be "real" for them. If you have children in your group who are frightened of puppets, emphasize the puppet's shyness or its small size, and consider allowing the child and their caregiver to handle and explore the puppet(s) individually after the program to alleviate future fears.

- Believe in your puppet while you are manipulating it.

- Watch the puppet when you are animating it; otherwise you are competing with it for the audience's attention. Looking at the puppet helps direct the audience's gaze toward it as well, and it also can help you make the puppet move more realistically.

- Practice with the puppet! It is particularly helpful to practice with the puppet in a mirror, so you begin to understand how various movements will appear to your audience. Remember that your audience will be seated on the floor, so make sure that the puppet looks slightly downward to maintain eye contact with the children at that height.

- If you wish to give a puppet a unique character voice, practice the voice intensively when you're all alone, until you can use it for extended periods of time as well as switch in and out of it comfortably. It is imperative that you are able to maintain the character voice confidently while the puppet is talking; otherwise it is very confusing for the audience.

- See Resources for listings of puppetry books and Web sites that can help you learn puppet manipulation techniques. I also included finger puppet, stick puppet, and hand puppet manipulation guidelines in *Books in Bloom: Creative Patterns & Props That Bring Stories to Life* (ALA Editions, 2003).

## Publicize

- Publicize your library's programs and services through traditional and nontraditional methods. For example, visit an immigrant group at a site where they typically host gatherings and share information about the library's services. In return, invite participants to a reciprocal event especially for them at your library. Get to know the leaders of the various groups in your community, and make sure they are aware of the library's resources and that it is a welcoming place. Make sure the library truly does welcome immigrants by making materials available in multiple languages; ensuring staff feel ready and confident to serve these groups by preparing them with practical and sensitivity training; hiring staff who speak multiple languages; and so forth.

- High-quality storytimes are one of a library's best public relations tools. Word of mouth can be your most effective publicity. If you present quality, enthusiastic, enjoyable, educational programs, participants will tell their friends about it and invite them! This method can inform individuals about your library's services that traditional publicity methods might not reach.

## Evaluation

- Make it a point to keep comprehensive notes about all of your programs—attendance statistics; what materials you used; what worked particularly well and what did not work as well; comments from the children and/or caregivers; what you might do differently another time; and so forth. Create a method to document this quickly and easily, or it is easy to let it slide. Good notes will save you time down the road when you want to repeat a program, track attendance trends, or figure out which particular book a storytime participant is remembering and requesting. Evaluate yourself regularly, and give your audience the opportunity to make anonymous comments on a regular or periodic basis as well. You may wish to keep these documents on the computer, but see pages 20–22 for some sample paper format evaluations and ideas on what you may wish to track.

- Although it is important to gather feedback from regular storytime attendees, make a point of publicizing your programs to and gathering information from people who do not typically attend. The times that you are currently offering the program are obviously fairly good for the people who already attend! How might you be able to accommodate families who are currently unable to attend the program? Can you augment your outreach efforts to reach children in organized day care settings or other groups? Can you offer evening and weekend storytime programs to accommodate the realities of working families?

- Remember to celebrate your successes. Write down special comments from program attendees, and save special thank you notes from school children. Share these with the Library Board and Administration or with your principal; real-life examples of the power of stories can play an important role in securing funding and determining institutional priorities.

- Always look for practical ways to improve your services.

# Sample Self-evaluation Form

## Program Evaluation

Type of Program _____

Title (if any) _____

Date(s) _____    Time(s) _____

Place _____

Target Age Group _____ Registration Limit (if any) _____

Presenter(s): _____

Materials Used: _____

_____

_____

_____

_____

_____

_____

_____

Total Attendance _____

Number of Children _____    Number of Adults _____

Comments/Observations/Evaluation (regarding attendance, format, theme, materials used, parent involvement, craft, etc.)

_____

_____

_____

_____

_____

_____

Would you do this program again? What changes, if any, would you make?

Additional Comments (e.g., from participants)

_____

_____

_____

# Sample Group Visit Tracking Form

Today's Date _____

## School/Day Care/Other Group Visit Request sheet

Name of Group _____

Contact Person _____

Telephone _____

E-mail _____

Visit Date Scheduled _____

If this group visits regularly, what are the other dates they will be visiting?

Please make up a separate sheet for each date, and cross-reference here:

_____

Time(s) Scheduled _____

Number in Group _____

Attending Adults _____     Age/Grade _____

Visit will be HERE _____ THERE _____

To Be Covered (Stories, Tour, Research Skills, etc.)

_____

_____

_____

Special Considerations (e.g., mobility, vision, hearing disability; English as a Second Language; etc.)

_____

_____

_____

Staff Person Presenting _____

Confirmed? (Please initial if okay) _____

Materials Used in Program _____

_____

_____

Total Attendance _____ # of Children _____ # of Adults _____

Comments _____

_____

# Sample Public Evaluation Form

## Preschool Storytime

**Summer 2009 Comment Form**

Thank you for bringing your child to PRESCHOOL STORYTIME at the library!

Please take a few moments to help us evaluate the program and plan for the future.

1. What days of the week and times of day would you especially like to have children's programs available at _____ Public Library?  (Mark as many days/times as you like.)

   **MONDAY** mornings _____ afternoons _____ evenings _____

   **TUESDAY** mornings _____ afternoons _____ evenings _____

   **WEDNESDAY** mornings _____ afternoons _____ evenings _____

   **THURSDAY** mornings _____ afternoons _____ evenings _____

   **FRIDAY** mornings _____ afternoons _____

   **SATURDAY** mornings _____ afternoons _____

   **SUNDAY** afternoons _____

2. Please rate your overall satisfaction with the Preschool Storytime programs.

   Extremely Satisfied          Satisfied          Not Satisfied

   Comments and Suggestions:

   _____

   _____

3. Have you noticed any particular areas of development in your child's pre-reading behaviors (such as interest in the alphabet, trying to sound out letters, saying rhymes, wanting to practice writing his/her name, excitement about books) since attending Preschool Storytime?

   _____

   _____

4. What is your CHILD's favorite part of Preschool Storytime? _____

   _____

   What is YOUR favorite part of Preschool Storytime? _____

   _____

5. How did you hear about the Preschool Storytime programs?

   Library Flyer or Brochure _____          Library Web Site _____          Library Staff _____

   Posters in the Library _____          Newspaper _____          Friend _____          Other _____

6. Additional Comments: _____

   _____

# Many Mittens
## January

## Early Literacy Activities

### Name Tags

Mitten stamp or sticker

### Storytime Clue(s)

Miniature pair of craft, doll, or toddler mittens

### Mailbox "Letter" of the Day

"M" and "m"

Mitten, Mom, Mouse, Moon, Milk, Man, Macaroni, Me

### Mother Goose Rhyme Time

**Baa Baa Black Sheep**

*"Baa baa, black sheep,*
*Have you any wool?"*
*"Yes sir, yes sir,*
*Three bags full.*
*One for my master,*
*And one for my dame,*
*And one for the little boy*
*Who lives down the lane."*

### Rhyming Basket

Mitten/Kitten; Mouse/House; Bear/Chair

### Early Literacy Skill: Letter Knowledge

Learn to recognize and identify letters, knowing that they have different names and sounds and that the same letter can look different.

- Mailbox "letter" of the day.

- Notice and talk about the letters on the giant mittens, and draw the letters in the air. Know that letters have names and sounds.

- Mitten Matching: Developing children's abilities to notice what is alike and different is one of the beginning steps toward letter knowledge.

## Program Summary and Theme

Whether or not you live in a place that has cold weather and snow, you can enjoy sharing some mitten adventures! Make giant felt mittens and pin them to a clothesline across your storytime area, facing the audience and behind where you will sit. Affix a letter to each mitten to spell out the word: M-I-T-T-E-N-S. (See patterns and instructions on pages 32–33 and 37–38.) Produce the next book or activity from the next mitten on the line.

(You can also stitch or glue letters to regular-size mittens and simply pull out a small-size representative clue for the next story or activity.) Make sure to wear brightly colored mittens yourself as you begin storytime!

Prepare the props and puppets ahead of time so you can use them throughout the program. Please see patterns and directions on pages 32–41. See additional suggested titles on pages 31–32 to substitute for older or younger audiences.

## Music

Play "winter" or "mitten weather" music as the audience is gathering in your storytime area. Possibilities include "Hot Chocolate" and "Wintersong" on *Wintersongs* by John McCutcheon (Rounder, 1995), "Let's Play in the Snow" on *Sing A Song of Seasons* by Rachel Buchman (Rounder, 1997), "I'm A Little Snowflake" on *Whaddaya Think of That?* by Laurie Berkner (Two Tomatoes, 2000), and many others.

# Sample Program

Please adjust content and length as needed.

## Introduction

*(Wearing your brightly colored mittens, wave enthusiastically at your audience.) Say:* Today we are sharing stories about MITTENS. When do we usually need to wear mittens on our hands? *(Take ideas—all guesses are good guesses.)* When it's really cold, we need to wear mittens like these *(show your mittens, then pull one off)*, or gloves *(put on one glove, hold it up so the audience can see)* that have a place for each finger, to keep our hands warm. We don't usually need to wear mittens or gloves inside the library, but I wanted to put them on today to give you an extra clue to what our stories are about. Do you see any other mittens around here? *(Act surprised by the giant mittens hanging behind you.)* Oh, my goodness! Those mittens are huge! They must be special storytime mittens.

*Say:* I see some letters of the alphabet *(point to the letters)* written on them! Let's see if we can say these letters together. *(Point to each letter as you go along; make sure to stand behind the mittens or next to them so you aren't blocking the children's view.)* M-I-T-T-E-N-S. That spells "mittens." Can you say it with me? *(Point to the whole word and "read" it together.)*

*Say:* We definitely are doing mitten stories today. Let's find out what the first story is going to be. *(Facing forward so you do not have your back to the audience, reach into the first giant mitten and dramatically produce your first book or representative item.)*

## Read Aloud: M

*(Point out that the letter "M" is for Mittens and also for Minerva in the book's title, and for Morgan in the author's middle name; draw the capital letter "M" in the air together.)*

*A Hat for Minerva Louise* by Janet Morgan Stoeke. Dutton, 1994. Toddler–Grade 1. Minerva Louise the chicken loves to be outside in the snow, but she gets very cold. Deciding that she needs warm winter clothes, she goes in search of some. When Minerva Louise discovers a pair of mittens near a snowman, she mistakes the mittens for two hats and proudly wears one on each end to keep warm.

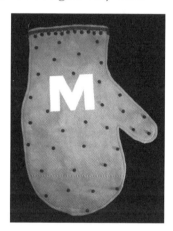

## Segue: I

*Say:* Minerva Louise found not one, but two mittens! That's called a pair of mittens, when two mittens go together like that. The mittens that Minerva Louise found were hooked together by a string. Some people wear their mittens with their coats, with a long string through the arms of their coat so they can't lose their mittens. *(Demonstrate this if possible.)* But often mittens aren't hooked on or clipped on to your coat, and then they can get lost. Let's see what is going to happen next. We are looking in the mitten with the letter "I" on it—let's draw the capital letter "I" in the air. *(Rummage around in the "I" mitten on the clothesline and quizzically produce a single, mateless, regular-size mitten.)* It's a mitten inside a mitten!

## Mitten Matching

*Say:* Usually a pair of mittens or a pair of socks look the same as each other, but it can also be fun and special to wear two that don't look alike! Today we are going to try and match some mitten pairs, and figure out where this mitten's other mitten has gone.

Play a mitten-matching game, deciding as a group whether or not two particular mittens make a pair. Manipulate the mateless mitten as a puppet, singing the "Pair of Mittens" song to the tune: "Did You Ever See a Lassie?"

Mitten 1 sings:

"Please find my other mitten, my mitten, my mitten.
Please find my other mitten,
So I'll be a pair."

Look carefully at Mitten 1 as a group. Talk about its color, pattern, shape, size, and so forth. Mitten 1 can make silly comments while you are talking about it! Have Mitten 1 explain that it is exhausted and needs to take a nap; hide it behind your flannel board or in a story box.

Put the Mitten Match box on your lap and hold up one mitten at a time. Talk about what you remember about Mitten 1, and compare those details to these mittens. Look at four or five mittens, some slightly similar to Mitten 1, before you pull out the mitten that actually matches Mitten 1. Call Mitten 1 back and compare details until your group decides they are definitely a pair. Sing to Mitten 1.

Group sings:

"Oh, here's your other mitten, your mitten, your mitten.
Oh, here's your other mitten,
Now you are a pair."

Mitten 1 and 2 sing:

"We're glad to be together, together, together.
We're glad to be together,
To help you keep warm."

The mittens kiss each other and bow to the audience. Put them together into the giant "I" mitten.

## Segue: First T

*Say:* Thank goodness we found that other mitten! Let's see what our next story will be about. Here's our first "T" mitten—let's draw the capital letter "T" *(draw "T" in the air).* What do you think will be in here? *(Take ideas— all guesses are good guesses. Produce your next storytime book or representative item from the first "T" mitten.)*

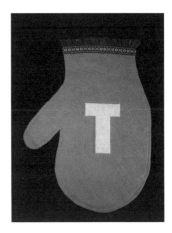

## Read Aloud

*Under My Hood I Have A Hat* by Karla Kuskin, illustrated by Fumi Kosaka. Laura Geringer Books, 2004. Toddler–K. A child describes the many layers of clothing needed to stay warm in the winter.

Before you begin reading, talk about vocabulary in the story that may be new to the children, such as the word "muffler" or "gloves" (if you didn't talk about gloves in your introduction). Bring real items to show.

OR

*Missing Mittens* by Stuart J. Murphy, illustrated by G. Brian Karas. HarperCollins, 2001. (MathStart series). PK–2. As a farmer tries to find the correct number of mittens for his various farmyard animals, the reader is introduced to odd and even numbers.

## Segue: Second T

*Say:* This next storytime mitten *(point to next "T" mitten)* is "T" again—let's draw it *(do so in the air).* It will probably have some shoes in it, right? Oh! Maybe

not—maybe something about mittens. I wonder what it will be. *(Dramatically reach far down into the mitten, so your arm disappears into it. If you have "The Mitten Song" sound recording in the mitten, tap on the plastic case so the children can hear the sound, and then pull it out. If you will do "The Mitten Song" as a rhyme instead, pull out a mitten-shaped paper with the poem written on it.)*

## Action Rhyme (Standing)

Share "The Mitten Song" by Marie Louise Allen while jumping in place. The children can help you repeat "thumbs in the thumb-place" while sticking up their thumbs, and "fingers all together" while showing their fingers together as if they are wearing mittens.

The text of the poem is available in *A New Treasury of Children's Poetry* selected by Joanna Cole (Doubleday, 1984) and in *The Poetry Break* by Caroline Feller Bauer (H. W. Wilson, 1995). It is also available on the following sound recordings: *Sing a Song of Seasons* by Rachel Buchman (Rounder Kids, 1997) and *H.U.M. All Year Long: Highly Usable Music* by Carole Peterson (Macaroni Soup, 2003).

> ### "The Mitten Song"
>
> *"Thumbs in the thumb-place,*
> *Fingers all together!"*
> *This is the song*
> *We sing in mitten-weather,*
> *When it is cold,*
> *It doesn't matter whether*
> *Mittens are wool,*
> *Or made of finest leather—*
> *This is the song*
> *We sing in mitten-weather:*
> *"Thumbs in the thumb-place,*
> *Fingers all together!"*
>
> —Marie Louise Allen

OR

Do "The Snowkey Pokey" (adapted by Gayle Selsback) to the tune: "The Hokey Pokey." "You put your MITTENS in; you put your mittens out …" Then repeat the song with other articles of winter clothing.

## Segue: E

*(Point to the "E" mitten.) Say:* Here is our next mitten, with the letter "E." *(Draw "E" in the air. Pull out a kitten puppet or plush with the* Three Little Kittens *book.)* In this next book, there are some lost mittens, too! Some of you may know this rhyme about three little kittens who lost their *(pause for the children to have a chance to supply the word)* mittens. If you know it, say it with me as we read the book.

## Read Aloud

*Three Little Kittens* illustrated by Paul Galdone. Clarion Books, 1986. PK–1. Three little kittens lose, find, soil, and wash their mittens.

## Segue: Action Song (Standing)

*Say:* I know a song about those three little kittens! Let's all stand up.

"Three Little Kittens"
*(Sung to the tune: "Three Blind Mice.")*

Three little kittens, three little kittens.
*(Hold up three fingers.)*

Lost their mittens, lost their mittens.
*(Hands out, empty.)*

They all ran around with their tails in the air.
*(Run around in little circles.)*

They looked for their mittens most everywhere! *(Pretend to look.)*

Then they saw that those mittens were under the chair!
*(Jump up with arms overhead, looking pleased.)*

Three little kittens, three little kittens.
*(Hold up three fingers.)*

## Segue: N

*Say:* We are almost to the end of our row of mittens. Here is the capital letter "N." *(Draw the letter "N" in the air. Pull out copies of both Jan Brett's and Alvin Tresselt's books,* The Mitten.*)*

We have one more lost mitten in this last story. Some of you may know this book about *The Mitten. (Show Jan Brett's version—many children are familiar with it.)* The story I am going to tell you is a lot like that story, but it comes out of this book *(show the Alvin Tresselt version).* In this book *(hold up the Brett version),* the mitten gets very stretched out at the end, but in this one *(hold up the Tresselt version)* something else happens!

## Prop Story

Share an abbreviated version of "The Mitten" with your story props. See pages 33–36 and 39–41 for patterns and instructions for making the props, and pages 29–31 for a storytelling script. The script is adapted from various versions of the traditional story, including the classic *The Mitten: An Old Ukrainian Folktale* retold by Alvin Tresselt, illustrated by Yaroslava, adapted from the version by E. Rachev. Lothrop, Lee & Shepard, 1964. PK–1. In this version of the traditional tale, the mitten explodes when all of the animals shove their way inside!

Also see:

*The Mitten: A Ukrainian Folktale* adapted and illustrated by Jan Brett. Putnam, 1989. Several animals sleep snugly in Nicki's lost mitten until the bear sneezes. (Available as a BIG Book.)

See Jan Brett's wonderful Web site at www.janbrett.com, with coloring sheets and activities featuring *The Mitten.*

The following song is fun to sing as you tell "The Mitten" with your puppets and props. Variations are included on many winter and mitten curriculum Web sites, and I've adapted it slightly yet again; I've been unable to determine the original adaptor.

"The Mitten"
*(Sung to the tune: "The Farmer in the Dell")*

The mitten on the ground.
The mitten on the ground.
Heigh-ho, it's cold in the snow!
The mitten on the ground.

Sing as a group:

The (mouse) snuggles in.
The (mouse) snuggles in.
Heigh-ho! It's cold in the snow!
The (mouse) snuggles in.

And so forth ...

## Conclusion S

*Say:* We have one last mitten to look inside. Here is the capital letter "S" *(draw "S" in the air as a group).* What do you think will be inside? Maybe a whole bunch of animals? *(Pull out a sample of your mitten craft and the craft supplies if you are making a craft. If you will not be doing a craft, pull out a sign that says "The End!")*

## Craft Ideas

- Make a pair of fancy decorated paper mittens with the pattern template provided (see page 37). Decorate with crayons, markers, stickers, lace, yarn, felt, and so forth. Paper punch the mittens at the wrists and join them together with yarn.

  Note: Avoid using buttons or pompoms if working with very young children, as the items could be a choking hazard. Also, use shortened lengths of yarn so they can't become wrapped around little necks.

- Make mitten pockets with all of the animals from *The Mitten*. See Jan Brett's Web site's "Mitten Line Drawings" at: www.jan brett.com/put_the_animals_in_the_mit ten.htm.

## "The Mitten" Storytelling Script

### Prop Pieces

*(Please note that the story prop pieces are designed as professional resources, not as playthings. They do not conform to child safety play standards, and they could easily become damaged if used in a manner other than that for which they were intended.)*

- cardboard box theater with fake fur snow
- mouse felt figure or finger puppet
- frog felt figure or finger puppet
- owl felt figure or finger puppet
- rabbit felt figure or finger puppet

- bear felt figure or small hand puppet
- cricket felt figure, plastic figure, or finger puppet
- three knit or sewn mittens, one very stretchy
- pieces of mitten fabric
- medium-size white balloon
- piece of fake fur snow to cover the balloon
- T-pin or safety pin to pop the balloon

Use with a copy of the book to show the audience both before and after presenting the story.

### Set-up

1. Inflate the balloon and hide it inside the box theater with the T-pin nearby so the pin is accessible but won't pop the balloon prematurely! You may need to masking tape the balloon in place if it threatens to roll out of the theater. Cover the mitten with the piece of fake fur snow to help conceal its existence.

2. Hide the mitten pieces inside the box theater.

3. Hide the mittens inside the box theater.

4. Hide the characters inside the box theater until it is time for their entrance.

### Presentation

1. Story narration is delineated in regular type; movement notes and miscellaneous directions are shown within the script in *italics*.

2. Learn the story and tell it to your audience from memory, using the prop pieces.

3. The script calls for you to be the voice of eight characters: the Narrator, Little Boy, Mouse, Frog, Owl, Rabbit, Bear, and Cricket.

4. Although it is not essential to use different character voices when presenting the story, it can truly engage the children's interest as well as help them distinguish which character is talking. Try out different voices to figure out which sounds the best for the different characters. All voices must feel natural for you after

practice so that you will be able to use and maintain them successfully during an actual performance.

Note: The following script is an adapted story version for telling as a prop and participation story, and includes notes for the storyteller on how and when to manipulate the prop pieces. Please look at the book(s) so that you know what adaptations have been made in this script. Show a copy of the book(s) to your audience both before and after sharing the story with the props, and give the complete title, author/illustrator, and publication information.

## Script

It was the very coldest day of winter. The wind blew. *(Blow and wave windy hands as a group.)* The snow swirled. *(Swirl hands as a group.)* And everyone shivered. *(Shiver as a group.)* A little boy was outside in the morning on this cold, frosty day, gathering firewood for his grandmother. As he picked up sticks, he accidentally dropped one of his mittens in the snow. *(Drop one mitten onto the lap theater's snow covering, draped slightly over the front so the audience can see it clearly.)* The snow swirled around him, and he couldn't find where he had dropped it, so he took the firewood and ran back home. "I will go and look for my mitten this afternoon," he said. Meanwhile, the mitten lay there in the snow. *(Point to the mitten.)*

Sing as a group: *(Sung to the tune: "The Farmer in the Dell.")*

The mitten on the ground.
The mitten on the ground.
Heigh-ho, it's cold in the snow!
The mitten on the ground.

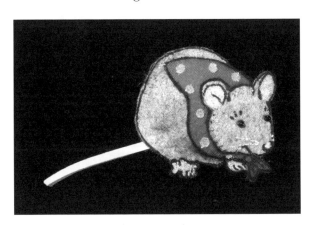

Before long, a little mouse came scurrying by. *(Scamper the mouse across the snow.)* She was very cold on this frosty day, and she was delighted to see that cozy mitten lying there in the snow. *(Make mouse peer at the mitten.)* "Why, look!" she squeaked. "What a warm, woolly mitten. I believe I'll just snuggle in and warm up." And that's exactly what she did. *(Snuggle mouse into mitten.)*

Sing as a group:

The mouse snuggles in.
The mouse snuggles in.
Heigh-ho! It's cold in the snow!
The mouse snuggles in.

Soon a little green frog came slippety-slidey-hopping by. *(Hop-slide the frog across the snow.)* His legs creaked when he hopped, because he was so cold! When he saw that toasty warm mitten with the little mouse inside, he hopped right over. *(Hop frog over to the mitten.)* "May I join you in that warm, woolly mitten on this cold, frosty day?" croaked the frog. "Come right on in," squeaked the mouse. "Quickly! Before you freeze!" So the little green frog snuggled into that mitten right next to the little mouse. *(Snuggle frog into mitten.)*

Sing as a group:

The frog snuggles in.
The frog snuggles in.
Heigh-ho! It's cold in the snow!
The frog snuggles in.

They had just settled themselves near the mitten's opening when an owl flew down. *(Swoop owl down to the mitten.)* "Whoooooooo is in that warm, woolly mitten?" hooted the owl. "May I join you on this cold, frosty day?" The mouse and the frog were a little bit nervous around owls, but they couldn't say no on this coldest

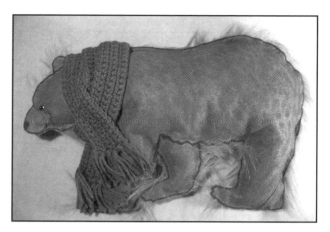

day of winter. So they moved over inside the mitten, and the owl snuggled in next to the frog. *(Snuggle owl into mitten.)*

Sing as a group:

The owl snuggles in.
The owl snuggles in.
Heigh-ho! It's cold in the snow!
The owl snuggles in.

Before too long a rabbit came hopping through the forest. *(Hop rabbit across the snow.)* Her ears had icicles hanging from them, she was so cold, but they twitched when she saw that warm, woolly mitten lying in the snow. *(Twitch rabbit and have her look into the mitten.)* "Is there room for me in that mitten?" asked the rabbit. "I'm so cold I have ear-cicles!"

"It's pretty crowded in here already," said the mouse and the frog and the owl, "but come on in. We'll snuggle closer together." *(Snuggle rabbit into mitten.)*

Sing as a group:

The rabbit snuggles in.
The rabbit snuggles in.
Heigh-ho! It's cold in the snow!
The rabbit snuggles in.

By now that mitten was extremely crowded, but it was toasty warm. A bear who was rambling by *(galumph the bear across the snow, pause at the mitten)* saw it lying there in the snow. The bear was very big and very cold and very cranky. "Why, what a nice woolly mitten," rumbled the bear. "I think I'll climb inside and warm up."

The other animals all squeaked, "No room! No room!" when they saw that enormous bear trying to climb into the mitten, but the bear pushed and shoved *(shove bear into the mitten)* and grunted and poked and managed to get most of himself into the mitten anyway! I'm afraid that he was used to getting his own way, and he never listened to anyone else.

Sing as a group:

The bear snuggles in.
The bear snuggles in.
Heigh-ho! It's cold in the snow!
The bear snuggles in.

While all of this was going on, a tiny little black cricket came chirping by. *(Totter cricket across the snow.)* She was very old, with creaky legs and tired wings, and she was colder than she had ever been in her life on this coldest day of winter. When she saw that warm, woolly mitten lying there in the snow, she decided to try and squeeze in too! (*Squeeze cricket into the very edge of the mitten.*)

Sing as a group:

The cricket snuggles in.
The cricket snuggles in.
Heigh-ho! It's cold in the snow!
The cricket snuggles in.

But oh, dear! That tiny cricket in addition to the bear and the rabbit and the owl and the frog and the mouse was just too much for the little boy's mitten! The mitten was packed too tight. It began to wobble and to wiggle and to shake (*shake mitten gradually and then more intensively*), and it flipped right over in the snow. (*Flip loaded mitten down so it is hidden inside the lap theater and grab your T-pin to pop the balloon.*) Where ... BANG! It exploded into pieces! (*Toss the little mitten fabric pieces up in the air.*)

The animals all jumped up and ran away to their cozy animal homes—the mouse to her little mouse hole. (*Scamper the mouse across the snow and hide her inside the box theater.*) The frog to his mud house near the river. (*Hop the frog across the snow the opposite way and hide him inside the box theater.*) The owl to his nest high in the tree. (*Fly the owl high into the air, hooting, and swoop him down inside the box theater.*) The rabbit to her hole under ground. (*Hop the rabbit across the snow and hide her.*) And the big old bear to his bear cave ... (*galumph the bear across the snow and hide inside the box theater*) ... where he snuggled up and snored for the rest of the winter. (*Snore loudly.*)

And what happened to the little cricket? (*Hold her up for the audience to see that she is safe.*) Well, she waited until the little boy came back for his mitten, and then she told him what had happened. (*Hold the cricket up by your ear as if she is talking to you and you are listening.*) He took her home to his own nice warm house, where they wrote down this story while the little boy's grandma made him a new mitten. (*Put on a pair of knitted mittens and hold up your mittened hands to show the audience.*)

So be careful when you are wearing your mittens. Try not to drop either of them, because you never know what could happen!

# Additional Resources

***All You Need for a Snowman*** by Alice Schertle, illustrated by Barbara Lavallee. Silver Whistle, Harcourt, 2002. PK–2. Lists everything that you need to build the perfect snowman, from the very first snowflake that falls.

***Clementine's Winter Wardrobe*** by Kate Spohn. Orchard Books, 1989. PK–2. Clementine the Cat chooses the clothes she will wear next winter.
**Extension Idea:** This makes a wonderful flannel board story! The children love to pick out what Clementine should wear.

***The First Day of Winter*** by Denise Fleming. Henry Holt & Company, 2005. Toddler–Grade 1. A child builds a snowman throughout the first ten days of winter, adding pieces gradually to bring the snowman to life.

***Flip's Snowman*** by Petr Horacek. Candlewick Press, 2002. Toddler–K. Flip the penguin dresses in mittens, a hat, and warm boots before going outside to build a snowman on a snowy day. The next day is sunny and the snowman melts, but then the snow begins to fall again! Includes flaps, die-cut pages, and a pull-tab snowfall.

***Froggy Gets Dressed*** by Jonathan London. Viking, 1992. PK–2. Rambunctious Froggy hops out into the snow for a winter frolic but is called back by his mother to put on some necessary articles of clothing, including underwear. (Available in Spanish and as a BIG Book.)

***The Missing Mitten Mystery*** by Steven Kellogg. Dial, 2000. Re-worked edition of *The Mystery of the Missing Red Mitten*, 1974. PK–2. Annie searches the neighborhood for her red mitten, the fifth she's lost this winter! At last she discovers it stuck in the snowman she built in Miss Seltzer's yard, showing up as its heart.

***The Mitten Tree*** by Candace Christiansen, illustrated by Elaine Greenstein. Fulcrum Kids, 1997. K–2. Old Sarah knits mittens for all the children waiting for the school bus and hangs them on the blue spruce tree at the bus stop.

*One Little Lamb* by Elaine Greenstein. Viking, 2004. Toddler–K. Simple text describes how a lamb's coat is made into yarn, which is made into mittens worn by a little girl when she visits the lamb on the farm.

*One Mitten* by Kristine O'Connell George, illustrated by Maggie Smith. Clarion Books, 2004. Toddler–K. One mitten can do many things, but when the second mitten is found, it is time to go outside and have fun.

*Runaway Mittens* by Jean Rogers, pictures by Rie Muñoz. Greenwillow Books, 1988. K–2. Pica's mittens are always turning up in strange places, but when he finds them keeping the newborn puppies warm in their box, he decides to leave them where they are until spring.

*Snow Play* by Kate Spohn. Scholastic, 2001. Toddler–K. A little bear embarks on a snow-filled walk to Grandma's house, enjoying snowy activities and building some snow creatures along the way. Snow falls on everything, including mittens.

*Snowballs* by Lois Ehlert. Harcourt Brace & Company, 1995. Toddler–Grade 1. Children create a snow family and decorate each figure with household and natural objects they have saved. A clothesline of mittens and gloves from around the world is included in the endpapers.

*Three Little Kittens* retold and illustrated by Lorianne Siomades. Boyds Mills Press, 2000. Toddler–K. A shortened version of the classic rhyme (there's no soiling of the mittens here), reinterpreted with Siomades' signature brightly colored illustrations. At the end, Mother Cat can't find the pie, which the mice have hidden, but all ends happily.

*Too Many Mittens* by Florence and Louis Slobodkin. E. M. Hale, 1963. K–2. Everyone in town knows that the twins have lost a red mitten, so any time a red mitten turns up anywhere it is brought to the twins' house! Although the book is not visually dramatic like many modern publications, it is still a good story and makes a nice read-aloud for slightly older audiences.

*Winter Is the Warmest Season* by Lauren Stringer. Harcourt, 2006. PK–2. A child describes pleasant ways to stay warm during the winter, from sipping hot chocolate and eating grilled cheese sandwiches to wearing woolly sweaters and sitting near a glowing fireplace.

# Story Prop and Craft Directions

## Giant "M-I-T-T-E-N-S" Display Mittens

### Tools and Supplies

- scissors
- pinking shears
- felt: sparkly white (for letters); miscellaneous colors for mittens as desired
- colored thread to match the mitten colors
- sewing machine or hot glue (OR may be hand-sewn)
- trim: miscellaneous decorative trim and embellishments as desired
- Tacky Glue® craft glue

### Directions

1. On a photocopier, enlarge the mitten pattern to various enormous sizes as desired, piecing the patterns together as necessary. Cut out the giant patterns.

2. Using pinking shears, cut a double mitten layer for each mitten. Stitch the two layers together around the edge, making sure to leave the wrist open.

3. Copy and cut out the letter patterns. Pin the letters to a single layer of sparkly white felt, and cut them out with pinking shears.

4. Arrange the mittens in a row along the floor, with their wrists along the same horizontal height (as if they are hanging from a clothesline). Measuring down from the tops of the mittens so the letters will all line up horizontally despite the varying mitten sizes, glue one letter to each mitten. Allow the glue to dry completely.

5. Embellish the mittens as desired with trim, sequins, pompoms, and so forth. Glue or stitch the embellishments to the mittens. Allow the glue to dry completely.

## "The Mitten" Felt Characters

Note: Small-size mouse, frog, owl, rabbit, and bear puppets or plush animals and plastic crickets are fairly easy to find and relatively inexpensive to purchase. Alternately, make the following double-layer stuffed felt characters and highlight their features with craft paint, button eyes, and trimmings: mouse, frog, owl, rabbit, bear, and cricket.

### Tools and Supplies

- scissors
- hand-sewing needle and thread
- Tacky Glue® craft glue
- colored felt
- polyester fiberfill
- fake fur (optional)
- googly eyes, stuffed animal eyes, and shiny black beads or button eyes
- feathers for owl (optional)
- pompom for owl's hat (optional)
- pompom tail for rabbit
- patterned vest fabric for rabbit (optional); Fray Check™ to seal fabric edges
- yarn or leather lacing tail for mouse
- 3 mm black pipe cleaners for cricket's legs
- small-size craft paintbrush
- acrylic craft paint or puffy paint: black and white (for outlining figures)

- acrylic craft paint or puffy paint: misc. colors (for highlighting figures as desired)

### Directions

1. Photocopy the animal patterns, adjusting sizes as desired. Pin the animal patterns onto the felt and cut out the figures.

2. If you wish to add real patterned fabric clothing or contrasting felt layers to the animals (mouse's kerchief; owl's hat; rabbit's vest; and cricket's kerchief, mittens, and boots), cut the photocopy pattern apart to the next level. This will enable you to cut out the clothing pieces separately from the body of the character and then glue them on. The bear's scarf may be made from a strip of felt or fabric and knotted around him like a doll's scarf after you have finished painting and decorating him.

3. Glue each character's layers together by drawing a thin line of Tacky craft glue around the edge of the bottom layer of felt and then pressing it together with the top felt layer. Make sure to leave a small opening through which you can later stuff the piece with fiberfill. Reinforce the rabbit's ears by gluing a bit of pipe cleaner between the layers. If the figure has multiple layers (such as clothing), glue all of the layers onto the base layer and allow the glue to dry completely.

4. Lightly stuff polyester fiberfill between the layers until the character is as fat as you would like, and then glue the opening shut. Hold the opening together with clip clothespins until the glue dries completely.

5. After the figures are assembled, paint outlines and highlights onto them with acrylic craft paint. Allow the painted pieces to dry completely.

6. Add any final details that could enhance the piece such as bead or button eyes, feathers, fur, trim, etc.

## "The Mitten" Box Theater With Snow Covering

### Tools and Supplies

- medium-size, open-topped cardboard box that you will be able to hold comfortably on your lap, and that is big enough to hide the balloon and all of the story pieces

- white spray paint or craft paint

- utility knife

- white fake fur, enough to cover the front, sides, and part of the top of your box, as well as an extra piece to cover the balloon

- Tacky Glue® craft glue OR hot glue gun

- package of white balloons (you will need a new balloon each time you tell the story!)

- T-pin for popping the balloon

### Directions

1. Paint the outside and inside of the cardboard box white. Allow the paint to dry completely.

2. Lay the box on one of its long sides, and cut off half of what is now the box top with your utility knife.

3. Glue white fake fur "snow" to the front, sides, and top of the box.

4. Save a piece of the fake fur snow to conceal the balloon when you hide it in the back of the box for the story.

## "The Mitten"

Note: A simple knitting pattern as well as a sewing pattern option are both included below in an effort to accommodate a range of skills and abilities.

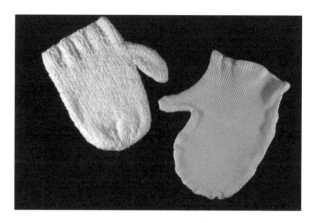

### Knit "The Mitten"

Pattern designed by Jess Bandelin, Punky Patterns

Difficulty level: Easy

### Materials

- approx. 300 yards of cotton/elastic yarn, such as Cascade Fixation

- size 7, 9, and 15 needles

- stitch markers

- stitch holders

- tapestry needle

*Abbreviations:*

K: knit, P: purl, M1: make one by placing a backward loop on the right needle, K2tog: knit 2 together, PM: place marker

*Cuff:*

Using size 7 needle, cast on 46 stitches. Work in K2, P2 rib for 13 rows.

Change to larger size needle and work 4 rows of stockinette stitch.

*Thumb Gusset:*

Row 1: K 22 stitches, PM, M1, K2, M1, PM, K 22 stitches.

Row 2: Purl.

Row 3: K 22 stitches, slip marker, M1, K4, M1, slip marker, K 22 stitches.

Row 4: Purl.

Continue this pattern of increase row then purl row, having 2 more stitches between the markers each time. Work until there are 14 stitches between the markers, and purl back.

*Dividing Row:*

K 22, slip to a piece of yarn or a holder, K 14 (these are the thumb stitches). Slip the remaining stitches to a piece of yarn or a holder without knitting them.

Purl back across the thumb stitches and cast on 2 stitches at the beginning of the next row.

Work back and forth on the thumb stitches until the piece measures 1.5 inches.

*Decreases:*

K1, K2tog. Repeat across row ending with a K1.

Purl back.

K2tog across row ending with a K1.

Purl back.

K2tog across row ending with a K1. (4 stitches)

Break off yarn leaving a tail about 8 inches long.

Draw yarn through remaining stitches and sew up thumb seam.

Place the stitches from the holders back on your needles, having them point to the center.

Pick up and knit 2 stitches from the bottom of the thumb. If you need to pick up more to assure that there are no holes, don't fret; you can decrease over the next few rows to get back to your target number of stitches, which is 46.

Work mitten even until it is 6.5 or 7 inches long, depending on the size of your hand. A good indicator is to make the mitten as long as your hand to the top knuckle on your middle finger.

*Decreases:*

K1, K2tog, repeat across row ending with a K1.

Purl back.

K1, K2tog, repeat across row ending with a K1.

Purl back.

K2tog across row ending with a K1.

Purl back.

K2tog across row ending with a K1. (6 stitches)

Break off yarn leaving a tail about 15 inches long.

Draw yarn through remaining stitches and sew side seam, and weave in ends.

For the mitten that will be full of animals, follow the preceding directions, but use size 15 needles all the way through. This mitten can be stretched big enough to let in all of the animals necessary, but the elastic springs it back to a nice manageable size when it is empty. I suggest getting the mitten damp and allowing it to dry flat after every use. That will allow it to return to its pre-stretched size.

## For the mitten pieces:

*Cuff (Make 2):*

With size 7 needles, cast on 22 stitches.

Work K2, P2 rib for 13 rows.

Bind off.

*Body (Make 2):*

With size 9 needles, cast on 22 stitches.

Work in stockinette stitch, K 1 row, P 1 row, for 5 inches.

K1, K2tog. Repeat across row.

Purl back.

K2tog across row.

Purl back.

K2tog across row.

Break off yarn and draw through stitches.

## Thumb:

Cast on 2 stitches.

Knit into the front and back of the first and last stitch on the needle.

Purl back.

Repeat these last two rows until there are 14 stitches on your needle.

Work these 14 stitches in stockinette stitch for 1.5 inches.

K1, K2tog. Repeat across row.

Purl back.

K2tog across row.

Purl back.

K2tog across row.

Break yarn and draw through remaining stitches.

Sew seam, leaving the wedge shape at the bottom open.

OR

## Sew "The Mitten"

### Tools and Supplies

- ¼ yard of extremely stretchy white fabric, such as nylon ribbing or swimsuit fabric
- white thread
- sewing machine (or may be hand-sewn)
- scissors
- dressmaker's pins

### Directions

1. Photocopy the mitten craft/sewing pattern, adjusting the size as desired. Cut six mitten outlines (to make three mittens total) from the fabric.

2. Stitch the mitten together. Seam allowance is ¼". Trim seams.

3. Cut small pieces of the fabric scraps to be bits of the mitten after it explodes.

# Giant Mitten and Mitten Craft

Enlarge as desired.

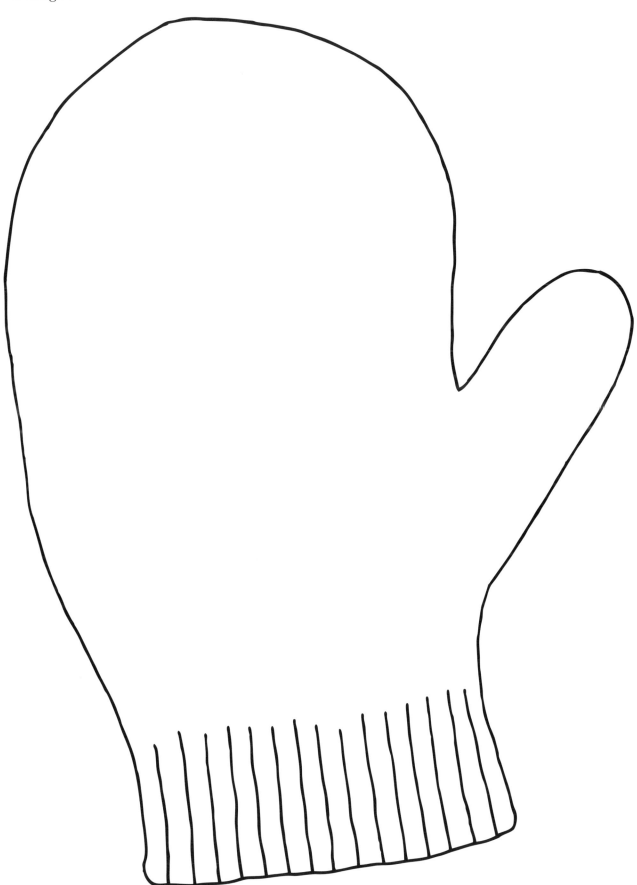

# Mitten Letter Patterns

Enlarge as desired.

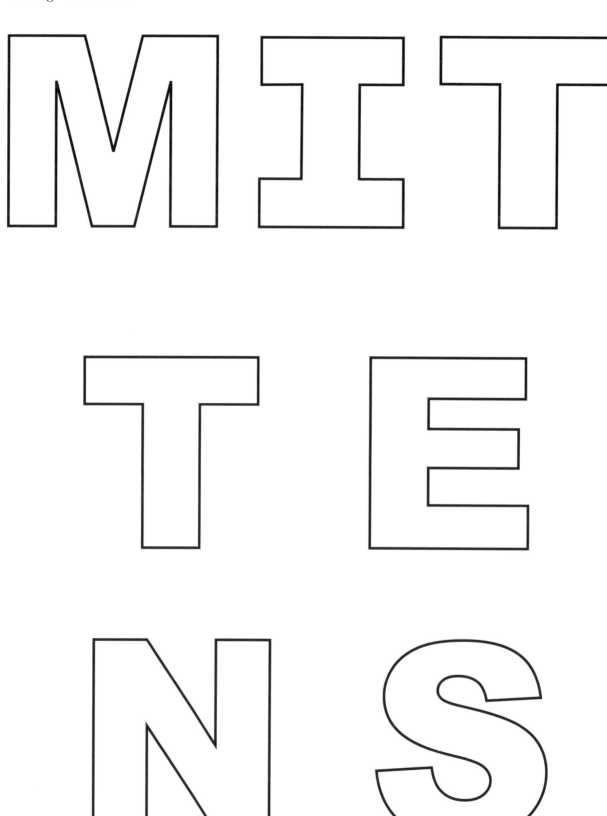

# Mitten Felt Characters

# Mitten Felt Characters

# Mitten Felt Characters

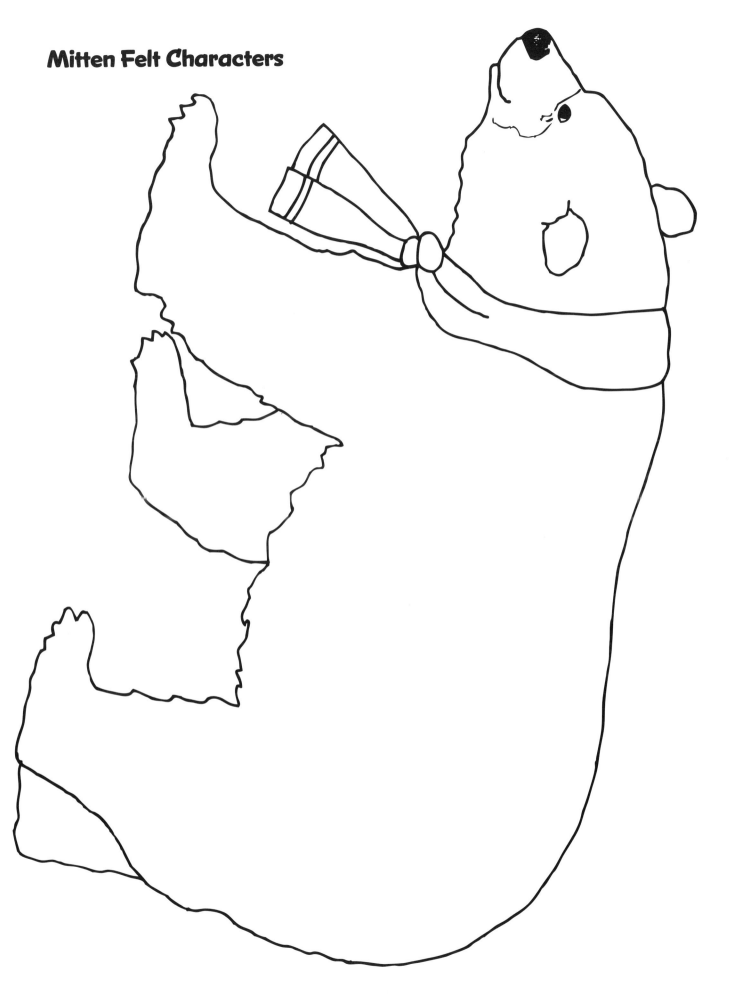

# Be My Valentine
## February

## Early Literacy Activities

### Name Tags

Heart stamp or sticker

### Storytime Clue(s)

Small decorated envelope with valentine card inside

### Mailbox "Letter" of the Day

"V" and "v"

Valentine, Vacuum, Violin, Violet, Vinegar, Vase, Van, Vacation

*(Define new vocabulary as needed.)*

### Mother Goose Rhyme Time

*Here Am I*

*Here am I,*
*Little Jumping Joan.*
*When nobody's with me,*
*I'm all alone.*

### Rhyming Basket

Heart/Tart; Spoon/Moon; Van/Man

## Early Literacy Skill: Print Awareness

Notice print and know how to handle books and follow the written word on a page.

- Hold up some of the storybook characters' valentines upside down, sideways, and so forth as you prepare to "read" them together, and see if the children detect the problem.

- Follow the text of the valentines with your finger as you read them aloud.

- Incorporate the words to "Valentine From a Bear" and the Mother Goose jumping rhyme "Early in the Morning" by writing them out ahead of time on a piece of grid board so attending adults can follow along. Point out to the group that the poem is written on the poster. Repeat each rhyme several times, encouraging the audience to say it with you. For at least one of the repetitions, follow the printed text on the poster with your finger as you read from left to right to reinforce print directionality as well as the concept that print stands for spoken language.

## Program Summary and Theme

Before the children enter the room or story-time area, suspend cutout paper hearts from the ceiling on 4-lb. test fishing line, attaching the hearts to the lines with slip-knots so they'll slide off easily when pulled. Make sure there are enough hearts so that there is at least one per child. These hearts can either be used for a craft following storytime or for the children to take home as they are. Please note that hanging the paper hearts from the ceiling takes awhile, but it is very exciting for the children to "catch" their heart raindrop(s). If your ceiling isn't an option for hanging hearts, consider taping them to walls, shelves, or furniture around your storytime space.

February is the perfect time to celebrate friends, family, valentines, and mail. Cover your storytime table with a red cloth, and display the books you plan to share. Make valentines from a character in each of your storytime books or reflecting a planned activity (see possibilities outlined on page 51 to match the suggested titles). Hide the storybook valentines in the "Letter of the Day" mailbox along with the letter "V" and "v" envelope before the program begins in the order in which you intend to share the stories and activities. Keep an eye on the time, and skip a book or activity if you need to. Read the valentines one by one as a group to introduce the next book or activity as you progress through the storytime program; encourage the children to help you visually match the valentine image to the book cover, or to figure out clues from the valentine to determine which book or story might be next.

Prepare the props and puppets ahead of time so you can use them throughout the program. Please see patterns and directions on pages 51–58. See additional suggested titles on pages 47–51 to substitute for older or younger audiences.

## Music

Play "friendship" or "families" music as the audience is gathering in your storytime area. Possibilities include "The More We Get Together" on *Singable Songs for the Very Young* by Raffi (Troubadour, 1976) and *Raffi in Concert* (Troubadour, 1989), "I Like You" on *Bert and Ernie's Greatest Hits* (Sony Wonder, 1996) and *Songs from the Street: 35 Years of Music* (Sony Wonder, 2003), "Is My Family" and "How Many People" on *Family Garden* by John McCutcheon (Rounder, 1993), "Friends Forever" on *We All Live Together*, vol. 5 by Greg and Steve (Youngheart, 1994), "Love Grows One by One" on *I'm Gonna Reach!* by Tom Pease (Tomorrow River, 1989) and *Daydreamer* by Priscilla Herdman (Music for Little People, 1993), "Family Tree" on *Family Tree* by Tom Chapin (Sony, 1992), and many others.

# Sample Program

Please adjust content and length as needed.

## Introduction

*Say:* Today we are celebrating our friends and families who love us, and talking about valentine cards! *(Hold up an example.)* To whom do you think you might give a valentine? *(Take suggestions—all are good ideas.)* Yes, we might give a valentine to a friend or to someone in our family; maybe to the grocery store worker who helps us or to the postal worker who delivers our mail every day; maybe to a teacher; maybe even to your pets! Valentines help us to say, "I care about you." I think our storytime group has received some valentines today, too. *(Hold up the mailbox.)* Let's see what has arrived! *(Open the mailbox and take out the top valentine.)* This first one is in a long skinny envelope. I wonder who it could be from? Do you notice any clues? *(pawprints, return address)* Well, it says it's for us— "Storytime Friends"—so let's open it and see. *(Open envelope and remove bone valentine; then hold it up.)* Look! This valentine is shaped like

a *(pause for children to say the word)* bone! It says *(follow the words with your finger as you read them),* "Happy Valentine's Day to our story-time friends. We hope you can read our book first! From your waggy digger friends." *(Match the bone to the one on the front of* Be Mine, Be Mine, Sweet Valentine *by Sarah Weeks.)*

## Read Aloud

*Be Mine, Be Mine, Sweet Valentine* by Sarah Weeks, illustrated by Fumi Kosaka. HarperCollins, Laura Geringer Books, 2006. PK–1. A variety of animals and a child offer valentines to their sweethearts in rhyming text. Open the flaps to supply the final word in each rhyming couplet.

Pause as you open each flap for the children to supply the rhyming word, then repeat that word as a group as you run your finger under the text.

*Extension Idea: This rhyming valentine is fun to retell with puppets and props as well.*

## Segue

*Say:* There were a lot of rhymes in those valentines, words that sound the same at the end. I wonder if the next valentine in our mailbox will have rhyming words in it. *(Open the mailbox and take out the next valentine; hold it up.)* This valentine feels very sticky. There are some bees on it! I wonder who might have sent it? *(Open envelope and remove bee valentine, opening it so you can read whom it is from.)* It's a valentine from a bear! Why do you think a bear would send a sticky valentine with bees on it? *(Take suggestions; all guesses are good guesses.)* I think this bear right here might be able to explain and teach us his little valentine poem!

## Poem with Props

Use a bear puppet or stuffed teddy bear with a basket containing an artificial red rose, artificial blue violets, and a honey bear container to share this valentine from a bear. Repeat it several times with the audience.

"Valentine From a Bear"

Roses *(hold up artificial red rose)* are red.
Violets *(hold up artificial blue violets)* are blue.
*(Hold up honey bear.)* Honey is sweet,
And so are you. *(Have bear blow kisses to the audience.)*

Ahead of time, write out the words to "Valentine From A Bear" on a piece of grid board so attending adults can follow along. Point out to the group that the poem is written on the poster. Repeat the rhyme several times, encouraging the audience to say it with you. For at least one of the repetitions, follow the printed text on the poster with your finger as you read from left to right to reinforce print directionality as well as the concept that print stands for spoken language.

*Extension Idea: Repeat the poem as if it was from other animals. For example, a valentine from a rabbit might say, "Carrots are sweet;" a dog might bark, "Bones are sweet;" a panda might think, "Bamboo is sweet;" and so forth. If the children come up with some unusual suggestions, go ahead and say the poem using those ideas too—there aren't right or wrong answers.*

## Segue

*Say:* There were rhyming words in the bear's poem, weren't there? The words BLUE and YOU sound the same at the end. I wonder what our next valentine will be. *(Open the mailbox and take out the next valentine; hold it up, discuss clues on the envelope if you like, and open it.)* Look! It's a waving hand valentine. It says, "Dear Skinnamarinks, Please sing my song before you're through. If you'll wave to me, then I'll wave to you!" Do some of you know the Skinnamarink song? It's a little bit silly, but let's see if we can do it.

## Action Song (Standing)

"Skinnamarink"

The song can be found on the following children's recordings, and many more:

- *Great Big Hits 2* by Sharon, Lois & Bram. Casablanca Kids, 2002.

- *If You're Happy & You Know It … Sing Along with Bob #1* by Bob McGrath. Bob's Kids Music, 1996.

- *One Elephant, Deux Eléphants* by Sharon, Lois & Bram. Casablanca Kids, 2002. Alternately titled and released as *One Elephant Went Out to Play* by Sharon, Lois & Bram. Drive Entertainment, 1995.

- *Sing Around the Campfire* by Sharon, Lois & Bram. Drive Entertainment, 1995.

Actions are adapted from those suggested in *Crazy Gibberish and Other Story Hour Stretches from a Storyteller's Bag of Tricks* by Naomi Baltuck, drawings by Doug Cushman. Linnet Books, 1993.

CHORUS:

Skinnamarinky dinky dink! *(Wave enthusiastically with one hand.)*
Skinnamarinky doo! *(Wave enthusiastically with other hand.)*
I *(point to self)* love *(cross fists over chest)* you *(point to group)*.

(REPEAT CHORUS)

I love you in the morning, *(Arms over head to make round circle sun high in the sky.)*
And in the afternoon. *(Lower circled arms to waist level.)*

I love you in the evening, *(Lower arms further and rock them briefly.)*

Underneath the moon. *(Dominant hand makes sign language letter "c" hand shape up high and to the side.)*

(REPEAT CHORUS)

*(Write out the words to "Skinnamarink" ahead of time so attending adults may follow along. Point out that the words are written on the poster.)*

## Segue

*(Open the mailbox and take out the next valentine; hold it up. Discuss clues on the envelope if you like, and open it.) Say:* This looks like a valentine from the whole world, or maybe to the whole world! I believe it belongs with this book called *What A Wonderful World*. First the words were a song, and then Mr. Ashley Bryan made pictures for the words and it was made into this book. The children in the pictures are putting on a puppet show to match the words of the song. We'll listen to the music together while I turn the pages.

## Sing Aloud

*What A Wonderful World* by George David Weiss and Bob Thiele, illustrated by Ashley Bryan. Atheneum, 1995. Toddler–Grade 4. Children put on a puppet show, using the words to the song, "What a Wonderful World."

Play a sound recording of "What A Wonderful World" to accompany the book as you turn the pages. Possibilities include *The Very Best of Louis Armstrong* by Louis Armstrong (Universal Music Special Projects, 2000) and *What A Wonderful World* by Louis Armstrong (Rock Bottom, Inc., 2003) as well as many other artists' renditions.

## Segue

*Say:* Wow, we've received a lot of valentines so far! I think there may be some more, but first let's see if we can remember how many we have already opened. *(Remember details of each valentine together and then hold each one up as you remember it. Count the total number of valentines on your fingers—FOUR.)* That's FOUR valentines—that means we get to do the FOUR VALENTINES jumping rhyme! Everyone who would like to can stand up and start jumping!

## Jumping Rhyme (Standing)

*(Jump enthusiastically throughout, jumping HIGH with arms in the air on the word "Up." When you reach the last line, continue jumping while holding up one hand to count to four on your fingers.)*

Early in the morning at eight o'clock
You can hear the postman's knock;
Up jumps Ella to answer the door,
One letter, two letters, three letters, four!

*Write out the words on a piece of grid board so attending adults can follow along, and point out to the group that the poem is written on the poster.*

*Extension Idea: If you have a small group, repeat the rhyme using each child's name.*

## Segue

*(Open the mailbox and take out the next valentine; hold it up. Discuss clues on the envelope if you like, and open it.) Say:* This valentine looks kind of like a piece of *(pause for input)* cheese! I wonder who it might be from? Hmmm, I think it might be from someone really little. There's not any writing on it. *(Guess together whom the valentine could be from.)* I think it is from Little Mouse!

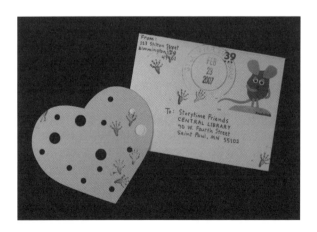

## Read Aloud

*Mouse's First Valentine* by Lauren Thompson, illustrated by Buket Erdogan. Simon & Schuster Books for Young Readers, 2002. Toddler–PK. Little Mouse follows his big sister Minka around the house and wonders what she is making as she collects red paper, lace, ribbon, and paste. He discovers at the end of the story that Minka has made him a valentine!

*Extension Idea: Retell the story with props and puppets. (See page 57.) Use a mouse hand puppet as big sister Minka mouse and have her hold up each of the (real) craft supplies she finds. As she does so, hold up your stick puppet Little Mouse and collectively ask, "What could it be?" in squeaky little voices just like Little Mouse does in the story. At the end of the story, hold up Minka's valentine for Little Mouse.*

*Extension Craft: Make Little Mouse and his valentine from big sister Minka!*

## Segue

*Say:* I think we have two last valentines waiting for us in our mailbox. This one is from someone named Cornelia Augusta. *(Point to return address.)* That must be this girl right here. *(Point to the cover of your remaining storytime book on display.)* Let's see what she wrote to us. *(Open envelope and remove valentine. Read it aloud, following the text with your finger.)* "Dear Storytime Friends, Guess what? One day it started raining hearts where I live! I will tell you all about it in my story. Love, Cornelia Augusta."

## Read Aloud

*The Day It Rained Hearts* by Felicia Bond. Laura Geringer Books, 2002, 1983. PK–2. On the day it rains hearts, Cornelia Augusta makes Valentine cards from the "heart rain" for four of her friends. Originally published in 1983 under the title *Four Valentines in a Rainstorm*, this new edition is larger in size and more easily visible for group viewing.

*Extension Craft: If you hung heart raindrops from the ceiling or taped them around your storytime space ahead of time, have each child "catch" one after storytime is done. Provide glue sticks, safety scissors, hole punches, cotton balls, colored paper, ribbon or yarn, paper lace doilies, markers, and crayons for the children to make their own valentines from the "heart raindrops."*

## Segue

*(Open the mailbox and take out the last valentine.) Say:* Here is the very last valentine card in our mailbox. There don't seem to be many clues on the envelope about who it's from, except some numbers. I see the numbers *(point to each number and say it together as a group)* 1-2-3-4-5. *(Look quizzical, then open the envelope.)* Oh! There are FIVE valentines in this envelope, and they have a little goodbye poem for you!

## Poem with Props

Share "Five Little Valentines" with your five valentines in their envelope and a mailbox.

"Five Little Valentines"

Five little valentines were having a race.

The first little valentine was covered with lace.

The second little valentine had a happy face.

The third little valentine was red and blue.

The fourth little valentine said, "I love you!"

The fifth little valentine was sly as a fox—

He ran the fastest to your valentine [mail]box!

In *Ring A Ring O'Roses: Finger Plays for Preschool Children* (11th ed.) compiled and edited by Charles Hansen and Cynthia Stilley. Flint Public Library, Michigan, 2000.

*Extension Craft: Make a five little valentines craft to match the poem. Glue or tape a copy of the poem to the outside of a large envelope and place the valentines inside for families to share together at home.*

## Conclusion

Prepare valentines ahead of time for the children in your group, and hide them in the mailbox to which the fifth little valentine runs at the end of "Five Little Valentines." Have the valentine open the mailbox and say in a squeaky valentine voice, "Look! There's a valentine for each of you to take home!" Allow the children to each select a valentine from the mailbox. Make sure to have plenty of extras in case they need to take one for a sibling.

## Additional Resources

*Alexander and the Wind-Up Mouse* by Leo Lionni. Pantheon, 1969. PK–1. Alexander the mouse makes friends with a toy mouse named Willy and wants to be just like him until he discovers that Willy is to be thrown away.

*Bill and Pete* by Tomie de Paola. Putnam, 1978. K–2. When Bill the Crocodile is captured with the intent of being turned into a suitcase, his good friend and toothbrush Pete the Plover comes to the rescue. (Available in Spanish.)

***Do You Want to Be My Friend?*** by Eric Carle. Crowell, 1971. Toddler–Grade 1. A mouse searches everywhere for a friend. (Available as a BIG Book.)

***Friends*** by Helme Heine. Atheneum, 1982. Translation of: Freunde. PK–2. Three friends who love to be together come to the realization that sometimes it's just not possible. (Available as a BIG Book.)

**George and Martha books** by James Marshall. Houghton Mifflin. PK–2. Classic stories about two best friends.

***The Giant Hug*** by Sandra Horning, illustrated by Valeri Gorbachev. Knopf, 2005. PK–2. When Owen sends a real hug to his grandmother for her birthday, he inadvertently brings cheer to the postal workers as they pass the hug along.

***Hug Me*** by Patti Stren. HarperCollins, 2002, 1977. PK–2. Porcupine Elliot Kravitz is unhappy that nobody is willing to hug him because of his sharp quills.

**Extension Ideas:** This story is fun to share with puppets and props. Introduce with the poem "The Porcupine" by Karla Kuskin, in *The Family Read-Aloud Holiday Treasury* selected by Alice Low, illustrated by Marc Brown. Little, Brown and Company, 1991, and show the children some African porcupine quills (they're pointed but not sharp). Share selected photographs and information about porcupines from a nonfiction title before you begin.

***I Love You: A Rebus Poem*** by Jean Marzollo, illustrated by Suse MacDonald. Scholastic, 2000. Grades 1–4. In this poem with a rebus format, the author professes love equal to that of a bird for a tree, a flower for a bee, and a lock for a key.

Before you begin, explain that a rebus is a type of riddle for a reader to solve. The rebus is made up of symbols or pictures that suggest the sounds of the words or syllables they represent. For example, a picture of an eye would represent "I." The letter "U" would stand for "you." A picture of a dog would represent the word "dog." "Bookworm" would be shown by a picture of a book + (plus sign) a picture of a worm.

**Extension Craft:** Have your students make their own rebus valentine mini-books.

**"I Made My Dog a Valentine"** in *It's Valentine's Day* by Jack Prelutsky, pictures by Yossi Abolafia. Greenwillow Books, 1983. K–4. A young boy wonders if it's really worth making valentines for his pets since they don't seem to appreciate them very much!

**Extension Craft:** What kind of valentine would you make for an animal? For example, what kind of shape or picture might a dog like on his valentine? If your school or library has a pet animal, make valentines for it. Make valentines for pets at home. Assign animals from each letter of the alphabet, and have each student make a valentine for his or her assigned animal; arrange the finished valentines alphabetically on a bulletin board.

**"The Lion and the Mouse"** by Aesop. Many versions of this story are available in collections of Aesop's Fables. PK–2. A tiny mouse helps a mighty lion, who had once showed him mercy, escape from a trap. "Little friends may prove to be great friends!"

**Extension Idea:** Tell this story with a lion hand puppet, a little mouse finger puppet, and a piece of net.

***Larabee*** by Kevin Luthardt. Peachtree Publishers, 2004. PK–1. The mailman's dog, Larabee, helps deliver letters and packages to everyone on the route except himself.

***Little Blue and Little Yellow*** by Leo Lionni. McDowell, Obolensky, 1959. A little blue spot and a little yellow spot are best friends. When they hug each other they become green!

**Extension Idea:** Cut out blue and yellow acetate circles for yourself and for each of the children in your group. (Colored acetate is available at art supply stores.) Share Margaret Read MacDonald's poem about Little Blue and Little Yellow in the "Color Me Red!" section of her storytime planning book *Booksharing: 101 Programs to Use with Preschoolers* (Library Professional Publications, 1988). Supply a copy of the poem and an envelope for each child so they may take their colored circles home after storytime.

***Love and Kisses, Kitty: A Lift-the-Flap Valentine*** by Max Haynes. Dutton Children's Books, 1999. Toddler–K. Kitty delivers valentines to each of her friends. The reader lifts the flap of each valentine to discover who receives it.

**Extension Idea:** Make valentines to match each of Kitty's, and retell the story with puppets.

**Extension Craft:** Provide animal-shaped paper cutouts or animal stickers, paper hearts, glue sticks, crayons, and markers for the children to make valentines for one of Kitty's animal friends or for Kitty.

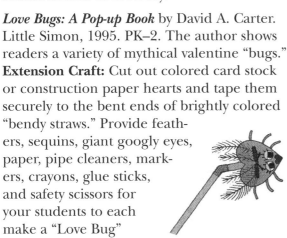

*Love Bugs: A Pop-up Book* by David A. Carter. Little Simon, 1995. PK–2. The author shows readers a variety of mythical valentine "bugs."

**Extension Craft:** Cut out colored card stock or construction paper hearts and tape them securely to the bent ends of brightly colored "bendy straws." Provide feathers, sequins, giant googly eyes, paper, pipe cleaners, markers, crayons, glue sticks, and safety scissors for your students to each make a "Love Bug" stick puppet.

**"Mail Myself to You"** by Woody Guthrie. Available on the following sound recordings: *Mail Myself To You* by John McCutcheon (Rounder Records Corp., 1988) and *This Land Is Your Land* by Woody and Arlo Guthrie (Rounder Records Corp., 1997). K–4. The singer mails himself to a friend!

**Extension Craft:** We can't really send ourselves through the mail in real life, but we can send letters and cards to let people know that we love them. Have the children draw a picture of themselves on heavy paper, or decorate a pre-cut child cutout to look like themselves. Have the children fold their self-portraits and put them in envelopes. Address to the children's home(s) and mail to their parents/caregivers, or send the envelopes home with the children. Keep in mind that children with multiple residences may want or need to make multiple copies of the craft.

*Making Friends* by Fred Rogers, photographs by Jim Judkis. Putnam, 1987. PK–K. Explains what it means to be friends and some of the easy and difficult aspects of friendship.

*Mama, Do You Love Me?* by Barbara M. Joosse, illustrated by Barbara Lavallee. Chronicle Books, 1991. PK–2. A child living in the Arctic learns that a mother's love is unconditional. (Available as a BIG Book.)

*Max's Valentine* by Rosemary Wells. Viking, 2003. Toddler–PK. Ruby uses all the candy to make her Valentine cards, but Grandma makes sure that Max ends up with some candy of his own. (Board Book.)

*May I Bring a Friend?* by Beatrice Schenk de Regniers, illustrated by Beni Montresor. Atheneum, 1965. PK–1. What could be more natural, when invited by the king and queen to tea, than to ask to bring a friend? The gracious king and queen welcome all of the friends over a series of days, including giraffes, lions, hippos, and monkeys. On the seventh day, the king and queen have tea at the zoo. The illustrations are a combination of small-size black-and-white drawings and larger pictures with minimal colors due to the book's older publication date, but the story is still delightful.

**"The More We Get Together"** on the sound recordings *Singable Songs for the Very Young* by Raffi (Troubador Records Ltd., 1976) and *If You're Happy & You Know It ... Sing Along with Bob #1* by Bob McGrath (Bob's Kids Music, 1996). Words and music are in Tom Glazer's *Eye Winker, Tom Tinker, Chin Chopper: Fifty Musical Fingerplays*. Doubleday, 1973. Toddler–Grade 2.

**Extension Idea:** Use sign language for MORE, TOGETHER, HAPPY, YOUR, MY, and FRIEND as you sing.

**"Mother's Chocolate Valentine"** in *It's Valentine's Day* by Jack Prelutsky, pictures by Yossi Abolafia. Greenwillow Books, 1983. K–3. The author inadvertently eats all of the valentine chocolates he bought for his mother, so he hopes that she will like the empty box!

**Extension Idea:** Purchase a fancy heart-shaped box of chocolates and remove all of the chocolates ahead of time, leaving most of the paper wrappers in the box. As you say the poem, position the lid of the box so the audience can't see that it is actually already empty, and pretend to eat the candy while you say the poem. Appear slightly dismayed but hopeful as you show everyone the empty box and wrappers at the end of the poem.

*My Best Friend* by Pat Hutchins. Greenwillow Books, 1993. PK–1. Despite differences in abilities, two little girls appreciate each other and are "best friends."

*My Daddy* by Susan Paradis. Front Street, 1998. Toddler–PK. A young boy marvels at the things his daddy can do, including cross the street alone, run outside without a coat, stay up way past midnight, and wander in the deepest woods.

*My Very Own Octopus* by Bernard Most. Harcourt Brace Jovanovich, 1991. PK–1. Having a pet octopus would offer its owner many advantages, including being able to take out more books from the library because the octopus could help carry them.
**Extension Idea:** Share the following Valentine's Day riddle—What did one octopus say to the other octopus on Valentine's Day? (ANSWER: I want to hold your hand hand hand hand hand hand hand hand!)

*Never Too Little to Love* by Jeanne Willis, illustrated by Jan Fearnley. Candlewick Press, 2005. PK–1. Tiny Too-Little loves somebody who's very, very tall, and Tiny really needs a kiss. Turn the pages to see Tiny make himself taller and taller.

*One Zillion Valentines* by Frank Modell. Greenwillow Books, 1981. PK–2. When Marvin shows Milton how to make valentines, they decide to make one for each person in their neighborhood.

*Our Valentine's Day Book* by Jane Belk Moncure, illustrated by Mina McLean and Carole Boerke. The Child's World, 1987. K–4 (for the craft). A child describes the kindergarten's activities as they prepare for Valentine's Day. In one segment, the students make a "Valentine Animal Park," creating a Leopartine, Lionatine, Elephantine, Giraffetine, and a Whaletine, among other valentine animals.
**Extension Idea:** What would an animal look like if it was made entirely out of hearts? It would be an "animal valentine," or maybe an "animaltine." Provide your students with lots of multi-size heart shapes or have them cut hearts out on their own; then try creating your own "Valentine Zoo" using the heart shapes to make each animal. Paste the shapes down onto paper; then add features

with markers or crayons. Older children can try partially slitting the valentine shapes so that they will fit together and make stand-up three-dimensional animals. Please note that the valentine shapes must be cut from sturdy paper such as card stock for the stand-up animals.

*Papa, Do You Love Me?* by Barbara M. Joosse, illustrated by Barbara Lavallee. Chronicle Books, 2005. PK–2. When a Masai father in Africa answers his son's questions, the boy learns that his father's love for him is unconditional.

*Play with Me* by Marie Hall Ets. Viking, 1955. PK–1. A little girl goes to the meadow to play, but each animal she tries to catch runs away from her until she sits quietly by the pond, and they all come back.

*Skidamarink: A Silly Love Song to Sing Together* illustrated by G. Brian Karas. HarperFestival, 2001. PK–K. Playful pictures of a penguin and polar bear couple ice-skating are a fitting accompaniment to this familiar love song.

*Swimmy* by Leo Lionni. Pantheon, 1963. PK–2. A little black fish in a school of red fish figures out a way of protecting them all from their natural enemies. (Available as a BIG Book.)

*This Is My Friend* by Mercer Mayer. (Little Critter.) Western Publishing Company, 1989. PK–1. Two friends experience the vicissitudes of friendship.

*The Valentine Bears* by Eve Bunting, pictures by Jan Brett. Clarion Books, 1983. K–2. Mrs. Bear plans a surprise Valentine's Day celebration for Mr. Bear despite their usual hibernating habits at that time of year.

**"A Valentine for Kitten"** in *Paper Stories* by Jean Stangl. Fearon Teacher Aids, 1984. The farm animals team up to cut a red valentine for Kitten's arrival on February 14.

*Valentine Friends* by April Jones Prince, illustrated by Elisabeth Schlossberg. Scholastic, 2007. Toddler–K. One group of animals teams up to make paper valentines while the other group bakes valentine cakes—then the two groups share!

*Valentine's Day At the Zoo: A Pop-Up Book* by Nadine Bernard Westcott. Little Simon, 2002. Toddler–Grade 1. The zoo animals bring various craft supplies to make a valentine for the reader.

**Extension Craft:** *Ask:* "If the animals at the zoo were making you a valentine, what do you think it would look like?" Provide the children with the same craft materials that the animals in the story bring to make their valentine for the reader: red and yellow paper, glue (sticks), crayons, and white paper doilies. Consider pre-cutting the paper and doilies into hearts or animal shapes for very young crafters.

*Yo! Yes?* by Chris Raschka. Orchard Books, 1993. PK–1. Two lonely children meet and become friends.

*We Are Best Friends* by Aliki. Greenwillow Books, 1982. K–2. When Robert's best friend Peter moves away, both are initially unhappy but learn that they can make new friends and still remain best friends.

# Story Prop and Craft Directions

## Valentines from the Storybook Characters

### Tools and Supplies

- colored card stock
- colored pencils, markers or crayons
- thematic stickers or decorations as desired
- pen
- envelopes, various sizes to match valentines
- cancelled postage stamps or postage stamp-like stickers

**Directions**

1. Copy the valentine patterns from pages 53–58 onto colored card stock, or design your own valentines to match your storytime selections.

   - *Be Mine, Be Mine, Sweet Valentine*: bone valentine
   - "Valentine from a Bear": beehive heart with bear
   - "Skinnamarink": hugging valentine
   - *What A Wonderful World*: earth valentine
   - *Mouse's First Valentine*: cheese heart
   - *Four Valentines in a Rainstorm*: heart letter
   - "Five Little Valentines": five hearts, cut one with leg holes as shown on the pattern

2. Decorate the valentines as desired, and insert valentines into appropriately sized envelopes. Address the envelopes accordingly, and decorate with doodle or sticker "clues" about their contents.

## Mouse's First Valentine Storytime Prop and Student Craft

### Tools and Supplies

- safety scissors
- paper punch
- glue sticks
- crayons and colored pencils
- cellophane tape
- double-stick tape
- red paper
- white paper lace doilies
- pink ribbon or yarn
- gray construction paper or card stock
- gray yarn
- wooden craft or Popsicle® sticks
- baggies or paper bowls

## Prepare in Advance
## (if your group is very young):

Photocopy or trace the heart pattern from page 57 onto red paper for each child and cut the hearts out. Cut one 12" length of pink ribbon or yarn for each child. Punch two holes near the center top of each heart as shown. Photocopy the mouse pattern from page 57 onto gray paper for each child. Cut them out. Cut one 6" length of gray yarn for each child. For ease of distribution, pre-package the craft supplies into a baggie or bowl craft kit for each child: one red heart, one white paper lace doily, one 12" length of pink ribbon or yarn, one mouse, one 6" length of gray yarn (mouse tail) and one wooden craft or Popsicle stick in each kit. Make a sample of the finished product to show the children, but encourage them to be creative and make the craft in their own way.

## Directions

1. Distribute one craft kit to each child.

2. Have the children put the yarn or ribbon through the holes in the paper heart, and help them tie it in a bow if they wish.

3. Have the children decorate the valentines however they wish and glue them to the paper lace doily.

4. Have the children color their mouse and tape his yarn tail to his body from behind.

5. Glue or double-stick tape the finished mouse to the craft or Popsicle stick.

# "Five Little Valentines" Story Prop and Student Craft

## Tools and Supplies

- scissors
- red and blue card stock or poster board
- paper lace doilies
- markers, colored pencils, or crayons
- enhancements such as stickers, pipe cleaners, googly eyes, fake fur, and so forth
- large envelope with poem affixed

## Directions

1. Copy the "Five Little Valentines" pattern from page 58 and trace five copies of the heart onto card stock or poster board.

2. Cut out the two leg/finger holes on the pattern and trace the holes onto one of the five hearts to be the "sly as a fox" running valentine. Cut out the holes and make sure they are large enough for the storyteller's index and middle fingers!

3. Decorate the valentines as desired, applying special features such as lace, the words "I Love You," and so forth to match the text of the poem.

4. Affix a copy of the "Five Little Valentines" poem to the outside of a large envelope for each student, and place the five valentines in the envelope.

# Valentine Patterns

Be Mine, Be Mine, Sweet Valentine

HAPPY VALENTINE'S DAY TO OUR STORYTIME FRIENDS. WE HOPE YOU CAN READ OUR BOOK FIRST! FROM YOUR WAGGY DIGGER FRIENDS

**The Day It Rained Hearts**

Dear Storytime Friends, Guess what? One day it started raining hearts where I live! I will tell you all about it in my story. Love, Cornelia Augusta

BEE MINE

Roses are red
Violets are blue
Honey is sweet
And so are you!
XOXO from
BEAR

# Valentine Patterns

"Skinnamarink"

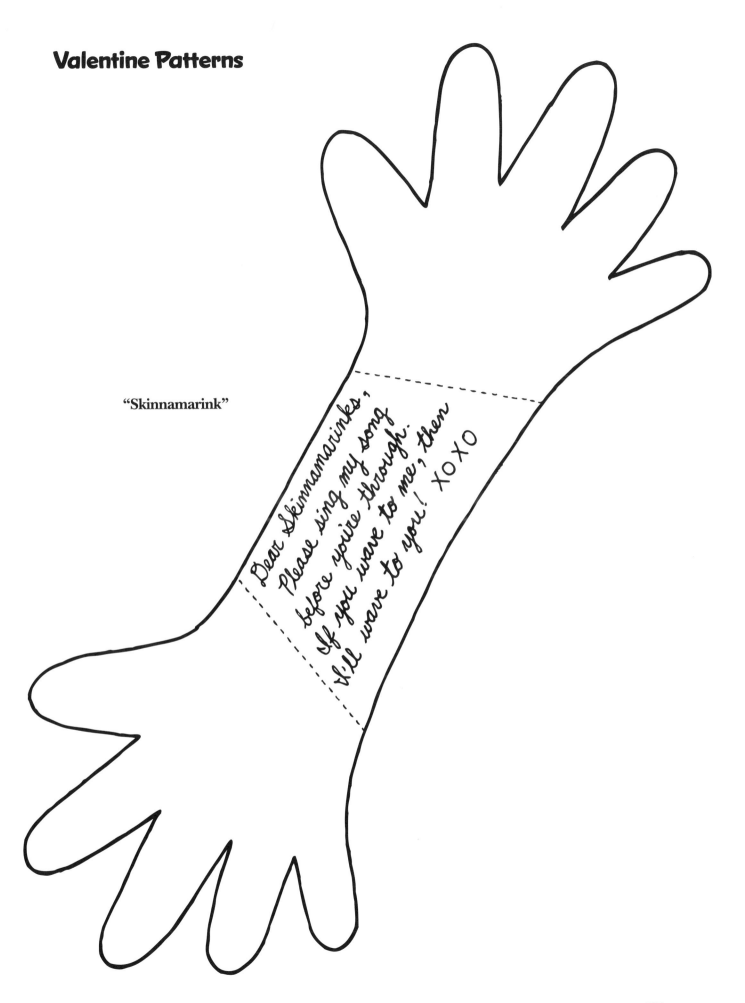

Dear Skinnamarinks,
Please sing my song
before you're through.
If you wave to me, then
I'll wave to you! XOXO

# Valentine Patterns

"What a Wonderful World"

# Valentine Patterns

"Mouse's First Valentine"
Heart Pattern

"Mouse's First Valentine"
Mouse Pattern

"Mouse's First Valentine"
Cheese Valentine

**"Five Little Valentines"**

"Five Little Valentines"

# Five Little Valentines

Five little valentines were having a race.

The first little valentine was covered with lace.

The second little valentine had a happy face.

The third little valentine was red and blue.

The fourth little valentine said, "I love you!"

The fifth little valentine was sly as a fox—

He ran the fastest to your valentine [mail]box!

# Extraordinary Eggs
## March

## Early Literacy Activities

### Name Tags

Egg stamp or sticker

### Storytime Clue

Plastic craft or toy egg

### Mailbox "Letter" of the Day

"E" and "e"

Egg, Elephant, Elbow, End, Everyone, Elevator, Enter, Empty

### Mother Goose Rhyme Time

*Hickety Pickety*

*Hickety Pickety, my black hen,*
*She lays eggs for women and men.*
*Sometimes ONE,*
*And sometimes TEN!*
*Hickety Pickety, my black hen.*

### Rhyming Basket

Egg/Peg; Hen/Pen; Block/Clock

### Early Literacy Skill: Phonological Awareness

Play with rhymes, practice breaking words apart and putting them back together, and listen for beginning sounds and alliteration.

- Play with the rhyming basket, and give clues for more rhyming words for which you don't have representative objects in the basket. For example, "I'm thinking of something that rhymes with 'egg' and 'peg' from our rhyming basket. This rhyming word is part of my body. It's not my arm, it's my _____. *(Leg.)* 'Egg, peg, leg.'" And, "I'm thinking of something that rhymes with "hen" and "pen" from our rhyming basket. It's the number that comes after nine—_____. *(Ten.)*

- Write out the words to the rhyme "Hickety Pickety" on a piece of grid board, and clap once for each word in the rhyme. Introduce variety by stomping feet or jumping once for each word.

- Share *Big Fat Hen* by Keith Baker (Harcourt Brace, 1994) rhythmically, emphasizing the rhyming words as you reach them.

- Blend word parts in several ways. For example, <u>Onset sound</u>: /h/ ... en. What's the word? *(Hen.)* What other words start with /h/? <u>Syllables</u>: buck ... le. What's the word? *(Buckle.)*

# Program Summary and Theme

Hatch some springtime stories together with your audience. If possible, purchase a few giant three-dimensional plastic lawn ornament eggs for decoration, or cut some large egg shapes from heavy poster board. Make a big nest from a large basket or bowl lined with raffia, and put the eggs into it! Arrange your storytime books and props around and in the nest, or hide some of them inside a large egg that comes apart in the middle.

Prepare the props and puppets ahead of time so you can use them throughout the program. Please see patterns and instructions on pages 66–74. See additional suggested titles on pages 64–66 to substitute for older or younger audiences.

## Music

Play "egg" or "chicken" music as the audience is gathering in your storytime area. Possibilities include "Baby Chickie" on *SO BIG: Activity Songs for Little Ones* by Hap Palmer (Hap-Pal, 1994); "Philadelphia Chickens" on *Philadelphia Chickens* by Sandra Boynton (Boynton, 2002); "Cluck, Cluck, Red Hen" on *The Corner Grocery Store* by Raffi (Troubadour, 1979); "C-H-I-C-K-E-N" on the sound recording *Your Shoes, My Shoes* by Tom Paxton (Red House Records, 2002); "The Mack Chicken Dance" on *Big Fun* by Greg & Steve (Youngheart, 1997); "The Chicken Song" on *Wee Sing in the Car* by Pamela Conn Beall and Susan Hagen Nipp (Price Stern Sloan, 2002); and many others.

# Sample Program

Please adjust content and length as needed.

## Introduction

*Say:* I brought some storytime surprises to show you. *(Hold up the four "Egg Surprise" eggs in a basket; see pages 66–72 for patterns and directions on how to make them.)* These are storytime eggs, not real eggs. If they were real eggs, we should leave them alone, but since they're pretend storytime eggs we can touch them and hold them! What do you think might hatch out of this one? *(Hold up one of the eggs. Take guesses; all guesses are good guesses.)* We might need to learn a little bit about eggs and what different ones look like before we can really figure out what might be inside.

## Read Aloud

Share a few selected pictures and facts from an informational book with good color photographs of different types of eggs, such as *Egg: A Photographic Story of Hatching* by Robert Burton, photographed by Jane Burton and Kim Taylor. Dorling Kindersley, 1994. PK–4. Photographs show various creatures that hatch from eggs.

## Segue

*Say:* Now that we've seen pictures of some different eggs, we might be able to figure out what's inside these storytime eggs!

## Poem with Props

Share "Egg Surprise" with your four egg props.

Eggs come in many sizes.
*(Hold up basket with four eggs in it.)*

Eggs hold some big surprises.
*(Nod and look mysterious.)*

Speckled, orange, white, or blue;
*(Hold up each egg in turn, encourage audience to name orange, white, and blue colors with you.)*

Eggs hold babies that are new!
*(Gently open each egg to reveal its surprise baby inside, guessing as a group what it might be. Note that Araucana chickens lay blue eggs.)*

If desired, sing a little "hatching song" as each egg hatches:

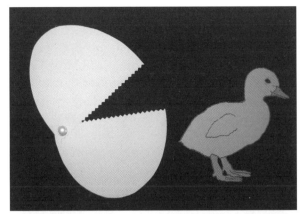

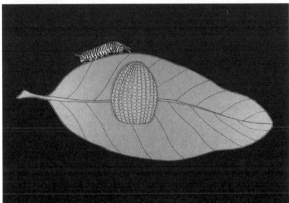

*(Sung to the tune: "The Farmer in the Dell")*

It's time for you to hatch,
It's time for you to hatch.
Peck-peck (OR nibble-nibble), crack-crack!
It's time for you to hatch.

## Segue

*Say:* Imagine if YOU were a little baby bird or reptile or fish or insect in an egg, how would your body be positioned in there? Would you have lots of room to stretch? *(Stretch your arms out wide.)* No! You'd be curled up tight like this. *(Crouch down in a ball with arms around your head.)* We get to pretend to be different creatures that hatch from eggs.

## Action Rhyme (Crouching/Standing)

Little chick in your egg,
*(Crouch down with arms curled over your head.)*
Sitting so still.
Little chick, will you hatch?
"Yes! I will!"
*(Jump up enthusiastically, mimicking the actions of the type of creature that just hatched. Encourage the children to call out their answer.)*

REPEAT with other creatures that hatch(ed) from eggs, such as duck, turtle, snake, dinosaur, platypus, caterpillar.

*(Make your voices sound "quacky" for the baby duck, speak and move slowly for the turtle, hiss "Yesssssss!" for the snake, and so forth!)*

*Extension Idea: Demonstrate the poem with your "Will You Hatch?" pop-up craft. See patterns and instructions on pages 67–68 and 73.*

Little chick
in your egg,
Sitting so still.
Little chick,
will you hatch?
"Yes! I will!"

## Segue

*Say:* The more we learn about eggs and what they look like, the more likely we will be able to tell what kind of creature might hatch out of each egg. In this next story, though, there's an egg that is a real mystery!

## Read Aloud

*I Want A Pet* by Lauren Child. Tricycle Press, 1999. PK–2. A girl tries to select a pet that will not eat her, be a copycat, make too much noise, or leave dirty footprints around the house.

Howl with the wolf, count the octopus' footprints, help Mom shrilly refuse to have a bat in the closet, and so forth.

*Extension Idea: Buy a giant plastic purple lawn ornament egg, or spray paint a differently colored one purple with "fusion" paint that adheres to plastic (available at craft and hardware stores). Make furry pointed ears or buy some ready-made from a costume shop or second-hand store to match those in the story, and hot glue them to the top of the egg as shown on the book's back endpapers. Produce the mysterious egg at the end of the story. Imagine together what could possibly be inside!*

## Segue

*Say:* We don't really know what will hatch out of that unusual story egg; the author doesn't tell us, so we can use our imaginations and have it be whatever we want it to be! Since that was kind of a silly book, I thought I would show you a REALLY silly book. It has riddles, or jokes, in it. See if you can guess the answers to some of these egg and chicken riddles.

## Riddles

Share several riddles from the early reader book *Chickie Riddles* by Katy Hall and Lisa Eisenberg, pictures by Thor Wickstrom. Puffin Books, 1997. PK–3.

For example:

Why should you never tell a joke to an egg? (ANSWER: Because it might crack up!)

What game do baby chicks love to play? (ANSWER: Peck-a-boo!)

What's the favorite game in the henhouse? (ANSWER: Chickers.)

## Segue

*Say:* I have a little hen I would like to introduce to you. Produce hen sitting in basket "nest." *(Hide the accordion-folded egg template*

*and a pair of safety scissors underneath her ahead of time.)* Her name is Hickety Pickety. *To hen:* Hickety Pickety, have you laid any eggs yet today? What? You're having a problem? Let me see … *(Reach under Hickety Pickety, clucking wildly for her, and remove the folded egg template and scissors. Hold them up for the audience to see.)* Oh! No wonder you were feeling uncomfortable! It doesn't look like those would be very smooth to sit on. Let's see what we can do about that.

## Mother Goose Rhyme

Share "Hickety Pickety" as a cut-and-tell rhyme (see pattern and instructions on page 74) with a hen puppet or plush, or see the *Mother Goose Rhyme Time: Animals* kit from UpstartBooks, 2006. If your hen isn't black, you can say "my little hen" instead of "my black hen."

### "Hickety Pickety" Cut-and-Tell

Hickety Pickety, my black hen,
*(Hold up hen and point to her; pat lap rhythmically.)*
She lays eggs for women and men.
*(Cut egg shape through all of the folded layers, following the egg outline. Make sure to leave the two flat sides attached!)*
Sometimes ONE,
*(Hold up single folded egg shape.)*
And sometimes TEN!
*(Dramatically open the folded egg panels; count them together the first time through.)*
Hickety Pickety, my black hen.
*(Hold up hen and point to her; pat lap rhythmically.)*

Fold the accordion egg back up again and repeat the rhyme several times together with the audience. Say it slowly, whisper it, sing it, then say it very quickly the last time through!

Return the now comfortably rounded egg(s) beneath Hickety Pickety for her to "hatch," and thank her for helping you with her rhyme. Put the safety scissors away in a secure location.

Write out the words to "Hickety Pickety" ahead of time on a piece of grid board so the adults in the audience can follow along. Try clapping once for each word in the rhyme.

## Segue

*Say:* This next book is about a mother hen and her ten baby chicks, as well. It's from a rhyme that begins "One, two, buckle my shoe ..." Some of you may already know it! If you do, please say it with me as we read the book.

## Read Aloud

*Big Fat Hen* by Keith Baker. Harcourt Brace, 1994. Toddler–Grade 1. Big Fat Hen counts to ten with her hen friends and all their chicks.

Read rhythmically, keeping a beat by patting your lap with your free hand as you go along. Encourage the audience to say the words with you if they already know the rhyme. Count the big fat hen's chicks together to make sure there are really ten.

*Extension Idea: If your group is really in a counting mood and you have plenty of time, you can count all of the hen's friends' fifty eggs or chicks!*

## Segue

*Say:* We have time for one more song and then one last story. This song is something that you may hear if you go to weddings where they dance afterwards. It is called "The Chicken." You'll probably need to know how to do this when you're a grown-up, so we'll practice it now!

Note: Some cultures and religions don't allow dancing, so you may want to describe this differently or substitute "I Know A Chicken" or an alternate activity if you have children in your group who would be unable to participate.

## Action Dance (Standing)

Do an adapted version of the "Chicken Dance" with your audience (instrumental "The Chicken") on the sound recording *All-Time Favorite Dances* (Kimbo Educational, 1991).

If your group is set up to successfully "swing partners," go ahead and try it. Otherwise do the beak, flap, shake tail, and clapping parts as usual; then simply flap and cluck noisily while revolving in place during the "swing your partner" part.

OR

Share the echo and action song "I Know A Chicken" from the sound recording *Whaddaya Think of That?* by Laurie Berkner (Two Tomatoes, 2000) with egg shakers. Use the CD, or sing it yourself with a variety of ways to shake each time you repeat the song: slow, high, low, up and down, in a circle, in a triangle, soft, loud, and so forth. You can also be the "shaky eggs" yourselves, and shake your bodies if you don't have access to egg shakers!

*Extension Craft: Older children can make egg shakers from plastic take-apart eggs and rice. Tape the eggs securely together with cloth tape or book tape.*

## Read Aloud OR Flannel/Prop Story

*Mrs. Hen's Big Surprise* by Christel Desmoinaux. Margaret K. McElderry Books, 2000. PK–1. When Mrs. Hen discovers a very large, strange-looking egg in her garden, she is sure it will hatch into the baby chick of her dreams. Her patience is rewarded when the egg hatches at last, although she is in for a bit of a surprise when her new baby turns out to be a dinosaur!

OR

Make storytelling props for *The Most Wonderful Egg in the World* by Helme Heine. Atheneum, 1983. PK–3. To settle a quarrel between three hens, the king must choose which one lays the most wonderful egg. Complete instructions and a storytelling script are included in *Books in Bloom: Creative Patterns & Props That Bring Stories to Life.* (ALA Editions, 2003.)

*Special Handout Idea: To accompany* The Most Wonderful Egg in the World, *punch out die-cut crowns from card stock or purchase gold foil cardboard crowns for the children to wear home, "just like the chickens." (See Resources, page 212.)*

## Conclusion

*Say:* Our storytime today had lots of EXTRAORDINARY eggs in it—that means they were special, remarkable, unusual, different—each in their own way. Each of you is extraordinary and wonderful in your own way, too, just like all of the eggs we learned about with their many surprises. You can give people some nice surprises this week—share a special story or picture or joke with your family and friends!

## Craft Ideas

- Make baby chicks with round egg-shaped bodies, attaching flappable wings to their sides with metal brad fasteners or knotted yarn. Give each chick googly eyes and a foamies beak, or draw them on. Provide colored craft feathers, felt, foamies, Tacky Glue, glitter, crayons, markers, and so forth for children to decorate their chicks as desired. Glue on orange feet that stick out below the body, or hole punch two leg holes and twist orange pipe cleaners through them for legs and feet. Use a hen puppet to comment approvingly in a chicken voice on the lovely chicken children as they are being made.

- Make egg-laying Hickety Pickety hens from styrofoam or paper cups. Glue craft feathers, eyes, a beak, comb and wattle to the upside-down cup to make Hickety Pickety. Give each child plastic Easter eggs to hide under his/her Hickety Pickety cup. Say the rhyme as you lift the hen to reveal her magically appearing eggs.

## Additional Extension Ideas

- Make an "Egg-Laying Black Hen." Complete instructions are included in the book *Crafts From Your Favorite Nursery Rhymes* by Kathy Ross (Millbrook Press, 2002).

- Adapt a "Little White Duck" craft as a "Baby Chick" simply by changing the shape of the bird's construction paper feet. The bird's body is made from the outline of the child's foot, and the two wings are made from tracings of the child's two hands. See "Little White Duck" in *Crafts to Make in the Spring* by Kathy Ross (Milbrook Press, 1998).

## Additional Resources

*Charlie Chick: A Pop-up Book* by Nick Denchfield and Ant Parker. Harcourt, 2007. (Reissue of *Charlie the Chicken.* Harcourt Brace, 1997.) Toddler–Grade 1. Charlie the chicken eats lots of healthy food so he will grow big and strong.

*Chickens Aren't the Only Ones* by Ruth Heller. Grosset & Dunlap, 1981. PK–2. An overview of oviparous (egg-laying) creatures.

**"Chicks"** by Eric Finney in *Here's A Little Poem: A Very First Book of Poetry* collected by Jane Yolen and Andrew Fusek Peters, illustrated by Polly Dunbar. Candlewick Press, 2007. PK–1. In this extremely brief yet visually descriptive poem, "warm, brown eggs" become fluffy baby chicks seemingly overnight!
**Extension Idea:** Share the poem with the illustrations, and then repeat several times with props. Spray paint plastic pull-apart eggs a light brown color. Make bright yellow pompom balls that will slip easily inside the eggs, and add orange pipe cleaner legs, orange felt beaks, and googly eyes to match the described "fluffy, yellow balls—on legs."

*The Cow That Laid an Egg* by Andy Cutbill, illustrated by Russell Ayto. HarperCollins Children's Books, 2008. PK–2. When Marjorie the cow feels depressed over her lack of any special talents, her chicken friends conspire to help her lay an egg! The other cows grow suspicious and everyone waits for the baby to hatch and prove that it is indeed Marjorie's. When the feathery baby appears, it seems clear that it is indeed a chicken after all; however, its first word of "Moooooooo!" reveals that it inarguably belongs to Marjorie.
**Extension Idea:** Paint black spots on a white plastic or hard-boiled egg to extend the story.

*Daisy and the Egg* by Jane Simmons. Little, Brown and Company, 1998. PK–1. Daisy the duckling eagerly awaits the arrival of a new brother or sister, even helping Mama Duck sit on the egg while they wait for it to hatch.

*Dora's Eggs* by Julie Sykes; pictures by Jane Chapman. Little Tiger Press, 1997. PK–K. As she goes around seeing the babies of the other farmyard animals, Dora becomes less and less proud of her first eggs—until they hatch into cute chicks.

*The Egg* by Dick Bruna. Routledge Kegan & Paul, 1975. Toddler–PK. When an egg mysteriously appears, the farm animals try to guess what will hatch out of it.

*The Egg Book* by Jack Kent. Macmillan, 1975. Toddler–K. In this wordless book, a hen discovers and subsequently sits on a variety of eggs (turtle, alligator, and ostrich) before finally laying and hatching an egg of her own.

*An Egg Is Quiet* by Dianna Aston, illustrated by Sylvia Long. Chronicle Books, 2006. K–4. Introduces readers to more than 60 types of eggs and an array of egg facts.

*Eggday* by Joyce Dunbar, illustrated by Jane Cabrera. Holiday House, 1999. PK–1. Dora the duck involves the other barnyard animals in a contest to find out who can lay the best egg.
**Extension Idea:** Decorate paper or three-dimensional eggs like the animals in the story. For example, paint an egg pink and attach a curly pink pipe cleaner tail for a "pig egg," and so forth.

*An Extraordinary Egg* by Leo Lionni. Knopf, 1994. K–3. Jessica the frog befriends the alligator that hatches from an egg she brought home, thinking it is a chicken. (Available as a BIG Book.)

*First the Egg* by Laura Vaccaro Seeger. Roaring Brook Press, 2007. Toddler–Grade 2. A fresh presentation of the concepts of transformation and creativity are depicted in this book with simple die-cuts that magically present change from egg to chick, tadpole to frog, seed to flower, caterpillar to butterfly, word to story, and so forth.

*Flap Your Wings* by P. D. Eastman. Random House, 2000. PK–2. Mr. and Mrs. Bird are surprised to find a very large egg in their nest, but are determined to hatch it. When Junior hatches at last, he is indeed a funny-looking baby bird since he is actually an alligator! The birds persevere, however, feeding Junior vast quantities and eventually working on teaching him to fly.

*The Golden Egg Book* by Margaret Wise Brown, illustrated by Leonard Weisgard. Golden Press, 1947. PK–1. A little bunny finds an egg and wonders what is inside of it.

*Good Morning, Chick* by Mirra Ginsburg, adapted from a story by Korney Chukovsky; pictures by Byron Barton. Greenwillow Books, 1980. Toddler–K. A newly hatched chick experiences many adventures, but is always protected and comforted by his loving mother, Speckled Hen.

*Guji Guji* by Chih-Yuan Chen. Kane/Miller, 2004. K–3. When an extra-large egg rolls right into Mother Duck's nest, she is too busy reading to notice the new addition. When her four eggs hatch, one youngster, Guji Guji, looks decidedly different (and more like a crocodile) than the others, but Mother Duck loves them all the same. When three duck-hungry crocodiles try to tempt Guji Guji into betraying his family, he comes up with a clever way to save the ducks once and for all.

*The Happy Egg* by Ruth Krauss; pictures by Crockett Johnson. HarperCollins, 2005. Toddler–K. A bird hatches from its egg and learns to fly.
**Extension Idea:** Hide a baby bird puppet inside a large plastic or cardboard take-apart egg. Make a mother bird headband or hat and act out the story with the props.

*Hatch, Egg, Hatch!* by Shen Roddie. Little, Brown and Company, 1991. PK–1. Mother Hen tries one silly thing after another to try to make her egg hatch. Includes textured and movable illustrations.

*Here A Chick, There A Chick* by Bruce McMillan. Lothrop, Lee & Shepard Books, 1983. Toddler–K. Photographs of baby chicks are used to illustrate such opposite concepts as inside/outside, asleep/awake, and alone/together.

*Horton Hatches the Egg* by Dr. Seuss. Random House, 1968. K–3. When a lazy bird hatching an egg wants a vacation, she asks Horton the elephant to sit on her egg, which he does through all sorts of hazards until he is rewarded for doing what he said he would.

*How Kind!* by Mary Murphy. Candlewick Press, 2002. Toddler–Grade 1. When Hen gives Pig an egg, she sets off a chain of events that brings kindness to all of the animals on the farm.

*Hurry! Hurry!* by Eve Bunting, illustrated by Jeff Mack. Harcourt, 2007. Toddler–Grade 1. All the animals of the barnyard community hurry to greet their newest member, who is just pecking his way out of an egg.

*Kipper and the Egg* based on the books by Mick Inkpen. Harcourt, 2001. Toddler. Kipper the dog has found an egg and wonders who it could belong to. In a surprise ending, it turns out to belong to a brontosaurus! The book is a touch-and-feel board book.
**Extension Idea:** Make flannel board cutouts to accompany the story.

*The Perfect Nest* by Catherine Friend, illustrated by John Manders. Candlewick, 2007. K–2. Jack the cat is building the perfect nest to attract the perfect chicken, who will lay the perfect egg, which will make the perfect omelet! Jack gets more than he bargained for when the chicken is joined by a duck and then by a goose. When the eggs unexpectedly hatch, Jack ends up as the doting "mother" to three feathered babies.

**"Ten Fluffy Chickens"** finger action rhyme

Five eggs
*(Hold up five fingers.)*
And five eggs,
*(Hold up other five fingers.)*
That makes ten.
Sitting on top is a mother hen.
*(Lock fingers together, knuckles up.)*

Crackle, crackle, crackle,
*(Clap hands.)*
What do you see?
*(Hands out questioningly.)*
Ten baby chicks, as yellow as can be!
*(Hold up ten fingers and wiggle them.)*
Peep! Peep! Peep! Peep! Peep! Peep! Peep! Peep! Peep! Peep!

*There Is A Bird On Your Head!* by Mo Willems. Hyperion, 2007. (Series: An Elephant and Piggie Book.) PK–2. Gerald the elephant discovers that there is something worse than a bird on your head—two birds on your head, plus a nest filled with hatching eggs!

*This Little Chick* by John Lawrence. Candlewick Press, 2002. Toddler– Grade 1. A little chick visits the other barnyard animals and is able to make sounds like each of them! The chick goes home to his mother at the end of the day and tells her all about it.
**Extension Idea:** Sing the text to the traditional tune for "I Went to Visit A Farm One Day"/"As I Went Down to the Farm One Day."

*Whose Chick Are You?* by Nancy Tafuri. Greenwillow Books, 2005. Toddler–Grade 1. Goose, Duck, Hen, Bird, and a little chick do not know to whom the newly hatched chick belongs, but Mother Swan knows.

# Story Prop and Craft Directions

## "Egg Surprise" Swivel Egg OR Three-dimensional Egg Props

### Swivel Eggs

### Tools and Supplies

- colored card stock or construction paper
- scissors
- pinking shears
- colored pencils
- four metal brad fasteners
- pictures of four oviparous (egg-laying) creatures (see pages 69–72, or find your own)
- envelope or basket large enough to comfortably hold all four eggs
- straw-like shredding or Easter grass in the basket

### Three-dimensional Eggs

### Tools and Supplies

- four three-dimensional take-apart "eggs"
- acrylic craft paint
- craft paintbrush
- four oviparous puppet/plush (duckling, caterpillar, turtle, chick)
- basket large enough to comfortably hold all four eggs
- straw-like shredding or Easter grass in the basket

## Ideas for Making Three-dimensional Eggs

These are a little bit trickier to produce than the flat paper swivel eggs, but the children love them! You'll be able to use them again and again.

- Speckled duck egg: Use a medium-size plastic or cardboard egg that comes apart and paint it gold or tan with brown speckles. Hide a duckling puppet/plush inside the egg.

- Orange butterfly egg: Purchase a tiny plastic toy holder from a gumball machine. Lightly sand the holder so paint will adhere to the plastic, or use plastic "fusion" paint. Paint the holder orange. Roll up a caterpillar finger puppet and insert it into the "egg." Consider hot gluing the base onto a felt "leaf" that you can stick to a Velcro board.

- White turtle egg: Use a spherical clear plastic Christmas ornament that comes apart and is made to be filled with miscellaneous decorations. Sand the outside of the plastic ball with sandpaper to dull the sheen, so it looks "milky." Paint the inside of the ornament white with plastic fusion paint, or sand it lightly so regular enamel paint will adhere to the smooth surface. Hide a turtle finger puppet/plush inside the egg.

- Blue Araucana chicken egg: Many light blue plastic Easter eggs are available; find one that fits your puppet or plush chick. If you can't locate a blue egg, paint one that's a different color with blue fusion paint. Hide the baby chick finger puppet/plush inside the egg.

### Directions

1. Color or paint one of your eggs tan with speckles; one orange; one white; and one blue to match the poem.

2. If making flat paper eggs, cut the flat edges of each with pinking shears. Trace the bottom egg half onto a plain piece of card stock and cut it out. Glue the piece to the back of the bottom egg around the edges, forming an open-topped "pocket."

Place the top and bottom egg halves together again, slightly overlapping the center edge. Make a small slit at one of the overlapping corners, through all layers of the egg. Insert a metal brad fastener into the slit so the egg swivels open and closed.

3. Cut out a picture of or find a baby oviparous plush/puppet creature for each egg.

4. Insert the babies into the egg pockets or into the eggs for "Egg Surprise."

## Pop-up "Will You Hatch?" Story Prop and Student Craft

### Tools and Supplies

- 8 oz. paper cups

- egg-shaped cutouts of "Will You Hatch?" rhyme

- flexible straws

- colored card stock or construction paper for chicks (cut into 2¾" squares or whatever size they need to be to fit easily down into the paper cups you are using)

- markers, stickers, pompoms, googly eyes, pipe cleaners, etc.

- Tacky Glue® craft glue

- double-stick cellophane tape

- cellophane tape

- scissors

- utility knife

### Directions

If making these crafts with a group, prepare the following ahead of time:

*Drill or cut a drinking-straw size hole in the center bottom of each paper cup. A small "x" slit with scissors or a utility knife will work if necessary. Glue the egg cutout with the "Will You Hatch?" rhyme (see pattern on page 73) to the outside of the cup, or stick it on with double-stick cellophane tape.*

1. Give each child small card stock or construction paper squares to make their chicks. (If you prefer to use a pattern, please see the chick patterns on page 73.) Have the children decorate the chicks as

desired with markers, stickers, pompoms, googly eyes, pipe cleaners, etc.

2. Glue or tape each chick to the end of the straw stem (the end nearest the flexible bend). Allow the glue to dry completely. Reinforce glued attachment points with tape if necessary.

3. Insert the end of the straw (the end furthest away from the flexible bend) down and through the inside of the cup. The straw should stop at the flexible bend and not go any further through the hole.

4. Gently pull the chicks straight down into the cups.

5. Say the poem and "hatch" the babies!

## Hickety Pickety's Folding Cut-and-Tell Egg

### Tools and Supplies

- strip of white paper, 31¼" long by 5½" wide (fadeless white roll paper works well)

- scissors

- pencil

### Directions

1. Accordion-fold the strip of paper at 3⅛" intervals (see the folding template on page 74), so that you have ten folded panels.

2. Photocopy the egg pattern and cut it out. Trace the egg outline lightly on the front panel of the folded strip.

3. Share "Hickety Pickety" as a cut-and-tell rhyme.

## "Egg Surprise" Turtle Egg

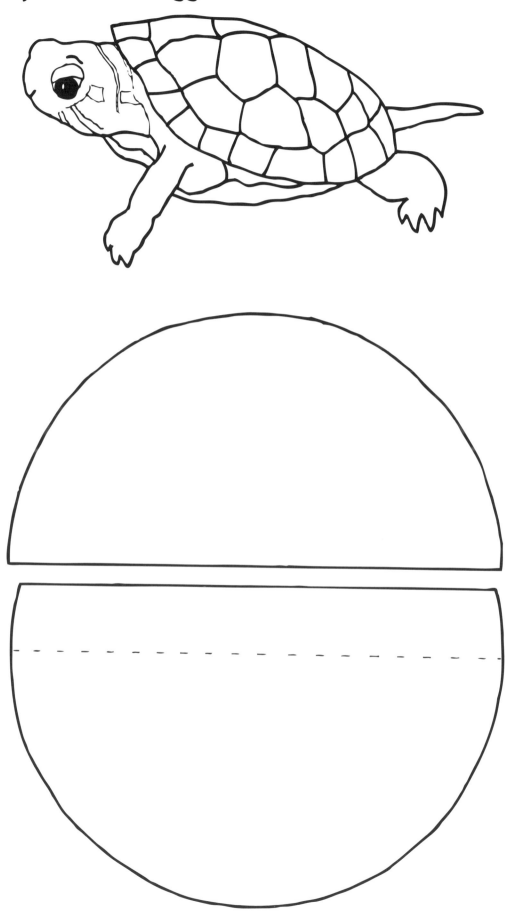

# "Egg Surprise" Chicken Egg

## "Egg Surprise" Duck Egg

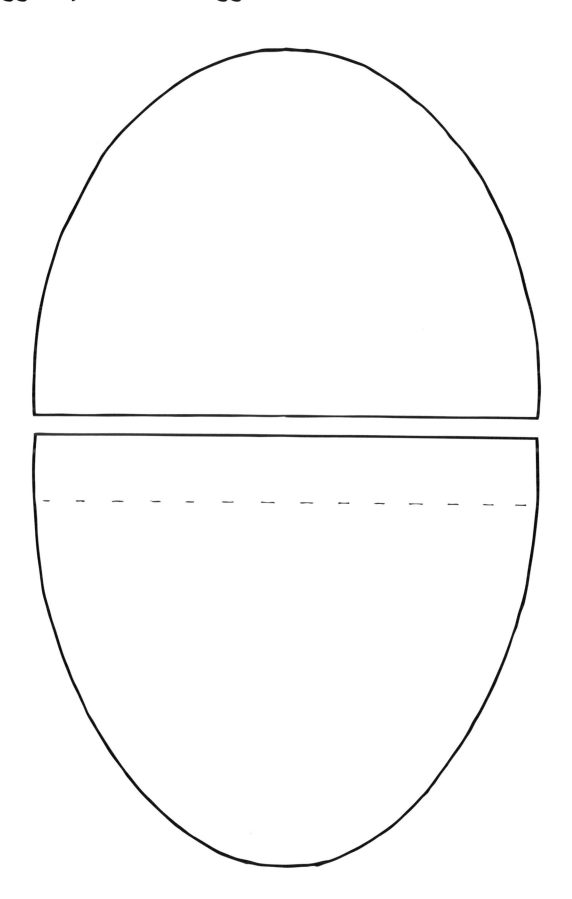

## "Egg Surprise" Caterpillar/Butterfly Egg

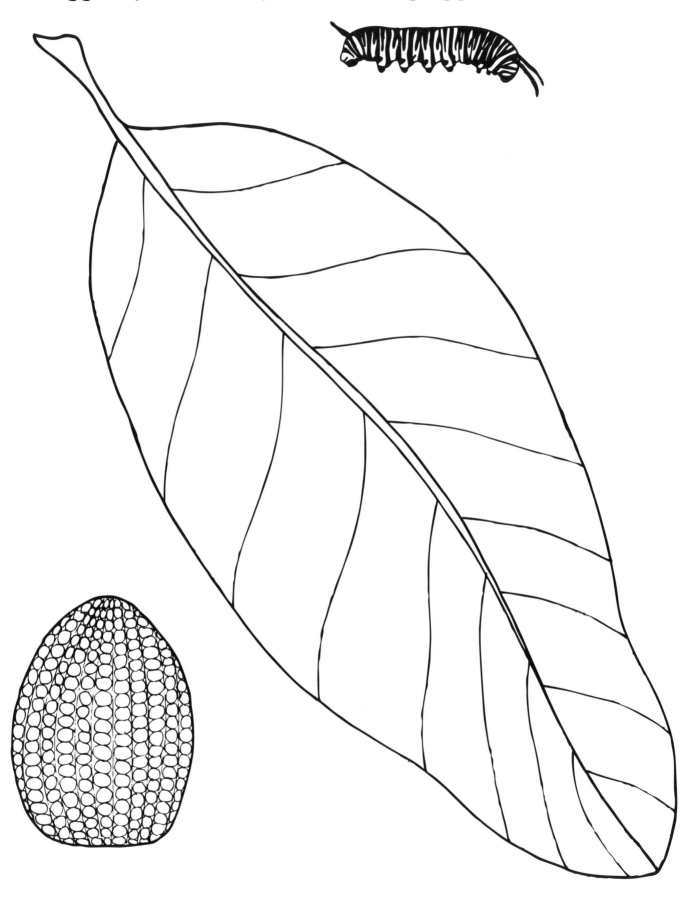

# Pop-up "Will You Hatch?" Story Prop and Student Craft

Little chick
in your egg,
sitting so still.
Little chick,
will you hatch?
"Yes! I will!"

"Will You Hatch?"
Chick Body

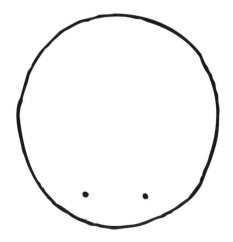

"Will You Hatch?"
Chick Beak

"Will You Hatch?"
Chick Wings

*(Cut 2 per chick.)*

# Hickety Pickety Folding 1-to-10 Egg Pattern

1. Cut a strip of white paper 31¼" long by 5½" wide. (Fadeless white roll paper works well.) Accordion-fold the strip at 3⅛" intervals (see the folding template below), so that you have 10 folded panels.

2. Photocopy the egg pattern below and cut it out. Trace the egg outline on the front panel of the folded strip.

3. Cutting through all of the folded layers, cut the rounded egg top and egg bottom. Make sure to leave the two flat sides attached!

4. Open your folding egg and make sure that there are 10 egg panels before using!

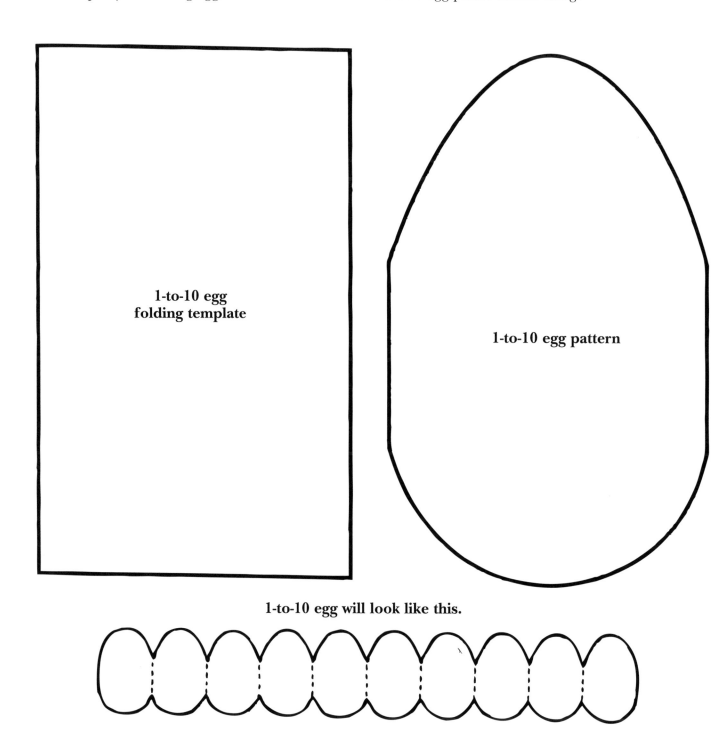

**1-to-10 egg folding template**

**1-to-10 egg pattern**

**1-to-10 egg will look like this.**

# Rainy Days
## April

## Early Literacy Activities

### Name Tags

Umbrella or raindrops stamp or sticker

### Clue(s)

Small doll umbrella

### Mailbox "Letter" of the Day

"R" and "r"

Rain, Run, Ravioli, Rip (demonstrate), Roar (roar together!), Raisin, Rice, Read

### Mother Goose Rhyme Time

*Rub-A-Dub Dub*

*Rub-a-dub dub,*
*Three men in a tub,*
*And who do you think they be?*
*The butcher, the baker, the candlestick-maker,*
*They all set out to sea.*

### Rhyming Basket

Boat/Goat; Bag/Flag; Fish/Dish

## Early Literacy Skill: Print Motivation

Encourage interest in and excitement about reading and books.

- Be delighted by the stories, poems, and activities that you share. Your enthusiasm will be infectious.

- Share Langston Hughes' beautiful poem "April Rain Song" liltingly, lyrically, and with feeling.

- Read *Rain Song* by Lezlie Evans (Houghton Mifflin, 1995) or *Listen to the Rain* by Bill Martin Jr. and John Archambault (Henry Holt & Company, 1988) with practiced rhythm and rhyme. Mirror the words' cadence and volume with your voice.

- Repeat "April Showers Bring May Flowers" and "Rain, Rain, Rain" several times with the children, encouraging their own enjoyment and internalization of the poems' lively rhythms.

- Lead the group in Laurie Berkner's action song "B-O-O-T-S" with joyful stomping, jumping, dancing, and splashing.

## Program Summary and Theme

Make a storytime splash on a rainy day! Create rainy day ambience by wearing a rain slicker and galoshes and carrying an umbrella as you welcome the audience. Dramatically produce books and props from a plastic bag or box so they don't "get wet."

Prepare the props and puppets ahead of time so you can use them throughout the program. Please see patterns and directions on pages 82–94. See additional suggested titles on pages 80–82 to substitute for older or younger audiences.

## Music

Play "rain" music as the audience is gathering in your storytime area. Possibilities include "Raindrops Keep Fallin' on My Head" instrumental on the sound recording *Teach A Toddler: Playful Songs For Learning* (Kimbo Educational, 1977), "After It Rains" on *Under a Shady Tree* by Laurie Berkner (Two Tomatoes, 2002), "Rhythm of the Rain" on *Put On Your Dancing Shoes* by Joanie Bartels (Purple Frog, 2001), "Robin in the Rain" and "Mister Sun" on *Singable Songs for the Very Young* by Raffi (Troubadour, 1976), "I Love Mud" and "It's A Rainy Day" on *Alligator in the Elevator* by Rick Charette (Pine Point, 1985), "Puddles" and "It's A Rainy Day" on *My Bear Gruff* by Charlotte Diamond (Hug Bug, 1992), "When the Rain Comes Down" on *Daydreamer* by Priscilla Herdman (Music for Little People, 1993), "What Do You Do on a Rainy Day?" on *Tot Rock* by Gary Rosen (Lightyear, 1993), "Hello Rain" by Marcia Berman on *Reaching for the Stars!* by Kathy Reid-Naiman (Merriweather Records, 2005), and many others.

# Sample Program

Please adjust content and length as needed.

## Introduction

*Say:* You've probably already guessed what our stories are about from the rainy day outfit I'm wearing. Do some of you like the rain? Sometimes when it rains really hard and we can't go outside and play, we sigh *(SIGH together as a group)* and groan *(GROAN together as a group)*. Have some of you heard the rhyme, "Rain, rain, go away, come again another day. I want to go out and play!"? Let's say it together. *(Chant the rhyme as a group, clapping or patting your knees to keep the rhythm.)* We sometimes feel that way, but rain is very important for many reasons. What do you think some of the reasons might be? *(All guesses are good guesses—talk about rain being good for the Earth, gardens, growing food, lakes and rivers, etc.)* Have some of you heard this little poem? "April Showers Bring May Flowers!"

*(Share "April Showers Bring May Flowers" several times with your paper plate umbrella/flower prop. Encourage the audience to say the rhyme with you.)* See pages 82–83 for patterns and instructions.

## Segue

*Say:* Some people love the rain because of the way it sounds. They say it is like music. Listen to this sound. *(Tilt your rain stick—purchase one from a music or educational store, or see directions for how to make one on page 83—so it sounds like a rain shower.)* Do you think it sounds a little bit like the rain?

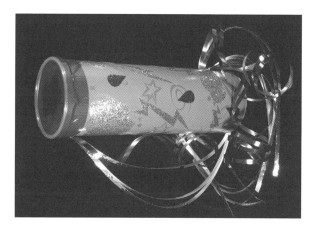

## Poem with Rainstick Accompaniment

Share the poem "April Rain Song" by Langston Hughes. The poem is included in many classic children's poetry resources, such as *Sing a Song of Popcorn: Every Child's Book of Poems* (Scholastic, 1988), *The Poetry Break* by Caroline Feller Bauer (H. W. Wilson, 1995), *A New Treasury of Children's Poetry: Old Favorites and New Discoveries* selected by Joanna Cole (Doubleday, 1984), and many more.

## Read Aloud

Rhythmically read one of the following two books, which describe the sounds and melodies of a rainstorm. Mirror the words' rhythm and volume with your voice.

- *Rain Song* by Lezlie Evans, illustrated by Cynthia Jabar. Houghton Mifflin, 1995. PK–2.

- *Listen to the Rain* by Bill Martin Jr. and John Archambault, illustrated by James Endicott. Henry Holt & Company, 1988. PK–2.

## Segue

*Say:* We can imitate, or copy, the sounds of a rainstorm right here in storytime. We'll do it together, so we can make a really big storm. Watch me and do what I do at the same time, and listen for the sounds of your very own rainstorm.

## Action Activity (Standing)

Lead the group in making the sound of a rainstorm.

1. Rub fingers of both hands together.

2. Rub open hands together.

3. Tap your index finger on the back of your other hand.

4. Tap back of hand, then slap leg with a staggered beat.

5. Slap both legs, becoming faster and faster.

6. While continuing to slap both legs, add foot stomping.

7. REVERSE backward through the steps until the "rainstorm" stops.

## Segue

*Say:* In the next story, several creatures try to hide under one tiny mushroom from a rainstorm that sounded just like the one you made. Do you think they will all be able to fit?

## Read Aloud

*Mushroom in the Rain.* Adapted from the Russian of V. Suteyev by Mirra Ginsburg, illustrated by Jose Aruego and Ariane Dewey. Macmillan, 1974. PK–2. An ant, butterfly, mouse, sparrow, and rabbit are all miraculously able to take shelter from the rain under the same mushroom, which was originally only big enough to shelter the ant. (Available as a BIG Book.)

When you repeatedly reach the line "the rain came down harder and harder," lay the book on your lap and slap your knees rapidly like #5 in the Action Activity at left. Encourage the audience to do this with you.

*Extension Idea: If you have a small enough group, consider acting out this story with creative dramatics. Make animal headbands for the creatures in the story if desired, and be the mushroom yourself with a giant umbrella that you gradually open while you narrate the story. Make sure that everyone gets a part. You can easily incorporate multiples of all of the animals. Call each of them under the umbrella/ mushroom in turn by singing the following song to the tune: "For He's a Jolly Good Fellow":*

*Join us under the mushroom,*
*Join us under the mushroom,*
*Join us under the mushroom,*
*There's surely room for you.*

*Sing the following song for the fox:*

*There's no room under the mushroom,*
*No room under the mushroom,*
*No room under the mushroom,*
*Especially not for you!*

## Segue

*Say:* Well, in that story there really was room for everybody under that mushroom, except for the fox that wanted to eat the rabbit! We don't usually hide under mushrooms when it rains; we hide under other things. Here is a poem about it!

## Poem with Props

Share "Rain, Rain, Rain" with your reversible paper plate story prop (or as a cut-and-tell poem as described in *Paper Stories* by Jean Stangl. Lake Publishing Co., 1984). See paper plate story prop directions on pages 82–83.

### "Rain, Rain, Rain"

*Raindrops on the hilltop,*
*Raindrops on the sea.*
*Raindrops on the green grass,*
*But no rain on me.*
*Why not? Because I have an umbrella!*

Write out the words to the rhyme ahead of time on a piece of grid board so attending adults can follow along, and point out to the group that the poem is written on the poster. Repeat the rhyme several times, encouraging the audience to say it with you. For at least one of the repetitions, follow the printed text on the poster with your finger as you read from left to right to reinforce print directionality as well as the concept that print stands for spoken language (encouraging the children's print awareness, another of the six early literacy skills).

## Action Song (Standing)

"The Itsy Bitsy Spider"

Sing the classic version of this well-loved action song, available on many sound recordings. "The Itsy Bitsy Spider" on the sound recording *Bathtime Magic* by Joanie Bartels (BMG, 1990) is one possible straightforward rendition. Next, share "The Eensy Weensy Spider" on the sound recording *Mainly Mother Goose* by Sharon, Lois & Bram (Elephant, 1984), where first the eensy weensy spider climbs the water spout, and then the BIG FAT SPIDER and the teensy-weensy spider follow. Adapt your actions to the words!

## Segue

*Say:* Our next story is about a boy named Pete who is about your age. He's grumpy because it's raining and he can't go outside to play. Let's see what happens.

## Read Aloud

*Pete's a Pizza* by William Steig. HarperCollins, 1998. Toddler–Grade 2. When Pete is stuck inside and miserable due to the rain, his parents come up with a fun game to turn him into a pretend pizza!

## Segue

*Say:* If Pete had gone outside when it was raining, what are some of the special things he could have worn or carried to keep him dry? *(Take guesses—all are good guesses.)* This next song is about something we can wear on our feet to keep them dry even if we stomp in the puddles! What are they? B-O-O-T-S *(spell it out on the board as you say each letter together).* Boots!

## Flannel Board and Action Song (Standing)

"Boots" by Laurie Berkner on the sound recording *Victor Vito* (Two Tomatoes Records, 1999). Use large-size magnetic or felt letters to point to as you spell out B-O-O-T-S!

Make felt or foamies black, brown, frog, dancing, and rain boots (or use real ones from the second hand store) to hold up or display as you sing and stomp, jump, dance, and splash your way through this lively action song. See patterns on pages 84–94.

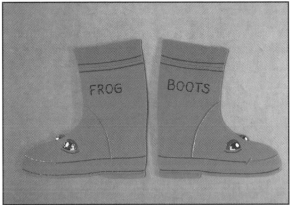

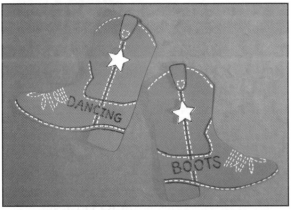

## Read Aloud

*The Napping House* by Audrey Wood, illustrated by Don Wood. Harcourt Brace Jovanovich, 1984. Toddler–Grade 2. In this cumulative tale, a wakeful flea atop a number of sleeping creatures causes a commotion with just one bite. The story begins during a gray downpour and ends with sunshine and a rainbow! (Available in Spanish and as a BIG Book.)

*Extension Idea: Extend the story with "The Napping House Song" from the sound recording that accompanies the 2004 reissued edition of the book (ISBN 0-15-205080-9).*

## Special Handout Idea

For a very special treat, give away inexpensive purchased "Rainbow Glasses" or "Rainbow Peepholes" after a Rainy Days Storytime.

Diffraction lenses mounted in cardboard frames enable the wearer to see rainbows shining from any light source. The glasses and peepholes are available from various discount toy catalogues or online (see Resources, page 216). Children adore them!

## Conclusion

*Say:* I have one last little song for you about the rain.

*Sing "If All the Raindrops." If the song is new to you,* listen to the tune on Mainly Mother Goose: Songs and Rhymes for Merry Young Souls *(Elephant Records, 1984). Musical notation for piano is included in* Sharon, Lois & Bram's Mother Goose: Songs, Finger Rhymes, Tickling Verses, Games and More *(Atlantic Monthly Press, 1985).*

*Sing:* If all the raindrops were lemon drops and gumdrops,
Oh what a rain it would be.
I'd stand outside with my mouth open wide;
I wouldn't care if I never went inside.

If all the raindrops were lemon drops and gumdrops,
Oh what a rain it would be.

Added verse:

If all the raindrops were POETRY and STORIES, oh what a rain it would be!
I'd run outside with my EARS open wide.
I wouldn't care if I never came inside.

If all the raindrops were POETRY and STORIES, oh what a rain it would be!

*Say:* Maybe you'll have some poetry and stories rain down on you this week! I hope so! If you do, don't get out your umbrella—just open up your EARS and listen as hard as you can!

# Additional Resources

***Bringing the Rain to Kapiti Plain*** by Verna Aardema, illustrated by Beatriz Vidal. Dial, 1981. K–2. Ki-pat pierces the clouds with an eagle feather arrow to release much-needed rain onto Kapiti Plain.

***Chicky Chicky Chook Chook*** by Cathy MacLennan. Boxer, 2007. Toddler–Grade 1. Brilliantly textured chicks, hens, bees, and kittens scamper through this wonderfully rhythmic text, until a thunderstorm crashes overhead and everyone gets "Wet. Wet. Wet." They all dry off in the ensuing "Sunny, sunny breeze and shine," and settle down to rest.

***Cloudy With a Chance of Meatballs*** by Judi Barrett, illustrated by Ron Barrett. Atheneum, 1978. K–3. In the tall-tale town of Chewandswallow, it rains soup and juice, snows mashed potatoes, and blows storms of hamburgers. Life is delicious until the weather takes a turn for the worse. (Available as a BIG book.)

***A Colorful Adventure of the Bee, Who Left Home One Monday Morning and What He Found Along the Way*** by Lisa Campbell Ernst, illustrated by Lee Ernst. Lothrop, Lee & Shepard, 1986. Toddler–K. A bee leaves its hive, passing many colors on its route before returning home through the rain and seeing a beautiful rainbow.

***Come On, Rain!*** by Karen Hesse, illustrated by Jon J. Muth. Scholastic, 1999. K–3. A young girl eagerly awaits a coming rainstorm to bring relief from the oppressive summer heat.

### "Five Umbrellas"

*Chant:* FIVE umbrellas by the back door,
The red one went out, and then there were FOUR.

FOUR umbrellas as pretty as can be,
The blue one went out, and then there were THREE.

THREE umbrellas with nothing to do,
The green one went out, and then there were TWO.

TWO umbrellas were having some fun, but
The yellow one went out, and then there was ONE.

Just ONE umbrella alone in the hall.
The purple one went out, and that was all!

*Gather five colored umbrellas, or make some for the felt board to share this classic backward counting rhyme.*

***Hello, Good-bye*** by David Lloyd, illustrated by Louise Voce. Lothrop, Lee & Shepard Books, 1988. Toddler–Grade 1. A bear, two bees, some birds, and other creatures meet at a tree and say hello until the rain begins and they say goodbye.

**"If All the Raindrops"** on *Mainly Mother Goose: Songs and Rhymes for Merry Young Souls.* Elephant Records, 1984. Musical notation for piano is included in *Sharon, Lois & Bram's Mother Goose: Songs, Finger Rhymes, Tickling Verses, Games and More.* Atlantic Monthly Press, 1985.

**Extension Idea:** Ask the audience: What would you like it to rain? Pizza? Chocolate cake? Money? Sing the song again with each set of ideas, adjusting wording as necessary. (e.g., "If all the raindrops were DOLLAR BILLS and PENNIES ... I'd run outside with my POCKETS open wide.") Consider singing some of the verses with your tongue sticking out as you pretend to try and catch the delicious "raindrops."

***In the Middle of the Puddle*** by Mike Thaler, illustrated by Bruce Degen. Harper & Row, 1988. PK–1. A frog and a turtle watch the rain gradually turn their puddle into an ocean before the sun comes along and returns things to normal.

***In the Rain with Baby Duck*** by Amy Hest, illustrated by Jill Barton. Candlewick Press, 1995. PK–1. Baby Duck hates walking in the rain until Grampa gives her Mother Duck's old boots and umbrella.

***Is There Room On the Feather Bed?*** by Libba Moore Gray, illustrated by Nadine Bernard Westcott. Orchard Books, 1997. PK–2. One rainy night a wee fat man and his wee fat wife are joined in their feather bed by a variety of animals, including a skunk.

**"It's Raining Pigs and Noodles"** in *It's Raining Pigs & Noodles: Poems* by Jack Prelutsky. Greenwillow Books, 2000. PK–4. Pigs, noodles, frogs, and hats are only a few of the many remarkable objects raining from the sky. The poet likes the unusual downpour "so much better than when it's raining rain."

**Extension Idea:** Use props to bring the poem to life for your audience. Securely hang an umbrella upside down by its handle from the ceiling. Hang the curved handle through a loop of string or a hook so you can easily lift it down when you are ready to present the poem. Gather clip-art pictures or three-dimensional toy versions of all the items listed in the poem and place them within the bowl of the umbrella in the order they appear in the poem. Type a copy of the poem and pin it inside the umbrella's fabric if you need it. When you are ready to begin, lift the umbrella down from the ceiling, keeping its handle pointing up, and peer into the bowl of the umbrella. Hold it high enough so the audience can't see into it. Look shocked and interested as you produce each item in turn. Keep the umbrella handle-side up throughout the poem until the end when you have emptied it of its "rain." Then turn it right side up over your head and hold out your hand to feel for more unusual raindrops that might be coming down from the sky as you say the last line of the poem.

*Kipper's Rainy Day* based on the books by Mick Inkpen. Red Wagon Books, 2001. Toddler–PK. Kipper the dog likes to splash in rain puddles. Lift flaps to find out who likes the rain and who does not.

*Little Cloud* by Eric Carle. Philomel Books, 1996. Toddler–Grade 1. A little cloud becomes all sorts of things—sheep, an airplane, trees, a hat, and so forth—before joining other clouds and raining.

**"Mr. Sun"** action song, available on the following sound recordings: *Singable Songs For the Very Young* by Raffi (Troubador Records Ltd., 1976) and *If You're Happy and You Know It ... Sing Along with Bob #1* (Bob's Kids Music, 1996).

*Mr. Gumpy's Motor Car* by John Burningham. Crowell, 1976. Toddler–Grade 1. Mr. Gumpy's human and animal friends squash into his old car and go for a drive until it starts to rain and the car gets stuck in the mud.

*Muddigush* by Kimberley Knutson. Macmillan, 1992. PK–1. Onomatopoeic text describes the squishy sounds and sensations associated with playing in the mud.

*One Rainy Day* by Valeri Gorbachev. Philomel Books, 2002. PK–1. A pig and various other animals crowd under a tree to escape the rain.

*The Piggy in the Puddle* by Charlotte Pomerantz, illustrated by James Marshall. Aladdin Books, 1989. PK–4. Unable to dissuade a young pig from frolicking in the mud, her family finally joins her for a mud party.

**Extension Idea:** Memorize this fabulous rollicking text if you can, and tell the story with felt board figures.

*The Puddle* by David McPhail. Farrar, Straus and Giroux, 1998. PK–1. A boy sets out to sail his boat in a rain puddle and is joined by a somewhat troublesome frog, a turtle, an alligator, a pig, and an elephant.

*Puddles* by Jonathan London, illustrated by G. Brian Karas. Viking, 1997. PK–1. When the rain stops falling and the skies clear up, it's time to put on boots and go outside to play in the puddles.

*Rain* by Manya Stojic. Crown Publishers, 2000. Toddler–Grade 1. A succession of African animals predict the coming rain and then enjoy its lush aftermath.

*The Rain Came Down* by David Shannon. Blue Sky Press, 2000. PK–2. A sudden rainstorm puts everyone on the block in a terrible mood and subsequently causes chaos. When the rain suddenly stops, everything and everyone becomes congenial once more.

*Rain Dance* by Kathi Appelt, illustrated by Emilie Chollat. HarperFestival, 2001. Toddler–K. In this counting book, various farm creatures hop, skitter, and prance in the rain.

**Rain Drop Splash** by Alvin Tresselt, illustrated by Leonard Weisgard. Lothrop, Lee & Shepard Books, 1946. PK–2. Raindrops fall until they become in turn a puddle, a pond, and a lake that spills over until it overflows into a river and finally joins the sea.

**Rain Play** by Cynthia Cotten, illustrated by Javaka Steptoe. Henry Holt & Company, 2008. K–3. Most people leave the park when rain begins to fall, while others enjoy the sights, sounds, and feel of the cool water—until thunder and lightning come near.

**A Rainbow of My Own** by Don Freeman. Viking, 1966. PK–1. A small boy imagines what it would be like to have his own rainbow with which he could play.

**Red Rubber Boot Day** by Mary Lyn Ray, illustrated by Lauren Stringer. Harcourt, 2000. Toddler–K. A child describes the many activities that may be enjoyed on a rainy day.

**Ruby's Rainy Day** based on the characters of Rosemary Wells. Grosset & Dunlap, 2004. Toddler–PK. Max wants to go outside and play baseball, but it's raining. Ruby insists that they put on their many colored rain clothes before going out, just in time for the sun to appear!

**Skyfire** by Frank Asch. Prentice-Hall, 1984. PK–1. When Bear sees a rainbow for the first time, he thinks that the sky is on fire and determines to put out the blaze. (Available as a BIG Book.)

**Thunder Cake** by Patricia Polacco. Philomel Books, 1990. PK–2. Grandma helps her granddaughter overcome her fear of thunderstorms by baking a "Thunder Cake" together.

**Today is Rainy** by Martha E. H. Rustad. Capstone Press, 2006. PK–1. Simple text and photographs present weather information, clothing choices, and activities for a rainy day.

**Wet World** by Norma Simon, illustrated by Alexi Natchev. Candlewick Press, 1995. PK–1. Describes a little girl's activities on a wet, wet, wet day.

**Yellow Umbrella** by Jae Soo Liu, music by Dong Il Sheen. Kane/Miller Book Pub., 2002. (Sound recording enclosed.) K–4. This remarkable wordless book and accompanying sound recording tell a story in pictures and music of children on their way to school on a rainy day. Needs to be used in an extended setting, but offers truly lovely possibilities.

# Storytime Prop and Craft Directions

## "April Showers"/"Rain, Rain, Rain"

### Tools and Supplies

- standard fluted paper plate
- acrylic craft paint
- foam paint brush
- adhesive flower foamies or flower stickers
- six black pipe cleaners
- two contrasting color pipe cleaners for the umbrella handle crook
- hot glue gun and hot glue sticks

### Directions

1. Fold the paper plate approximately in half, with one side being about ½" shorter than the other side. (The longer side is what will fold up in front to cover the smaller back side.)

2. Paint or color the top of the plate (where you would normally place your food) green. Paint or color the bottom side any color and decorate as the umbrella. Allow the paint to dry completely.

3. Stick or glue flowers to the green side of the plate, taking care not to place any directly along the fold. Make sure the flowers are flat enough so that the plate can close into an umbrella. Allow the glue to dry completely.

4. Braid three of the black pipe cleaners together to form a stiff handle. Wrap the other three black pipe cleaners around and around the braided handle to make it even more sturdy. Wrap the two contrasting pipe cleaners around the bottom of the handle and turn it up into a crook. Hot glue the pipe cleaner handle to the back of the short side of the paper plate. Make sure that a small piece of the pipe

cleaner handle will extend above the top of the umbrella and bend slightly over the top of the plate as a fastener. Allow the glue to dry completely.

## "April Showers" / "Rain, Rain, Rain" Student Craft

Decorate small paper plate folded umbrella halves with markers, glitter, and crayons. Cut out flower pictures from magazines to paste inside, draw flowers, or use foamies stick-on flowers. Make sure the children don't place flowers over the paper plate's fold. Glue pipe cleaner or flexible bend straw handles onto the umbrella backs. Glue or tape a copy of the poem(s) to the front of each umbrella for families to enjoy at home.

## Rain Stick

### Tools and Supplies

- one empty potato chip can with lid
- six plastic six-pack soda can holders
- ½ cup of rice, popcorn, or dried beans
- colored cloth tape
- scissors
- colored contact paper or construction paper
- markers, crayons, etc.
- decorative ribbons, stickers, and so forth as desired

### Directions

1. Fold six plastic six-pack can holders lengthwise and insert them into the potato chip can.

2. Pour approximately ½ cup of rice, popcorn or dried beans into the can among the plastic can holders. Seal can lid tightly with cloth tape.

3. Cover the outside of the can with colored contact paper or construction paper, and decorate with rain motifs or other designs as desired.

4. Turn the rain stick on end to hear the pattering "rain"; flip it again as necessary to keep the rain falling.

For an alternative way to craft a rain stick using aluminum foil and a long cardboard gift wrap tube, see "Pitter-patter Rain Stick" in *Crafts to Make in the Spring* by Kathy Ross, illustrated by Vicky Enright (Millbrook Press, 1998).

## "BOOTS" Magnet/Velcro®/ Flannel Board

(B-O-O-T-S; black boots; brown boots; frog boots; dancing boots; rain boots)

### Tools and Supplies

- scissors
- four sheets of black foamies, felt, or card stock (B-O-O-T-S letters and black boots)
- two sheets of brown foamies, felt, or card stock (brown boots)
- two sheets of green foamies, felt, or card stock (frog boots)
- two sheets of red foamies, felt, or card stock (dancing boots)
- two sheets of yellow foamies, felt, or card stock (rain boots)
- acrylic craft paint or puffy paint for embellishment as desired: white, brown, black, red, yellow, green
- hot glue gun and hot glue (if using foamies)
- self-adhesive magnet mounting squares or Velcro® dots

### Directions

1. Photocopy the letter and boot patterns on pages 84–94. Cut the pieces from colored foamies, felt, or card stock.

2. Highlight the pieces with colored craft paint or other decorations as desired for added interest. Allow the paint to dry completely.

3. If the letters and boots are made from foamies or card stock, hot glue small pieces of flexible magnet or a Velcro dot to the back of each cutout.

# Boot Letter Patterns

Enlarge as desired.

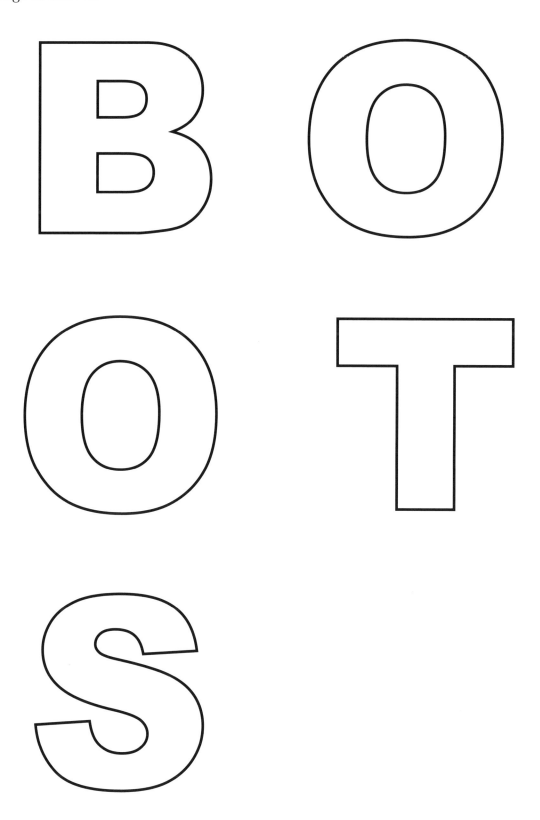

# Boot Patterns

BLACK

**Boot Patterns**

BOOTS

**Boot Patterns**

BROWN

# Boot Patterns

BOOTS

**Boot Patterns**

FROG

**Boot Patterns**

BOOTS

**Boot Patterns**

**Boot Patterns**

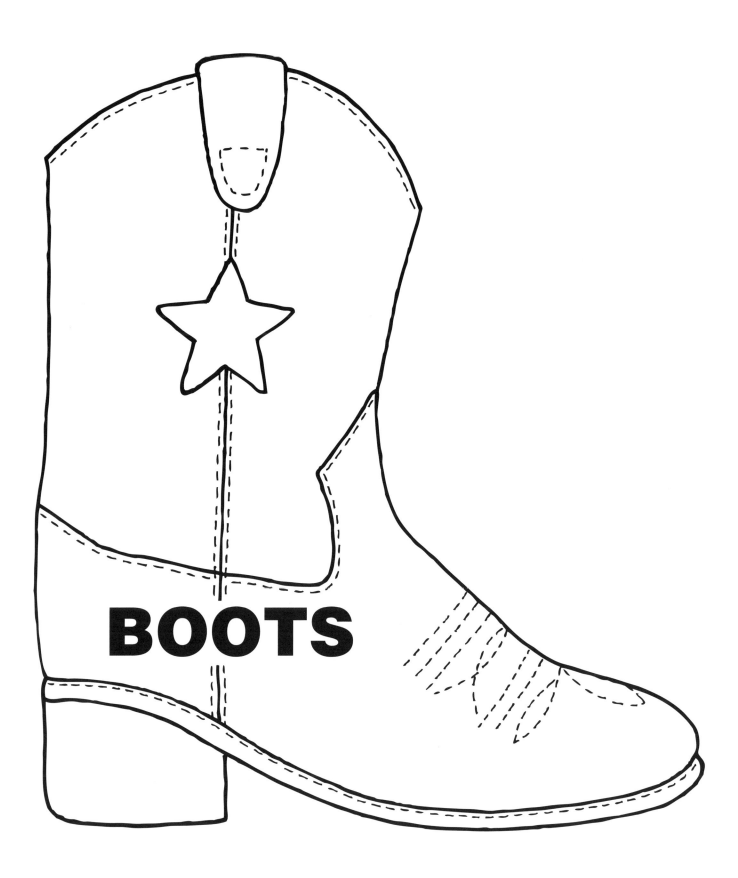

BOOTS

**Boot Patterns**

RAIN

**Boot Patterns**

BOOTS

# Growing Gardens
## May

## Early Literacy Activities

### Name Tags

Flower stamp or sticker

### Clue(s)

Packet of seeds; gardening miscellaneous

### Mailbox "Letter" of the Day

"G" and "g"

Garden, Girl, Game, Goat, Good, Gate, Grass, Giggle

### Mother Goose Rhyme Time

*Mistress Mary*

*"Mary, Mary, quite contrary,*
*How does your garden grow?"*
*"With silver bells and cockleshells,*
*And pretty maids all in a row."*

### Rhyming Basket

Seed/Bead; Carrot/Parrot; Bone/Phone

## Early Literacy Skill: Narrative Skills

Practice retelling stories or events, sequencing the order in which events happened, and adding descriptions.

- Talk about the sequence of events in *Sunflower* by Miela Ford (Greenwillow Books, 1995), or *The Carrot Seed* story by Ruth Krauss (Harper & Row, 1945). What happened first? What did the seeds need to be able to grow? What happened at the end of the story? What do you think the little boy in *The Carrot Seed* did with the carrot after it came up?

- If you have a small enough group and adequate time, act out "The Gigantic Turnip" with creative dramatics.

- Make miniature "Growing Flowers" crafts and say the poem together as a group while each child manipulates his or her flower puppet.

## Program Summary and Theme

Plant a garden of stories together with your audience. Cover the storytime table with brown "dirt" fabric, and display the books you plan to read alongside plastic gardening tools and peeking out from plastic flower pots. Wear a gardening hat, plastic shoes, and canvas gloves if desired. This gardening apparatus serves as visual storytime clues for the children—help them interpret what they see.

Prepare the props and puppets ahead of time so you can use them throughout the program. Please see patterns and directions on pages 101–106. See suggested titles on pages 99–101 to substitute for older or younger audiences.

## Music

Play "garden" music as the audience is gathering in your storytime area. Possibilities include "The Valley of Vegetables" on *Buzz Buzz* by Laurie Berkner (Two Tomatoes, 1998); "Family Garden" on *Family Garden* by John McCutcheon (Rounder, 1993); "The Garden" (Frog and Toad) on *Unbearable Bears* by Kevin Roth (Marlboro, 1985); "Little Seed" on *Woody's 20 Grow Big Songs* by Woody Guthrie (Warner Brothers, 1992); "The Garden Song" on *Peter, Paul, and Mommy, Too* by Peter, Paul, and Mary (Warner Brothers, 1993); "The Zucchini Song" on *A Friend, a Laugh, a Walk in the Woods* by Dan Crow (Allshouse, 2000); "Won't You Plant Your Seeds With Care" on *Say Hello to the Morning* by Kathy Reid-Naiman (Merriweather Records, 1999); and many others.

# Sample Program

Please adjust content and length as needed.

## Introduction

*(Hold up a real packet of vegetable seeds and shake it audibly.) Say:* We're going to plant some seeds today. They're not vegetable seeds like this, though, or even flower seeds. They're a special kind of seed—story seeds. We'll plant these seeds in our minds, and they will grow in our imaginations! Maybe some of you will tell and write stories some day, or even today after this storytime is over. In our first story today, I think the storyteller's story seed must have been the idea of a giant vegetable that grew so big it just wouldn't come out of the ground.

## Read Aloud

*The Gigantic Turnip* by Aleksei Tolstoy & Niamh Sharkey. Barefoot Books, 1999. PK–2. In this traditional Russian tale, a farmer grows a turnip so big that it takes the combined efforts of him and his wife, six canaries, five geese, four hens, three cats, two pigs, one cow, and one little mouse to pull it from the ground.

Talk about what the word "gigantic" means. Count the number of creatures in each new group as they join the line, and have the children help you repeatedly list everyone in the lineup as the characters try again and again to pull up the turnip. Mimic the "pulled and heaved and tugged and yanked" action vigorously as a group. When the turnip finally comes flying out of the ground, follow the word POP! with your finger and say it aloud, then repeat it loudly (a chance to shout in the library!) together with the children. All fall over and laugh like the animals at the end!

## Segue

*Say:* That tiny little seed grew into a huge turnip! We get to pretend we are tiny little seeds too, and then all of a sudden we will sprout, which means we'll start to grow.

## Action Rhyme (Crouching/ Standing)

"Little Seed"

Little seed in the ground,
*(Crouch down with hands cupped over your head.)*
Lying so still.
Little seed, will you sprout?
"Yes! I will!"
*(Stand up slowly and spread your arms up and out like plant tendrils growing. Encourage children to call out their answer.)*

If desired, extend this activity further by pretending to sprinkle water from an empty watering can on your "seeds" while they are crouched down "lying so still"; then have the sun shine on them (use your sun stick puppet, see pages 103–104) and the wind blow on them; then ask "will you sprout?"

## Segue

*Say:* I have a really short poem for you, and then one that is a little bit longer. They both have the month of May in them. Have some of you heard this little poem? "April showers bring May flowers!"

## Poem with Props

Share "April Showers Bring May Flowers" with props. For "April showers," wave your rain stick puppet over your tiny Growing Flower craft prop. As you say, "bring May flowers," pop up the flower puppet. Say the poem several times, encouraging the audience to say it with you.

## Segue

*Say:* Here is our other poem about May. The author made it sound as if it was written by a dog!

## Poem with Props

"May" in *Dog Days: Rhymes Around the Year* by Jack Prelutsky. Knopf, 1999. Toddler–Grade 1.

> **"May"**
>
> *How sweet to be a dog in May,*
> *And garden every single day.*
> *I dig up dirt, I dig up stones,*
> *And plant a row of lovely bones.*
>
> —Jack Prelutsky

Use a dog puppet to say the poem, or find/make yourself a dog hat or headband and be the dog narrator yourself. A headband with ears works great, or put tights on your head like Rob Reid's inspired version of "Do Your Ears Hang Low?" Make sure to incorporate doggie movements (e.g., scratching) as well as barking so that you are convincing!

Use your "May" Bone Planter (see directions on pages 102–103) to share the poem. Pretend to dig in the planter as you dig up "dirt"; hide one or two rocks in the planter ahead of time to dig up as "stones"; and then plant three plastic or cardboard cutout "bones" in the planter's three holes as you say "plant a row of lovely bones." After planting the bones, "water" them with a small watering can, then put in a garden marker to show what you planted.

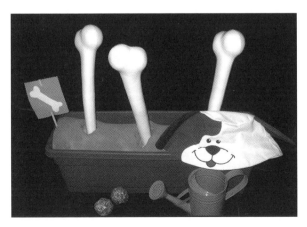

## Segue

*Say:* In this next story, a child plants a REAL seed. Here is what happens.

## Read Aloud

*Sunflower* by Miela Ford, pictures by Sally Noll. Greenwillow Books, 1995. PK–1. A young girl plants a sunflower seed, waters it, and watches it grow.

Before you begin, show the children a real, striped sunflower seed!

OR

*The Carrot Seed* by Ruth Krauss, pictures by Crockett Johnson. Harper & Row, 1945. Toddler–K. A little boy plants and carefully tends a carrot seed with fantastic results. (Available as a BIG Book.)

Make a giant fabric carrot (see patterns and directions on pages 101–102 and 105) and pull it from a hiding place at the end of the story.

## Segue

*Say:* Growing seeds into flowers or vegetables or stories takes a lot of hard work! Here is a song about some of the things that happen before and after a seed sprouts and becomes a plant.

## Action Song (Standing)

Share the song:

"In My Garden" by Alan Arkin and Jeremy Arkin, on the sound recording *One Light, One Sun* by Raffi (Troubador Records Ltd., 1985). Words and music are also available in *The Second Raffi Song Book* (Crown Publishers, 1986).

Perform the actions suggested by the words—energetically pretending to dig the ground; hoe the weeds; plant the seeds; and grow, pick, and eat the resultant peas.

OR

"Planting Seeds" *(Sung to the tune: "The Farmer in the Dell"; mimic the actions suggested by the words.)*

The children plant the seeds,
The children plant the seeds,
High-ho the derry-o
The children plant the seeds.

Verse 2: The sun comes out to shine ...
Verse 3: The rain begins to fall ...
Verse 4: The seeds begin to grow ...
Verse 5: We eat the yummy food ...

Write out the words ahead of time on a piece of grid board so attending adults can follow along, and point out to the group that the song is written on the poster.

## Segue

*Say:* We've already learned that a seed needs to be planted for it to even begin to sprout or grow. We've also learned about some of the things that help a seed grow into a plant. What do you think a seed needs? *(Water, sunshine, pulling the weeds, etc.—but all guesses are good guesses.)* Well, the girl in this next story didn't know those things, so here is what she tried!

## Prop Story

*Grow Flower, Grow!* by Lisa Brucc, illustrated by Rosalind Beardshaw. Scholastic, 2001. (Originally titled: *Fran's Flower*, HarperCollins, 2000; Bloomsbury, 1999.) Toddler–Grade 1. When Fran and her dog Fred find a tiny green tip growing in a flowerpot filled with soil, they try to help it grow by bringing it indoors and giving it some of their own favorite foods (e.g., ice cream, pizza, spaghetti, cookies, and one of Fred's bones). The tip stays tiny until Fran becomes disgusted and puts it out of doors, where the rain falls, wind blows, and sun shines upon it. Unseen by Fran, the tiny green tip grows bigger and bigger until she is surprised one day by a beautiful flower!

Use your "Fran's Flower" switcheroo prop (see directions on page 103) to tell the story with other gathered props. Be Fran yourself, and use a dog puppet or plush as Fred. "Find" the pot with its flower tip "outdoors" *(produce it from a large box or other secure, hidden spot),* and then try to make it "grow" like Fran does in the story. Give the flower tip a piece of plastic pizza, or make a pizza slice from craft foamies. Use ivory-colored yarn for spaghetti, plastic or felt cookies, a giant plastic Halloween bone or a smaller rawhide one, and so forth. Repeat the phrase "Grow, flower, grow!" as a group as you try giving the plant each new food item. When you become disgusted that the green tip is not growing, put the pot back "outside" where you have already hidden the fully grown flower. Wave your giant sun and rain stick puppets (see directions on pages 103–104) over that general vicinity, and pretend to be the wind together with the audience using your collective hands and voices. Produce the beautiful flower on cue with excitement (and enthusiastic barking by Fred).

## Conclusion

*Say:* Now each one of you has story seeds in your head. Some are seeds from the stories we shared today, and some are seeds that you already had in your imaginations. I hope that some of those seeds will grow up into whole stories some day—maybe even today! Think about what stories you can share with your families and friends.

## Craft Ideas

• Make tiny "Growing Flowers" crafts using small paper cups and flower cutouts and leaves glued/taped to green drinking straws (see directions on page 104). Share the poem below using your "Growing Flowers." Glue or tape a copy of the poem to the outside of each cup for families to enjoy at home (see page 106).

**"Growing Flowers"**

*(Hold the cup in one hand, with the flower tucked down out of sight.)*
Plant some tiny little seeds,
*(Pretend to drop seeds in cup.)*
Water them and pull the weeds.
*(Make a tiny "rain shower" with your free hand; pretend to pull weeds from the cup.)*
Let the sun shine down below,
*(Make a tiny sun "o" circle with your free hand.)*
And little seeds are sure to grow!
*(Slowly pop up the flower so it gradually appears over the rim of the cup.)*
—Kimberly Faurot

The "Growing Flowers" crafts may also be used with the "Little Seed in the Ground" action poem from storytime.

## Additional Extension Ideas

- Cut out flannel board or shadow puppet figures for *The Gigantic Turnip.*

- Act out *The Carrot Seed* with a plastic watering can, the giant fabric carrot (hidden in "dirt" brown cloth), and a toy wheelbarrow.

- Make a "S is for ... Seed With a Secret" story prop from a pair of discarded shoulder pads! Complete instructions are included in the book *Kathy Ross Crafts Letter Sounds* by Kathy Ross, illustrated by Jan Barger (Millbrook Press, 2002).

## Additional Resources

*Big Yellow Sunflower* by Frances Barry. Candlewick Press, 2008. PK–1. Describes how sunflowers develop from seed to seedling to bright yellow flower. The pages unfold one at a time to form the petals of a sunflower.

*Bumpety Bump!* by Pat Hutchins. Greenwillow Books, 2006. Toddler–K. A boy helps his grandfather on the farm, showing the hen that follows them all that he can do.

*Carrot Soup* by John Segal. Simon & Schuster, 2006. PK–1. After working hard on his garden all spring and summer, Rabbit looks forward to harvest time when he can make soup. Every carrot disappears, however, and Rabbit must find out who has taken them. Includes a recipe for carrot soup.

*The Enormous Carrot* by Vladimir Vasilevich Vagin. Scholastic, 1998. PK–2. A group learns the value of teamwork as one animal after another joins in the effort to pull a giant carrot out of the ground.

*Flower Garden* by Eve Bunting, illustrated by Kathryn Hewitt. Harcourt, 1994. PK–K. Helped by her father, a young girl prepares a flower garden as a birthday surprise for her mother. (Available as a BIG Book.)

*Garden* by Robert Maass. Henry Holt & Company, 1998. K–2. This nonfiction title discusses the beauty and harmony of gardens, the different kinds, and how to care for them.

*The Giant Carrot* by Jan Peck. Dial, 1998. PK–2. Little Isabelle surprises her family with her unique way of helping a carrot seed grow and of getting the huge vegetable from the ground. Includes a recipe for carrot pudding!

*The Great Big Enormous Turnip* by Alexei Tolstoy; illustrated by Helen Oxenbury. Franklin Watts, 1968. PK–2. The mouse added just the necessary weight to the line formed by all those trying to pull up the giant turnip.

*Grow Little Turnip, Grow Big.* (I'm Going to Read! Series, Level 1.) Sterling Publishing, 2006. (Reissue of *The Turnip* retold by Harriet Ziefert, illustrated by Laura Rader. Viking, 1996. Toddler–K.) In this easy reader version of the traditional tale, each character calls "Yoo Hoo!" (or some variation thereof) for the next to come and help pull the enormous turnip out of the ground.

*Growing Colors* by Bruce McMillan. HarperCollins, 1988. Toddler–K. Photographs of green peas, yellow corn, red potatoes, purple beans, and other fruits and vegetables illustrate the many colors of nature.
**Extension Idea:** Bring some real produce to match the photographs for the children to touch.

*Growing Vegetable Soup* by Lois Ehlert. Harcourt, 1987. Toddler–Grade 1. A father and child grow vegetables and then make them into a soup.

***A Harvest of Color: Growing a Vegetable Garden*** by Melanie Eclare. Ragged Bears, 2002. K–3. Six young neighbors plant a vegetable garden together, recording their work along the way. They celebrate at the end of summer with a salad made from their own produce.

***How Groundhog's Garden Grew*** by Lynne Cherry. Blue Sky Press, 2003. K–1. Squirrel teaches Little Groundhog how to plant and tend a vegetable garden.

***I'm A Seed*** by Jean Marzollo, illustrated by Judith Moffatt. Scholastic, 1996. PK–1. A pumpkin seed and a marigold seed grow into plants side by side.

***In the Garden: Who's Been Here?*** by Lindsay Barrett George. Greenwillow Books, 2006. PK–1. As Jeremy and Christina pick vegetables for their mother, they see evidence of animals and insects that have been in the garden before them.

***Jasper's Beanstalk*** by Nick Butterworth and Mick Inkpen. Bradbury, 1993. Toddler–PK. A cat plants a bean that eventually sprouts.

***The Little Red Hen*** by Byron Barton. HarperCollins, 1993. PK–1. The little red hen finds that none of her lazy friends are willing to help her plant, harvest, or grind wheat into flour, but all are eager to eat the bread she makes from it.

***The Little Red Hen*** retold and illustrated by Paul Galdone. Seabury Press, 1973. PK–1.

***The Little Red Hen*** by Jerry Pinkney. Dial Books for Young Readers, 2006. PK–2. A beautifully illustrated version of the classic fable.

***Max Loves Sunflowers*** by Ken Wilson-Max. Hyperion, 1998. Toddler–K. Max plants seeds and waits. The seeds grow, and he dances when the sunflowers open. (Movable book.)

***Miss Rumphius*** by Barbara Cooney. Viking, 1982. K–4. Great-aunt Alice Rumphius plants lupines along the roads as she does her part to "do something to make the world more beautiful."

***Mole's Hill: A Woodland Tale*** by Lois Ehlert. Harcourt, 1994. PK–2. When Fox tells Mole she must move to make way for a new path, Mole finds an ingenious way to save her home. After Mole quietly enlarges her hill and

beautifies it by planting grass and flower seeds, the other animals decide they want to keep the lovely hill just as it is rather than removing it to make the path. Instead, Fox asks Mole to dig a tunnel through the hill!

***One Little Seed*** by Elaine Greenstein. Viking, 2004. Toddler–K. Follows a seed from the time it is planted until it grows into a beautiful flower.

***Over in the Garden*** by Jennifer Ward, illustrated by Kenneth J. Spengler. Rising Moon, 2002. PK–1. In this reworking of the traditional song "Over in the Meadow," mother insects and their children enjoy various activities from morning sun to evening moon. A simple musical score is included at the back.

***Planting a Rainbow*** by Lois Ehlert. Harcourt, 1988. Toddler–K. A mother and child plant a rainbow of flowers in the family garden. (Available as a BIG Book.)

**"Sarah Small"** in *The Frogs Wore Red Suspenders* by Jack Prelutsky. Greenwillow Books, 2002. PK–2. In her garden, Sarah Small grows a variety of clothing.
**Extension Idea:** Make flannel board cutouts to accompany the poem.

***A Seed Is Sleepy*** by Dianna Hutts Aston, illustrated by Sylvia Long. Chronicle Books, 2007. K–4. Information about many different types of seeds and how they germinate, accompanied by gorgeous, detailed watercolor illustrations.

***So Happy!*** by Kevin Henkes, illustrated by Anita Lobel. Greenwillow Books, 2005. K–3. Set in the Southwest, everything is dry and dusty at the beginning of this circular story about an amaryllis seed, a lost rabbit, and a restless boy. The coming of nourishing rain ultimately turns the story toward a happy resolution.

**"Spaghetti Seeds"** in *A Pizza the Size of the Sun* by Jack Prelutsky. Greenwillow Books, 1996. PK–3. Some seeds that were supposed to grow into spaghetti have only produced macaroni.
**Extension Idea:** Have a cloth bag or basket of raw macaroni that you have "harvested" from the fields.

***The Surprise Garden*** by Zoe Hall, illustrated by Shari Halpern. Scholastic, 1998. Toddler–K. After sowing unmarked seeds, three children wait expectantly for their garden to grow. (Available as a BIG Book.)

*Ten Seeds* by Ruth Brown. Knopf, 2001. PK–K. We see what happens to the ten flower seeds that a child plants in the soil. One is taken by an ant, one by a mouse; a slug consumes one seedling; one small plant is crushed beneath a stray ball; and so forth. One seed grows and thrives, however, and eventually drops ten new seeds for the child to plant again.

*This Is the Sunflower* by Lola M. Schaefer, illustrated by Donald Crews. Greenwillow Books, 2000. PK–K. Cumulative verse describes how a sunflower in a garden blossoms and, with the help of the birds, spreads its seeds to create an entire patch of sunflowers.

*This Is Your Garden* by Maggie Smith. Crown Publishers, 1998. K–2. A little girl, given good tools and seeds, begins to grow a garden that needs water, sun, weeding, and her encouragement.

*The Tiny Seed* by Eric Carle. Crowell, 1970. PK–1. A simple description of a flowering plant's life cycle through the seasons. (Available as a BIG Book.)

*Tops & Bottoms* adapted by Janet Stevens. Harcourt, 1995. K–3. Hare turns his bad luck around by striking a clever deal with the rich and lazy bear down the road.

*The Turnip* retold and illustrated by Janina Domanska. Macmillan Publishing, 1969. PK–2. This classic retelling of the story is somewhat involved, but incorporates exciting dialogue for participation such as "One, two, three, pull!" When all those in the line finally pull up the giant turnip, they fall backwards and the magpie, the last to join them, flies away thinking he caused the damage.

*Two of Everything: A Chinese Folktale* retold and illustrated by Lily Toy Hong. Albert Whitman, 1993. K–3. When a poor farmer finds a magic brass pot in his garden that doubles or duplicates whatever is placed inside it, his efforts to make himself wealthy lead to unexpected complications.

*Up, Down, and Around* by Katherine Ayres, illustrated by Nadine Bernard Westcott. Candlewick Press, 2007. PK–1. A garden produces a variety of edible plants, such as corn that grows up, onions that grow down, and tomato vines that twine all around. Peppers grow up. Potatoes grow down. Pumpkins vine around and around. (Available as a BIG Book.)

*Vegetable Garden* by Douglas Florian. Harcourt, 1991. Toddler–K. A family plants a vegetable garden and helps it grow to a rich harvest.

*What Does Bunny See? A Book of Colors and Flowers* by Linda Sue Park, illustrated by Maggie Smith. Clarion Books, 2005. PK–K. A rabbit wanders through the various flowers and colors of a cottage garden.

*What's This?* by Caroline Mockford. Barefoot Books, 2000. PK–1. A young girl, assisted by a bird and a marmalade cat, nurtures a seed until it grows into a beautiful sunflower. When the sunflower's head droops in the fall, the girl's teacher helps her save the seeds to share with her classmates in the spring.

*Who Is in the Garden?* by Vera Rosenberry. Holiday House, 2001. PK–1. A tour through a garden brings encounters with its inhabitants—including wrens, a praying mantis, a box turtle, and more.

*Zinnia's Flower Garden* by Monica Wellington. Dutton Children's Books, 2005. PK–1. Zinnia plants a garden, eagerly waits for the plants to grow, sells the beautiful flowers, then gathers seeds to plant the following year.

# Story Prop and Craft Directions

## Giant Carrot Prop

### Tools and Supplies

- orange felt, 1 yard of 45" wide
- light green felt, 1 yard of 45" wide
- orange thread
- polyester fiberfill stuffing (3½ 8 oz. bags)
- scissors
- dressmaker's pins
- sewing machine
- hand-sewing needle

### Directions

1. Photocopy the CARROT BODY, CARROT TOP, and CARROT FROND patterns on page 105 at 400% (or at 200% twice if necessary!). Tape the enlarged paper pattern pieces together. Cut the pieces from felt as directed on the patterns.

2. Fold the bottoms of two of the CARROT FRONDS lengthwise as shown on the pattern and pin. The third frond will remain flat. Pin one of the folded fronds on one side of the flat frond and the second folded frond on the other side of the flat frond. They should be positioned opposite of each other, with their outer edges lined up with those of the center flat frond. Stitch across the bottom edge of the fronds to secure them. Seam allowance is ½".

3. Position the two orange CARROT TOP halves exactly on top of each other, right sides together. Slide the stitched edge of the CARROT FRONDS between the CARROT TOP layers so the fronds are in the center with their bottom edge along the straight edges of the CARROT TOP halves, and pin. With orange thread, stitch across the straight edge. Seam allowance is ⅝". Press the CARROT TOP seam allowance open along the outer edges.

4. Baste a gathering stitch around the edge of the CARROT TOP, ½" in from the edge. This will help ease the top onto the carrot bottom later on.

5. Stitch small horizontal tucks all over the CARROT BODY with orange thread. (Fold carrot felt over, right sides together, and stitch a short seam. The beginning and end of the seams should be at the very edges of the fold; the inner part of the seam should be ¼" or so in from the fold.) This will help to shape the carrot body and give it ridges like a real carrot.

6. Right sides together, stitch the outer edge of the CARROT BODY using orange thread. Seam allowance is ⅝". Leave a 5" opening along the side (about 12" down from the top of the carrot), so that you can turn the carrot right side out later on. Trim seams.

7. Gather the CARROT TOP slightly so it will ease successfully onto the CARROT BOTTOM. With right sides together and green fronds pointing down into the carrot casing, pin the orange CARROT TOP to the CARROT BOTTOM all around; stitch with orange thread. Seam allowance is ⅝". Trim seams.

8. Turn carrot right side out and stuff with polyester fiberfill until firm. Stitch opening closed using orange thread.

## "May" Bone Planter

### Tools and Supplies

- plastic planter, approximately 24" long and 7½" deep
- polyester foam to fit inside the planter (use thick foam and cut it to fit using a bread knife, or roll up a larger piece of thin foam into a thick roll and wedge it into the planter)
- scissors
- hot glue gun and glue sticks
- brown craft paint
- paintbrush
- thin dowel rod (approximately ¼" diameter; 10" long)
- green card stock
- white paper
- pinking shears
- hole punch
- Tacky Glue® craft glue
- three giant plastic bones OR cut out 3 bone shapes from heavy cardboard and paint white
- utility knife

### Directions

1. Cut the foam to fit the planter, and position it securely (you can hot glue it if necessary).

2. In the foam, cut three evenly spaced holes in which to plant the "bones" (size the holes appropriately so the bones will stand upright when planted). Use scissors to cut the holes. Foam is difficult to cut; it is fine if the holes appear a bit ragged.

3. Paint the top of the foam with brown craft paint to look like "dirt." Allow the paint to dry completely.

4. If you do not have ready-made giant plastic bones, make three bone-shaped cutouts from the heavy cardboard and

paint them white. Allow the paint to dry completely.

5. Cut out a 4½" long x 4" wide rectangle from green card stock, using pinking shears. Hole punch the center top and center bottom, about ½" in from the edge. Cut out a small bone shape from the white paper and glue it to the center of the green card stock backing. Insert the dowel rod through the holes as shown in the "May" photo to create a "bone" garden marker.

6. Use the bone planter, bones, and garden marker together with a dog puppet, hat or headband; one or two rocks; and a watering can to share the poem as described on page 97.

## Grow, Flower, Grow! Switcheroo Prop

### Tools and Supplies

- two identical plastic flowerpots, approximately 11" diameter and 9" deep
- two flat Styrofoam disks (approximately 9" diameter; 1" thick), sized to fit snugly down into the tops of the flowerpots
- two Styrofoam cubes, approximately 5"
- brown craft paint
- paintbrush
- hot glue gun and glue sticks
- giant colorful artificial flower
- bottom tip of artificial flower, approximately 13" long
- heavy-duty wire cutters

### Directions

1. Paint both Styrofoam disks with brown paint. Allow the paint to dry completely.

2. Hot glue the Styrofoam cubes to the inside bottom of each flower pot. They will help provide some stability for the wire stems when you insert them and for the Styrofoam disks.

3. Hot glue the painted Styrofoam disks to the inner rim of each flowerpot so that the disks are level. There is often a ridge or indentation one or two inches

down from the flowerpot rim where the disk will fit snugly, or it can rest on the Styrofoam cube.

4. Stick the bottom stem tip in the center of the first flowerpot, pushing it down through the Styrofoam disk and Styrofoam cube to touch the bottom of the pot for stability. It should stick out 6½" or so above the "dirt" disk so it can be seen easily by the audience. Stick the artificial flower stem into the center of the second flowerpot, pushing it down through the Styrofoam disk and Styrofoam cube to touch the bottom of the pot for stability.

5. Use the flower switcheroo prop together with gathered fake food props and your giant sun and rain stick puppets to tell the story as described on page 98.

## Giant Sun and Rain Stick Puppets

### Tools and Supplies

- heavy yellow matte board or cardboard
- yellow and orange craft paint
- heavy gray matte board or cardboard
- silver craft paint
- paintbrush
- silver Christmas tree "icicles" for the rain, approximately 20" long
- sharp utility knife
- two ⅝" thick dowel rods (22" long for the sun; 30" long for the rain cloud)
- black craft paint
- clear gloss acrylic varnish
- hot glue gun and hot glue sticks
- black cloth "duck" tape or heavy-duty book tape

### Directions

1. Cut out a large circle shape from the yellow matte board or cardboard for the sun. Cut out a large cloud shape from the gray matte board or cardboard for the rain cloud.

2. Outline and paint the sun and rain cutouts as desired with the craft paint (see

photo for possible ideas). Allow the paint to dry completely.

3. Paint the dowel rods black. Allow the paint to dry completely. Varnish the dowel rods and allow to dry.

4. Hot glue and tape the silver rain "icicles" to the back of the cloud, approximately 3" up from the bottom cloud edge.

5. Hot glue a dowel rod to the center back of each cutout, high enough on the back so the rod will adequately support the figures. Reinforce the glued attachment point with black cloth tape or heavy-duty book tape.

Note: These stick puppets can be used to dramatize many stories, poems, and songs! For example, let the sun shine and the rain fall on an "itsy bitsy" spider finger puppet as you prepare to sing the song about the famous little spider. (See the sound recordings "The Itsy, Bitsy Spider" on *Bathtime Magic* by Joanie Bartels, BMG, 1990; and "The Eensy Weensy Spider" on *Mainly Mother Goose: Songs and Rhymes for Merry Young Souls* by Sharon, Lois, & Bram, Elephant, 1984).

## Tiny Growing Flower Story Prop and Student Craft

### Tools and Supplies

- 8 oz. paper cups
- poem cutouts of "Growing Flowers" and/or "Little Seed"
- flexible green straws
- light green card stock or construction paper for leaves (cut into 1¼" squares)
- colored card stock or construction paper for flowers (cut into 2¾" squares, or

whatever size they need to be to fit easily down into the paper cup)

- markers, stickers, pompoms, googly eyes, etc.
- craft glue
- cellophane tape
- scissors
- utility knife

### Directions

If making these crafts with a group, prepare the following ahead of time:

*Drill or cut a drinking-straw-size hole in the center bottom of each paper cup. A small "x" slit with scissors or a utility knife will work if necessary. Glue a copy of the "Growing Flowers" and/or "Little Seed" poems (see patterns on page 106) to the outside of the cup, or type and print the poems on adhesive labels and affix.*

1. Give each child a green straw stem; green card stock or construction paper for leaves; and colored card stock or construction paper for flowers. Have the children cut out leaves and flowers and decorate them as desired with markers, stickers, pompoms, googly eyes, etc.

2. Glue or tape each flower to the very end of the straw stem (the end nearest the flexible bend); glue or tape the leaves to the flexible bend section below the flower. Allow the glue to dry completely. Reinforce glued attachment points with tape if necessary.

3. Insert the end of the straw (the end furthest away from the flexible bend) down and through the inside of the cup. The straw should stop at the flexible bend and not go through the hole.

4. Gently pull the flowers straight down into the cups.

5. Say the poem(s) and "sprout" the flowers!

# Storytime Carrot Patterns

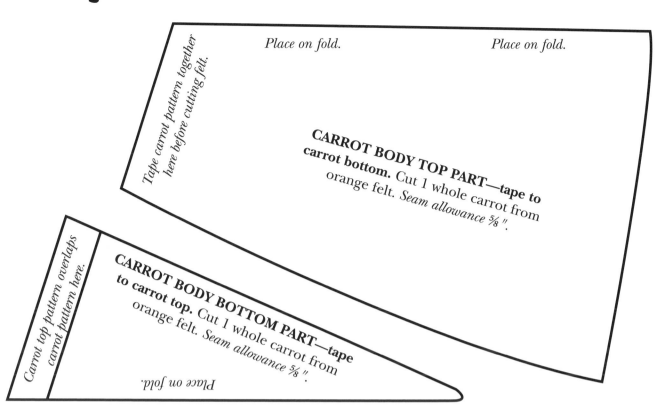

*Place on fold.*          *Place on fold.*

*Tape carrot pattern together here before cutting felt.*

**CARROT BODY TOP PART—tape to carrot bottom.** Cut 1 whole carrot from orange felt. *Seam allowance ⅝".*

*Carrot top pattern overlaps carrot pattern here.*

**CARROT BODY BOTTOM PART—tape to carrot top.** Cut 1 whole carrot from orange felt. *Seam allowance ⅝".*

*Place on fold.*

**CARROT TOP**
Cut 2 from orange felt.

## PHOTOCOPY THIS ENTIRE PAGE AT 400%.

**Tape the enlarged paper pattern pieces together as necessary.**

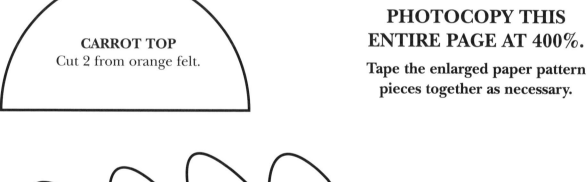

**CARROT FRONDS**
Cut 3 from light green felt.

*Fold line.*

# Poems for Tiny Growing Flowers Craft

## Growing Flowers

Plant some tiny little seeds,

Water them and pull the weeds.

Let the sun shine down below,

And little seeds are sure to grow!

## Little Seed

Little seed in the ground,

Lying so still.

Little seed, will you sprout?

"Yes! I Will!"

# I Like Bugs
## June

## Early Literacy Activities

### Name Tags

Insect stamp or sticker

### Clue(s)

Insect finger puppet(s) or plastic/rubber insect(s)

### Mailbox "Letter" of the Day

"B" and "b"

Bug, Bumblebee, Ball, Bear, Birthday, Boy, Bike, Book

### Mother Goose Rhyme Time

*Little Bo-Peep*

*Little Bo-Peep has lost her sheep,*
*And doesn't know where to find them.*
*Leave them alone, and they'll come home,*
*Wagging their tails behind them.*

### Rhyming Basket

Bug/Mug; Bee/Tee; Fly/Pie

## Early Literacy Skill: Language and Vocabulary

Introduce and explain new words or new meanings to familiar words.

- Use informational books and realia throughout storytime to illustrate and elaborate new words or concepts as you are learning about insects, such as thorax, exoskeleton, larva, pupa, nymph, cocoon, chrysalis, ommatidia, and so forth.

- Explain multiple terminologies in an engaging manner as appropriate; for example, inchworms are sometimes called measuring worms, or loopers. Demonstrate the inchworm's crawling motion with your rod puppet, showing how its body loops up in the middle when it crawls.

- When you tell your inchworm puppet that he "really used [his] wits" to figure out how to escape from the birds that wanted to eat him, explain to him and the children that it means he was really thinking hard and being smart.

- Rhyming basket: Clarify and define new words such as "mug" and "tee" with realia and explanations.

## Program Summary and Theme

Go on a "Bug Hunt" together with your audience! Consider creating a "tall, tall grass" environment around your entire storytime area, or behind the storyteller if your group is too big to be easily encircled. Cut tall grass frond outlines from sturdy green poster board (poster board is available in several thicknesses), and mount them on cardboard boxes or large bookends for stability (have a volunteer help you prepare this in advance). Hide copies of your books or other representative items around the storytime area ahead of time. "Discover" them with a magnifying glass and "catch" them in a butterfly net or a giant "bug bottle" as the storytime progresses.

Prepare the props and puppets ahead of time so you can use them throughout the program. Please see patterns and directions on pages 117–123. See suggested titles on pages 115–117 to substitute for older or younger audiences.

## Music

Play "buggy" music as the audience is gathering in your storytime area. Possibilities include *Songs About Insects, Bugs & Squiggly Things* created by Jane Murphy, musical arrangements by Dennis Buck (Kimbo Educational, 1998); "There Ain't No Bugs on Me" on *Not for Kids Only* by Jerry Garcia and David Grissman (Acoustic Disc, 1993); "Shoo Fly" on *On the Move* by Greg and Steve (Youngheart, 1997); and many others.

# Sample Program

Please adjust content and length as needed.

## Introduction

*Say:* Today we are going on a bug hunt in storytime! Before we begin, we need to make sure we know what a bug looks like.

*(Use informational books and realia to illustrate and elaborate facts about insects, arthropods, and "true bugs." Only explain as much as your group can handle.)*

FUN FACTS

- Instead of having a skeleton inside their bodies like humans, insects have a hard outer shell called an exoskeleton to protect their soft inside organs.

- Insects have six legs.

- Insects have three distinct body segments—abdomen, thorax, and head.

- During an insect's life, its body goes through a series of changes called metamorphosis. Some insects go through a complete metamorphosis, starting life as an egg, hatching into a larva (or caterpil-

lar), becoming a pupa (a butterfly's pupa is usually called a chrysalis; a moth's pupa is called a cocoon), and then emerging as an adult.

See these nonfiction titles for beautiful photographs of this process: *Life Cycle of a Butterfly* by Angela Royston (Heinemann Library, 1998) and *Butterfly* ("See How They Grow" series) photographed by Kim Taylor, written and edited by Mary Ling (Dorling Kindersley, 1992).

Other insects go through an incomplete metamorphosis, beginning as eggs but hatching to look like adult insects, only smaller. They are called nymphs at this stage. The nymph then sheds its skin as it grows, until it is its adult size.

- All bugs are insects, but not all insects are bugs! "True bugs," or hemipterans, have piercing and sucking mouthparts.

- Insects are arthropods, having an exoskeleton and jointed legs; however, not all arthropods are insects! For example, spiders are arthropods, but not insects.

*Say:* Many bugs are really small *(hold up an enormous plastic bug\* in one hand off to the side, outside your range of vision and deliberately not looking at it),* so we may need a magnifying glass *(hold up magnifying glass in other hand)* to be able to see its legs and body parts. *(The audience may be calling out to you that your bug isn't small!)* We'll take a look at this tiny, itsy bitsy little bug right now and make sure it is really an insect. *(Bring magnifying glass across to peer at bug, and jump back!)* Wow! This is definitely not a small bug, is it? We should be able to see it clearly even without a magnifying glass! *(Point out the body parts that you learned about in the informational books.)*

(\*Giant plastic bugs are frequently available at discount and toy stores, or in "prize" catalogues such as Kipp Bros., Oriental Trading Company, Rhode Island Novelty, U. S. Toy Company, Inc., and others. See Resources on page 216.)

## Segue

*Say:* Now that we know a little bit more about bugs, are you ready to go on a storytime bug hunt today? That's great, because a bug hunt is what our first book is all about.

## Read and Sing Aloud (With Adaptations)

*Bug Hunt: A Lift-the-Flap Book* by Neecy Twinem. Grosset & Dunlap, 1999. Toddler–Grade 1. A bee, ladybug, butterfly, grasshopper, and more hide behind leaf, grass, and flower petal flaps.

Note: Several of the creatures discovered are not actually bugs or even insects, for example the roly-poly "pill bug," an earthworm, a daddy-longlegs spider, and a snail. Depending on the level of your group, you can discuss together whether or not these discoveries are bugs or insects, or arthropods, or none of the above.

*CHANT while patting lap, collectively repeating throughout:*

We're going on a bug hunt,
a bug hunt, a bug hunt.
We're going on a bug hunt,
let's see what we can find.

*As you lift each flap to find out what is hiding beneath it, sing about where you are looking and what you found to the tune: "Mary Had A Little Lamb." For example:*

Let's look behind the flower petal,
flower petal, flower petal.
Let's look behind the flower petal.
What could be hiding there?
*Announce together:* "It's a LADYBUG!"

(Note: If you do not have access to the book, you can still share the story as a chanting/singing rhyme with puppets and props.)

## Segue/Action (Standing to Sitting)

*Say:* I think we should find out what our next buggy book is going to be. I'm sure it's hiding somewhere in this room. Do you think so? Let's try saying our "Bug Hunt" chant together and jump to keep the rhythm, okay? *(Jump while chanting the "Bug Hunt" chorus several times through, then dramatically "sssshhhhhh" the group and motion for them to be seated before you look behind the tall grass and hold up what was there. Creep detective-style around the storytime area, magnifying glass in hand.)* Let's chant "Bug Hunt" again softly:

We're going on a bug hunt,
a bug hunt, a bug hunt.
We're going on a bug hunt,
let's see what we can find.

*(Sung to the tune: "Mary Had a Little Lamb.")*

Let's look behind the tall grass,
the tall grass, the tall grass.
Let's look behind the tall grass.
What could be hiding there?

*Announce:* "It's *In the Tall, Tall Grass!* by Denise Fleming. This must be our next buggy book!"

## Read Aloud with Actions

*In the Tall, Tall Grass* by Denise Fleming. Henry Holt & Company, 1991. Toddler–Grade 1. A fuzzy caterpillar crawling through the tall, tall grass on a sunny afternoon sees many insects, birds, and small animals. (Available as a BIG Book.)

Munch, sip, buzz, and so forth as you revel in the world of the tall, tall grass. Encourage the audience to make the sounds with you, and incorporate actions as appropriate.

*Extension Idea: Song with flannel board or puppets*

*Make simple flannel board or stick puppet figures for the many creatures found in the captivating pages of Denise Fleming's In the Tall, Tall Grass. Share the song "The Twelve Days of Summer in the Tall, Tall Grass" with the audience, using your cutout figures. There are lots of pieces for everyone to play a part, or manipulate the pieces yourself while everyone sings together. If you are using stick puppets and need to manipulate them alone, you can mount each group of creatures in a long narrow block of foam and simply manipulate the block. On the final time through, sing it as fast as you can for a rousing conclusion!*

*For an additional extension, consider adding rhythm instruments for the various insects and creatures, with each having a distinct sound.*

"The Twelve Days of Summer in the Tall, Tall Grass" (The first day of summer is June 21.)

Adapted by Kimberly Faurot
*(Sung to the tune: "The Twelve Days of Christmas.")*

On the first day of summer,
The tall grass let me see:

A caterpillar crawling by me.

On the second day of summer,
The tall grass let me see:
2 hummingbirds
and a caterpillar crawling by me.

*Continue with the following:*

3 busy bees
4 flapping birds
5 busy ants
6 sliding snakes
7 scratching moles
8 hurried beetles
9 zapping frogs
10 hopping bunnies
11 fireflies
12 swooping bats

On the last day of summer,
The tall grass let me see:
100 million stars …

## Segue/Action (Standing to Sitting)

*Say:* Wow, there were sure a lot of bugs AND animals and other creatures in that tall, tall grass! I wonder what else there will be for us to find? Are you ready to jump? *(Chant the "Bug Hunt" chorus while jumping, then sit down again before looking beneath the flower so that everyone will be able to see what you discover.)*

We're going on a bug hunt, a bug hunt, a bug hunt.
We're going on a bug hunt, let's see what we can find.

*(Sung to the tune: "Mary Had a Little Lamb")*

Let's look beneath this flower, flower, flower.
Let's look beneath this flower.
What could be hiding there?

*(Peek your fabric inchworm rod puppet—see instructions and pattern on pages 119–121—around the flower so the audience can see part of him, then duck him back again. Have him peek out at the audience several times.)*

*Say to puppet:* What's the matter? Will you come out so we can see you? *(Puppet shakes head.)* Are you frightened? *(Puppet nods head vigorously.)* What? Some birds wanted to eat you? Oh, no wonder you're being extra cautious. Don't worry, we won't hurt you! *(Peek puppet out and inch him out so audience can see.)*

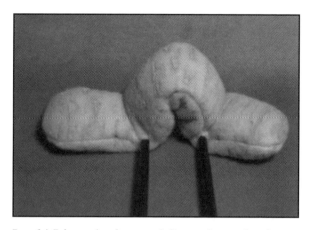

Look! It's an inchworm! Sometimes they're called measuring worms, or loopers. *(To puppet.)* Will you show us how you crawl, so we can see why you're called that? *(Demonstrate your inchworm rod puppet inching along: hold the puppet's front rod still with one hand while moving the back rod forward and toward it with the other hand, making the inchworm hump up in the middle. Move the front rod forward and away again so the inchworm is stretched out flat once more, and so forth.)* His body loops up in the middle when he crawls, doesn't it? That's why one of its names is a "looper." *(To puppet)* Will you bite us? *(Puppet shakes head vigorously.)* Inchworms don't bite or sting people, so they are often considered friendly and cute even though some inchworm species can damage crops and trees. There are even poems about inchworms. *(Invite an adult or older child volunteer to come forward and face the audience with his or her arm stretched out horizontally to their side. Inch your fabric inchworm rod puppet slowly up the volunteer's arm as you recite the poem "Inch-Worm" by Dorothy Aldis. Pause the puppet periodically as it goes to stretch its head around like an actual inchworm typically does as it crawls along. At the end of the poem, the rod puppet kisses the volunteer's cheek, then takes a bow along with the volunteer.)*

## Poem with Props

Recite Dorothy Aldis' poem "Inch-Worm" while manipulating your inchworm rod puppet as described above. "Inch-Worm" is included in various poetry anthologies, including *Flit, Flutter, Fly!: Poems About Bugs and Other Crawly Creatures* selected by Lee Bennett Hopkins (Doubleday, 1992).

> **"Inch-Worm"**
>
> *Little green inch-worm,*
> *Inch-worm, inch.*
> *You can't hurt me,*
> *You don't pinch.*
>
> *Never did anyone*
> *Any harm*
> *So take your little green walk*
> *Up my arm.*
>
> —Dorothy Aldis

An additional or alternate option is Douglas Florian's "The Inchworm" in his book of insect poems entitled *Insectlopedia* (Harcourt Brace, 1998).

## Segue

*Say to puppet:* We're so glad you didn't get eaten by any birds! We're going to read all about what happened in your story. *(Hold up the book* Inch By Inch *by Leo Lionni.)* You really used your wits to figure out what to do! That means you were really thinking hard about it, and you were being smart. *(Puppet nods vigorously; set him on a leaf while you read the book.)*

## Read Aloud

*Inch By Inch* by Leo Lionni. Astor-Honor, 1960. PK–3. When a little inchworm is accosted by some hungry birds, he uses his skill in measuring to save himself.

Share the story using different voices for the various birds. Sing the nightingale's comments with a lofty operatic voice, and when the nightingale begins to sing her song for the inchworm to measure, begin singing an operatic version of a well-known song such as "Twinkle, Twinkle, Little Star" or a popular radio hit song if you have older students. The audience will love it!

## Segue

*(After you have read the last page and closed the book, extend the idea by having your own inchworm puppet inch back and away out of sight. Call "goodbyes" to him as he goes, have him turn, nod, and blow kisses.) Say:* Thank goodness our inchworm escaped being eaten! Now he will be able to turn into a moth some day. I wonder who else is hiding in this tall, tall grass?

## Segue/Action
## (Standing to Sitting)

We're going on a bug hunt,
a bug hunt, a bug hunt.
We're going on a bug hunt,
let's see what we can find.

*(Sung to the tune: "Mary Had A Little Lamb")*

Let's look along a tree bough,
a tree bough, a tree bough.
Let's look along a tree bough.
What could be hiding there?

*Say:* It's a—*(produce branch with bottle cocoon or chrysalis and mailbox with raised flag containing a tiny letter hanging from it)*—wait a minute! This doesn't look like an insect, or even like a larva! I wonder if this little letter *(hold up letter)* might explain what is going on. Look! It's addressed to us. *(Point with finger to address and run your finger along the words as you read them aloud.)* TO: Library Storytime. That's us!

## Poem with Props

Share "Message from a Caterpillar" by Lilian Moore with your cocoon and moth OR chrysalis and butterfly. See patterns and instructions on pages 117–119 and 122–123. The poem is included in *The Poetry Break: An Annotated Anthology With Ideas for Introducing Children to Poetry* by Caroline Feller Bauer, illustrated by Edith Bingham (H. W. Wilson, 1994), *Something New Begins: New and Selected Poems* by Lilian Moore, illustrated by Mary Jane Dunton (Atheneum, 1982), *Itsy-Bitsy Beasties: Poems From Around the World* selected by Michael Rosen, illustrated by Alan Baker (Carolrhoda Books, 1992), and others.

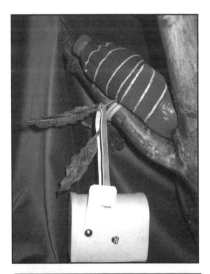

### "Message from a Caterpillar"

*Don't shake this
bough.
Don't try to
wake me
now.*

*In this cocoon
I've work to
do.
Inside this silk
I'm changing
things.*

*I'm worm-like now
but in this
dark
I'm growing
wings.*

—Lilian Moore

## Segue

*Say:* So this is the pupa. Since she says it's a cocoon *(OR chrysalis)*, she must be turning into a moth *(OR butterfly)*. Oh! It's hatching! *(Gently open the cocoon/chrysalis hatch and help your moth/butterfly puppet emerge. Remind the children that her wings need to pump up and dry before she can fly.)* She can sit and listen to our next story while her wings are getting ready. Then we'll check on her again and see if she is ready to fly!

## Segue

*Say:* We have time for one more story, so let's find out what it is. Just in case it's a bug that might get scared away if we are loud, let's whisper our chant very softly this time:

We're going on a bug hunt, a bug hunt, a bug hunt.
We're going on a bug hunt, let's see what we can find.

*(Sung to the tune: "Mary Had a Little Lamb")*

Let's look beneath this green leaf, green leaf, green leaf.
Let's look beneath this green leaf.
What could be hiding there?

*(Produce either a small plush Very Hungry Caterpillar doll\* if you have one, or a copy of* The Very Hungry Caterpillar.*)*

*Announce:* I think many of us know this story—it's all about a very hungry caterpillar!

*(\*Plush Very Hungry Caterpillar dolls are available from many children's bookstores or from* www.carlemuseum.org/shop.*)*

## Read Aloud OR Flannel OR Puppet Story

*The Very Hungry Caterpillar* by Eric Carle. Philomel Books, 1987. Toddler–Grade 1. A hungry little caterpillar eats his way through a varied and very large quantity of food. Full at last, he forms a cocoon around himself and goes to sleep—awakening as a beautiful butterfly. (Available in Spanish and as a BIG Book.)

Note: If you have clarified the differences between a cocoon and chrysalis during the program, you may wish to share Mr. Carle's Web site FAQ explanation about why the butterfly in *The Very Hungry Caterpillar* comes from a cocoon rather than a chrysalis (see www.eric-carle.com).

Count all of the foods together as a group, make munching noises, and so forth.

## Segue

*Say:* Check on your moth or butterfly with drying wings, and help her "fly" away. Sing a little song as you manipulate the puppet. *(Sung to the tune: "Twinkle, Twinkle, Little Star." Words by Kimberly Faurot.)*

MOTH

Little moth, the moon is high; *(hold your moon stick puppet from May "Growing Gardens" aloft)*

I think your wings are finally dry.
It is time for you to try,

To flutter, flutter, flutter fly!
Fly away into the sky,
Little moth—goodbye! Goodbye!

OR

BUTTERFLY

Hello, little butterfly!
I think your wings are finally dry.
It is time for you to try,
To flutter, flutter, flutter fly!
Fly away into the sky,
Little butterfly—goodbye!

## Conclusion

*Say:* She is off to have some moth/butterfly adventures, isn't she? We certainly had a buggy adventure of our own—we found lots of bugs and insect stories on our storytime bug hunt today! Keep your eyes and ears open, and you may see and hear some more insects on your way home today and as you go through the week. Since our bug hunt is over for now, though, let's do our "Bug Hunt" chant one last time—saying "We went on a bug hunt," and ending with "And we found lots of bugs!"

Chant the following slightly altered version of the end of *Bug Hunt: A Lift-the-Flap Book* by Neecy Twinem:

We went on a bug hunt,
a bug hunt, a bug hunt.
We went on a bug hunt,
and we found lots of bugs! Hooray!
*(Clap enthusiastically.)*

## Special Handout Idea

See the way many insects see with their faceted eyes by looking through faceted "prism scopes."* Butterflies' compound eyes are made up of many tiny eyes called ommatidia (om-a-tid-ee-a). (*Practice saying the word together.*) Share pages from informational titles that show an insect's faceted eyes, such as:

*Butterflies and Moths* by John Feltwell. Eyewitness Explorers series. Dorling Kindersley, 1997. (See pages 18–19.)

*Insects* by Steve Parker. Eyewitness Explorers series. DK Publishing, 1997. (See page 21.)

(*"Prism scopes" are frequently available at discount stores or in "prize" catalogues such as Kipp Bros.; Oriental Trading Company; Rhode Island Novelty; U. S. Toy Company, Inc.; and others. See Resources.)

## Craft Ideas

- Make a "Paper Caterpillar to Butterfly" craft from *Crafts for Kids Who Are Wild About Insects* by Kathy Ross, illustrated by Sharon Lane Holm (The Millbrook Press, 1997). A piece of paper is folded in half and cut to look like a fat caterpillar; when you open the paper, the resulting shape serves as a butterfly's wings. Extend the craft further by decorating the other side as a chrysalis, then share the following poem with your "Paper Caterpillar, Chrysalis, Butterfly" craft. Glue or tape a copy of the poem to the cutout for families to repeat together at home.

"Caterpillar, Chrysalis, Butterfly"

Roly-poly caterpillar
(OR "Very hungry caterpillar")

Into a corner crept.
*(Hold up caterpillar.)*

Spun himself a blanket,
*(Flip over to chrysalis side.)*

Then for a long time slept.
*(Snore!)*

Roly-poly caterpillar
(OR "Very hungry caterpillar")

Wakening by and by,
*(Open to show butterfly.)*

Found himself with beautiful wings—

Changed to a butterfly!
*(Flap butterfly gently.)*

- Make Inchworm Paper Puppets using the pattern and directions on pages 120–121.

Use colored paper for the inchworm's body, and two plastic drinking straws for the rods. Inchworms, or looper worms, come in a variety of sizes and colors, and with a wide variety of markings, so your students should decorate their puppets creatively! Use crayons and markers as well as yarn, pom poms, and stickers to personalize the top side of each inchworm first, and then affix the straw rods to the bottom side of the inchworm along the dotted lines with clear tape.

Play Frank Loesser's song "Inchworm" while the children are working on their inchworm puppets. The song is included on the following sound recordings: *A Child's Celebration of Song 2* (Music for Little People, 1996), *Singin' in the Bathtub* by John Lithgow (Sony, 1999), and *There's a Hippo In My Tub* by Anne Murray (Capitol, 1977).

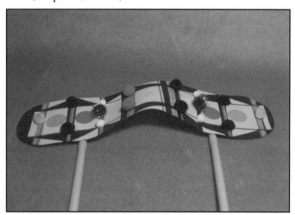

- Make a "Letter B" Butterfly. Complete instructions are included in *Kathy Ross Crafts: Letter Shapes* by Kathy Ross, illustrated by Jan Barger (Millbrook Press, 2002). Position two large letter "B" cutouts back to back form the butterfly's wings, with a colored craft stick in the middle for the butterfly's body.

## Additional Craft Ideas

- Make "Hatching Butterflies." See complete directions at: www.hhmi.org/coolscience/butterfly/index.html.

Cut out and color a butterfly from colored card stock or construction paper. Make a tiny hole in the butterfly's head, and twist a piece of pipe cleaner through

it to serve as antennae. Glue the butterfly to one end of a wooden craft stick. Allow the glue to dry completely. Color a toilet paper tube to look like a chrysalis. Curl the butterfly's wings and slide it into the chrysalis tube. Pull it out when it is time for the butterfly to "hatch!"

- Make "Handprint Wings Butterflies." See complete directions at: www.enchant edlearning.com/crafts/handprint/butterfly.

Trace the children's hands onto colored construction paper so you have a total of six hand shapes. Cut them out to be the butterfly's wings. Cut out a butterfly's body from dark construction paper, and glue or staple three handprints to each side of the body, with the fingers pointing outward. Decorate the butterfly with crayons, markers, or paint, and glue on googly eyes and pipe cleaner antennae.

## Additional Extension Ideas

- Make a "Tall, Tall Grass" caterpillar rod puppet with yellow fabric, following the Fabric Inchworm Rod Puppet directions on page 119–120. Decorate with paint, pompoms, and pipe cleaners to reflect the caterpillar in Denise Fleming's book *In the Tall, Tall Grass*.

- Cut out flannel board figures for *The Very Hungry Caterpillar*, or large poster board food pieces, each with a round hole in the middle for a caterpillar puppet to chomp its way through.

- Make "The Twelve Days of Summer in the Tall, Tall Grass" pieces as a group and perform the song for family members!

- Share "The Very Hungry Caterpillar" song with actions from *Literacy in Motion* by The Learning Station (Kimbo Educational, 2005).

- Fun Fact: Insects can taste their food too! We have taste buds on our tongues, and can taste salty, sweet, sour, and bitter flavors. Ants taste their food with their antennae. Butterflies have taste buds on their feet and taste their food by standing on it!

# Additional Resources

*Alpha Bugs: A Pop-up Alphabet* by David A. Carter. Little Simon, 1994. PK–2. Familiar objects such as a doughnut, hammer, umbrella, and so forth are given buggy eyes and features, transforming them into members of an odd but comical alphabet species.
**Extension Craft:** Imagine what other everyday objects would look like as "bugs," and create them from cut paper.

*Ant, Ant, Ant!: An Insect Chant* by April Pulley Sayre, illustrated by Trip Park. NorthWord Books for Young Readers, 2005. PK–4. Exuberant rhyming text lists numerous insect names, with details about each featured insect explained in a glossary.

*Arabella Miller's Tiny Caterpillar* by Clare Jarrett. Candlewick Press, 2008. PK–2. In this extension of the classic rhyme/song about little Arabella Miller, a little girl feeds a tiny caterpillar and watches him morph into a swallowtail butterfly. Listen to the classic version on the sound recording *Mainly Mother Goose: Songs and Rhymes for Merry Young Souls* by Sharon, Lois & Bram (Elephant Records, 1984) or *Wee Sing in the Car* by Pamela Conn Beall and Susan Hagen Nipp (Price Stern Sloan, 2002).
**Extension Idea:** Sing the entire book to the classic tune ("Twinkle, Twinkle, Little Star"). Make sure to practice ahead of time so you will be able to get the timing right!
**Extension Craft:** Share the first page of the book with a little paper caterpillar puppet, and make paper inchworm/caterpillar puppets as a group after finishing the story. If you would like to make miniature caterpillars, simply shrink the paper inchworm pattern on the copier, and use coffee stirrers or cocktail straws for rods.

*The Beauty of the Beast: Poems from the Animal Kingdom* selected by Jack Prelutsky, illustrated by Meilo So. Knopf, 1997. K–8. Insects are highlighted in section one. The poems reflect a wide range of difficulty levels and content.

*Beetle Bop* by Denise Fleming. Harcourt, 2007. PK–2. Illustrations and rhyming text reveal the great variety of beetles and their swirling, humming, crashing activities.

*Buggy Riddles* by Katy Hall and Lisa Eisenberg; pictures by Simms Taback. Dial Books for Young Readers, 1986. PK–3. An illustrated collection of insect riddles including "Why do bees hum? They don't know the words!" and "What is the best year for grasshoppers? Leap year!"

*"Bugs! Bugs!"* in *A Pizza the Size of the Sun* by Jack Prelutsky; pictures by James Stevenson. Greenwillow Books, 1996. K–4. The author is "bugs" for all sorts of bugs, keeping them in his pockets and even wearing them in his hair.
**Extension Idea:** Make felt or three-dimensional clay bugs to match the descriptions in the poem and share the props, enthusiastically hugging and kissing the bugs and bouncing them on your knee as directed!

*Bugs! Bugs! Bugs!* by Bob Barner. Chronicle Books, 1999. Toddler–Grade 1. Brief rhyming text introduces children to familiar bugs. Includes a section with fun facts.

*"Buzz, Buzz, Buzz," Went Bumblebee* by Colin West. Candlewick Press, 1997. Toddler–Grade 1. Bumblebee buzzes around bothering everyone until he comes to a gentle butterfly who understands that the busy bee is looking for someone to be his friend.
**Extension Idea:** Make flannel board cutouts to accompany the story.

*The Caterpillar and the Polliwog* by Jack Kent. Prentice-Hall, 1982. PK–2. Impressed by the proud caterpillar's boast that she will turn into a butterfly when she grows up, a polliwog determines to watch the caterpillar very carefully and turn into a butterfly too.

*The Caterpillow Fight* by Sam McBratney, illustrated by Jill Barton. Candlewick Press, 1996. PK–1. A rowdy pillow fight among young caterpillars causes the Big Caterpillar to step in and take action.

*A Colorful Adventure of the Bee Who Left Home One Monday Morning and What He Found Along the Way* by Lisa Campbell Ernst, illustrated by Lee Ernst. Lothrop, Lee & Shepard, 1986. Toddler–K. A bee leaves its hive, passing many colors on its route before returning home through the rain and seeing a beautiful rainbow.

*Crafts for Kids Who Are Wild About Insects* by Kathy Ross, illustrated by Sharon Lane Holm.

The Millbrook Press, 1997. PK–4. Projects reflect a variety of insects and difficulty levels.

**"Caterpillars"** poem in *A Cricket in a Thicket* by Aileen Fisher, illustrated by Feodor Rojankovsky. Scribner, 1963. PK–2. Caterpillars don't do or know much except how to chew and grow so they will become butterflies; however, that is more than the poet can do no matter how much she chews!

*Flit, Flutter, Fly! Poems About Bugs and Other Crawly Creatures* selected by Lee Bennett Hopkins, illustrated by Peter Palagonia. Doubleday Books for Young Readers, 1992. PK–4. A collection of poems by a variety of authors about bugs and other creatures that crawl.

*From Caterpillar to Butterfly* by Deborah Heiligman, illustrated by Bari Weissman. HarperCollins, 1996. (Let's-Read-and-Find-Out Science series.) PK–1. Drawings and explanatory text clearly describe a classroom caterpillar's metamorphosis into a Painted Lady butterfly.

*The Grouchy Ladybug* by Eric Carle. HarperCollins, 1996, 1977. PK–1. A grouchy ladybug, looking for a fight, challenges everyone she meets regardless of their size or strength. (Available in Spanish.)

*The Honeybee and the Robber: A Moving/Picture Book* by Eric Carle. Philomel Books, 2000, 1981. PK–1. After gathering nectar and making its way safely home, a lone honeybee saves the day when a bear attacks the hive. Includes tabs and pop-ups.

**"Hurt No Living Thing"** by Christina G. Rossetti in *Sing A Song of Popcorn: Every Child's Book of Poems* selected by Beatrice Schenk de Regniers, illustrated by Marcia Brown, et al. Scholastic, Inc., 1988. PK–4. An admonition to treasure all living things, including insects.

*I'm a Caterpillar* by Jean Marzollo, illustrated by Judith Moffatt. Scholastic, 1997. (Hello Reader! Level 1.) PK–1. Provides a simple explanation of what happens as a caterpillar changes into a butterfly—from the caterpillar's point of view. (Available as a BIG Book.)

**"I'm Off to Catch a Bumblebee"** in *Something Big Has Been Here; Poems* by Jack Prelutsky, drawings by James Stevenson. Greenwillow Books, 1990. PK–2. The poet has all sorts of disparate, wild apparatus to help him in his quest to catch a bumblebee.
**Extension Idea:** Gather props to tell this funny poem!

*Insectlopedia: Poems and Paintings* by Douglas Florian. Harcourt Brace, 1998. Grades 2–6. Presents twenty-one short poems about such insects as the inchworm, termite, cricket, and ladybug.

*Itsy-Bitsy Beasties: Poems From Around the World* selected by Michael Rosen, illustrated by Alan Baker. Carolrhoda Books, 1992. K–4. An anthology of short poems about insects and other small animals by authors from around the world.

*Joyful Noise: Poems for Two Voices* by Paul Fleischman, illustrated by Eric Beddows. Harper & Row, 1988. PK (listeners)–Grade 6 (performers). A collection of poems describing the characteristics and activities of a variety of insects.

**"The Last Cry of the Damp Fly"** by Dennis Lee in *A New Treasury of Children's Poetry: Old Favorites and New Discoveries* selected by Joanna Cole, illustrated by Judith Gwyn Brown. Doubleday, 1984. K–3. A fly swimming in a diner's soup requests removal, but ends up getting swallowed.

*Max's ABC* by Rosemary Wells. Viking, 2006. PK–1. When the ants from Max's ant farm escape, they cavort merrily through the alphabet as they take bites of his birthday cake, drink his cranberry juice, and kick their feet in the bathtub. All ends happily with the ants back in the ant farm at last, sound asleep and snoring ant snores.

*Miss Spider's Tea Party* by David Kirk. Scholastic, 1994. PK–2. When lonely Miss Spider tries to host a tea party, the other bugs refuse to come for fear of being eaten!

**"Mosquito"** in *The Llama Who Had No Pajama: 100 Favorite Poems* written by Mary Ann Hoberman, illustrated by Betty Fraser. Harcourt Brace, 1998. K–4. The poet implores Mrs. Mosquito to stop biting her.
**Fun Fact: Did You Know?**
If you hear a mosquito buzzing, you know that it's a female mosquito—she makes that noise with her wings. If you are bitten by a mosquito, you know that is a female as well, because male mosquitoes do not bite people

(their mouth apparatus can't pierce our skin). Source: *A Mosquito Is Born* by William White, Jr. and Sara Jane White (Sterling Publishing, 1978).

**"The Mosquito"** string story in *The Story Vine: A Source Book of Unusual and Easy-to-Tell Stories from Around the World* by Anne Pellowski. Macmillan Publishing Co., 1984. PK–4. A woman hears a buzzing sound while weaving cloth, but can't initially locate the source of the noise. At last the buzzing mosquito appears directly in front of her, and she claps her hands together—effectively dispatching it.

*Old Black Fly* by Jim Aylesworth; illustrated by Stephen Gammell. Henry Holt & Company, 1991. PK–4. A mischievous fly has a very busy, bad day romping through the alphabet, landing many places where he shouldn't. He ultimately meets his match and his demise, however, when he has the audacity to buzz around Mama. (Available as a BIG Book.)

"Patter Pitter Caterpillar" in *Beneath a Blue Umbrella: Rhymes* by Jack Prelutsky; pictures by Garth Williams. Greenwillow Books, 1990. PK–1. Patter Pitter Caterpillar ends up getting a tiny hug from a tiny bug.
**Extension Activity:** Share this brief poem using puppets.

*Ten Flashing Fireflies* by Philemon Sturges, illustrated by Anna Vojtech. North-South Books, 1995. PK–1. Two children catch fireflies on a summer night, putting them into a jar one by one until ten fireflies are caught. The insects blink slowly in the jar, and the children release them so they can fly away again.

*Two Bad Ants* by Chris Van Allsburg. Houghton Mifflin, 1988. K–4. When two bad ants desert from their colony, they experience a dangerous adventure that convinces them to return to their former safety.

*The Very Busy Spider* by Eric Carle. Philomel Books, 1984. Toddler–Grade 1. The farm animals try to divert a busy little spider from spinning her web, but she persists and produces a thing of both beauty and usefulness. The pictures may be felt as well as seen.

*The Very Clumsy Click Beetle* by Eric Carle. Philomel Books, 1999. PK–1. A clumsy young click beetle learns to land on its feet with encouragement from various animals and a wise old beetle. An electronic chip with a built-in battery creates clicking sounds to accompany the story.

*The Very Lonely Firefly* by Eric Carle. Philomel Books, 1995. PK–1. A lonely firefly goes out into the night searching for other fireflies. The final page has miniature flashing lights.

*The Very Quiet Cricket* by Eric Carle. Philomel Books, 1990. PK–1. A very quiet cricket who wants to rub his wings together and make a sound like many other animals do finally achieves his wish. The final page has a built-in sound chip.

*There Was An Old Lady Who Swallowed a Fly* by Simms Taback. Viking, 1997. PK–2. Presents the traditional version of a famous American folk poem first heard in the U.S. in the 1940s with illustrations on die-cut pages that reveal all that the old lady swallows. (Available as a BIG Book.)

*Waiting For Wings* by Lois Ehlert. Harcourt, 2001. PK–2. Follows the life cycle of four common butterflies, from their beginnings as tiny hidden eggs and hungry caterpillars to their transformation into butterflies.

*What's That Sound, Woolly Bear?* by Philemon Sturges, illustrated by Joan Paley. Little, Brown and Company, 1996. Woolly Bear caterpillar quietly shuffles along looking for a place to spin her bed and dream of tiger moths, while all around her other bugs buzz, chatter, zip, and whir.

# Story Prop and Craft Directions

## "Message From a Caterpillar" Moth OR Butterfly; Bottle Cocoon OR Chrysalis; and Mailbox with Letter

### Moth OR Butterfly

Note: Moth and Butterfly finger puppets and hand puppets are fairly easy to find and relatively inexpensive to purchase. (See Resources.) Alternately, make the following moth or butterfly.

## Tools and Supplies

- needle-nose pliers
- scissors

MOTH

- one 8½" x 11" sheet of tan or gold vellum
- one brown or tan "bump chenille stem"/ pipe cleaner
- puffy paint: dark brown, white, orange, tan

BUTTERFLY

- one 8½" x 11" sheet of orange vellum
- one black "bump chenille stem"/pipe cleaner
- puffy paint: white

## Directions

1. Photocopy the moth OR butterfly wing pattern on pages 122–123 onto the sheet of vellum as directed on the pattern, and cut it out.

2. Fold the wings in half along the center dotted line.

3. Highlight the body and wings with puffy paint if desired (see informational books for standard marking patterns: cecropia moth and monarch butterfly). Allow the paint to dry completely.

4. Cut a two-bump section from the "bump chenille stem"/pipe cleaner, making sure to retain the skinny lengths on the ends. Fold the section in half so the two bump sections match up to each other.

5. Apply a thin line of glue on the front of the wings along the fold, and another line of glue along the back side along the fold. Position the pipe cleaner bumps so one is along the butterfly's front and the other is along its back. Hold the pipe cleaner in place while it dries with clip clothespins if needed. Allow the glue to dry completely.

6. Twist the top of the pipe cleaner together and position the ends in a "V" at the top of the head as antennae. For the moth, bend the antennae back around so it is in a leaf shape; for the butterfly, curl the two antennae tips under to look like a butterfly's clubbed antennae. Twist the

folded pipe cleaner at the bottom of the body and curl it up and over the back.

7. Gently curl your moth or butterfly's wings around its body, in preparation for slipping into the cocoon or chrysalis bottle.

## *Cocoon OR Chrysalis*

### Tools and Supplies

- small clear plastic water or soda bottle, 12 oz., with its cap
- one knee-high nylon stocking (cocoon: opaque brown; chrysalis: black sheer)
- two small black elastic hair bands or rubber bands
- hot glue gun with hot glue sticks
- craft paint: brown and gold (cocoon) OR black, silver, and gold (chrysalis)
- utility knife to cut open the cocoon/ chrysalis "escape hatch"
- craft paintbrush
- brown or black string or ribbon to tie cocoon/chrysalis to a "branch" or leaf

### Directions

1. With the utility knife, cut an opening near the top of the plastic bottle, large enough so your moth/butterfly puppet will be able to slide in and out easily. The dimensions of the hole should be approximately 3" wide at the bottom, 1" wide at the top near the bottle neck, and 2" high.

2. Remove the bottle's cap and paint it brown (cocoon) or black (chrysalis). Allow the paint to dry completely.

3. Pull the knee-high nylon stocking up over the bottle so it is tight and smooth, though not stretched. Gather the nylon securely to the bottle neck with the two elastic bands, one at the base of the bottle neck and the other midway up the neck.

4. In the space where the nylon stocking stretches over the cut-out section of the bottle, cut away the nylon stocking. The edges will be rough, which is fine; it won't show when you are done. Hot glue the edges of the nylon hole to the edges of the hole in the bottle.

5. Cut off the nylon above the bottle neck so it extends approximately three inches above the top of the neck. Fold the length back down over the bottle so it will cover the top part of the bottle, including your cut-out "escape hatch" section.

6. Paint the cocoon/chrysalis as desired (see informational books for standard marking patterns). You may wish to also paint the part that will be hidden under the folded-down nylon, as it may show during storytime when you pull up the folded-down part to ease the moth/butterfly through the escape hatch. Allow the paint to dry completely.

7. Tie a string or narrow ribbon to the top of the cocoon/chrysalis to hang it from a storytime "branch" or leaf. Twist the bottle cap back onto the bottle, stopping about halfway—right above the top hairband.

8. Lift up the folded-down nylon covering, insert the moth/butterfly into the cocoon/chrysalis bottle, and pull the nylon back down over the escape hatch. Hang the cocoon/chrysalis so the escape hatch is facing you rather than the audience.

### Mailbox with Tiny Letter

- Tiny cardboard or metal mailboxes can be purchased from many craft or novelty stores, or paint a tiny cardboard box to look like a mailbox. See Resources (page 216–217) for mail-order options.

- Write out the poem "Message from a Caterpillar" by Lilian Moore in delicate writing on a tiny piece of paper, then insert the poem into a tiny envelope and place it in the mailbox.

## Inchworm Rod Puppet

### Fabric Inchworm

### Tools and Supplies

- lime green fabric (polar fleece works well)
- dressmaker's pins
- fabric shears

- sewing machine (*optional*—or may be hand-sewn)
- lime green thread
- hand-sewing needle
- polyester fiberfill stuffing
- black craft paint
- clear gloss acrylic varnish
- lime green craft paint
- craft paintbrush
- two wooden dowel rods, ¼" diameter and 10" long
- two wooden dowel rod end caps to fit ¼" dowel rods (candle cups or partially drilled wooden balls work well)
- Tacky Glue® craft glue

### Directions

1. Drill two small holes in each of the dowel rods, one inch and two inches from one end. Both holes on the rod should face the same direction. Paint the dowel rods and dowel rod end caps black; allow paint to dry. Glue one dowel rod end cap onto the non-drilled end of each dowel rod; allow glue to dry.

2. Photocopy the fabric inchworm pattern from page 121 and cut it out. Pin the pattern onto the green fabric and cut out as specified on the pattern.

3. With right sides together, pin and stitch the inchworm fabric along the stitching lines as shown on the pattern. Seam allowance is ¼". Trim the seams. Turn the inchworm casing right side out.

4. Stuff the inchworm casing loosely with polyester fiberfill so the inchworm will still be flexible and able to bend easily.

5. Insert the dowel rods one at a time into the openings along the side of the inchworm, with the holes pointing up and down. The 2" holes should be at the very edge of the inchworm casing. Stitch the dowels gently in place at the "x" points on your pattern. With green thread, insert your hand-sewing needle through the entire inchworm and 1" dowel rod

hole from bottom to top and then back through again several times. Don't pull the thread so tightly that there is a huge dimple at the spot, but make it secure. Hand-stitch the edges of the inchworm tightly to the dowel rods at the 2" hole points, and stitch the rest of the side opening closed.

6. Lightly paint cross-wise stripes on the inchworm with apple green paint, in varying widths and lengths. Allow paint to dry.

7. Your fabric inchworm rod puppet is ready to inch!

## *Paper Inchworm*

### Tools and Supplies

- colored paper, 24#
- safety scissors
- markers, crayons, or colored pencils
- colored stickers
- two plastic drinking straws (bendable or straight)
- cellophane tape
- Tacky Glue® craft glue
- pompoms, felt, lace, etc.

### Directions

1. Trace or photocopy the inchworm pattern from page 121 onto colored paper and cut it out.

2. Decorate the top side of the inchworm with markers, crayons, colored pencils, stickers, etc. (wait with the three-dimensional objects).

3. Affix the two drinking straws along the dotted lines on the bottom side of the paper inchworm with clear tape.

4. Decorate the top side of the paper inchworm with three-dimensional accoutrements such as pompoms, as desired.

### Manipulating Your Inchworm Puppets

Hold your inchworm puppet's front rod still with one hand while moving the back rod forward and toward it with the other hand, making the inchworm hump up in the middle. Move the front rod forward and away again so the inchworm is stretched out flat once more, and so forth.

# Inchworm Pattern

Tape straw along this line.

Tape straw along this line.

Inchworm Paper
Puppet Pattern

Stitch to here.

Insert dowel rod
along this line.

Stitch to here.

Stitch to here.

Insert dowel rod
along this line.

Stitch to here.

Inchworm Fabric
Puppet Pattern
*seam allowance ¼"*

# Moth

Photocopy at 100% on gold or tan vellum.

# Butterfly

Photocopy at 100% on orange vellum.

# Storytime Picnic
## July

## Early Literacy Activities

### Name Tags

Picnic basket OR ant stamp or stickers

### Clue(s)

Miniature picnic basket with checkered cloth; miniature picnic food; large plastic ant

### Mailbox "Letter" of the Day

"P" and "p"

Picnic, Popcorn, Peanut Butter, Purple, Pool, Pear, Princess, Puppy

### Mother Goose Rhyme Time

*Hey Diddle Diddle*

*Hey diddle diddle,*
*The cat and the fiddle,*
*The cow jumped over the moon.*
*The little dog laughed*
*To see such fun,*
*And the dish ran away with the spoon.*

### Rhyming Basket

Ants/Pants; Snail/Pail; Man/Can

### Early Literacy Skill: Phonological Awareness

Play with rhymes, practice breaking words apart and putting them back together, and listen for beginning sounds and alliteration.

- Play with the rhyming basket, and give clues for more rhyming words for which you don't have representative objects in the basket. For example, "I'm thinking of something that rhymes with "snail" and "pail" from our rhyming basket. When a dog is happy, it wags its _____." (*Tail.*)

- Write out the words to "Five Little Hot Dogs" on a piece of grid board, and clap once for each word in the rhyme. Introduce variety by stomping feet or jumping once for each word.

- Play together with the wonderful words in *Here Comes Henny* by Charlotte Pomerantz (Greenwillow Books, 1994). Is a "snicky-snacky" the same thing as a "snacky-snicky?" Make up real and nonsense words that rhyme, such as picky, chicky, snicky, licky, ticky, bicky, nicky, and so forth.

- Rhythmically sing "The Ants Go Marching," encouraging participation and emphasizing the rhyming words as you reach them.

- Blend word parts in several ways. For example, <u>Onset sound</u>: /p/ … ig. What's the word? (*Pig.*) What other words start with /p/? <u>Syllables</u>: pic … nic. What's the word? (*Picnic.*)

# Program Summary and Theme

Take a break with a picnic of stories! Spread "picnic blankets" or red-and-white checked tablecloths on the floor for your audience to sit upon, load your storytime books and props into a picnic basket or cooler, and you'll be ready for a storytime picnic. Produce the next book or prop item from the basket as you segue between the stories and activities.

Prepare the props and puppets ahead of time so you can use them throughout the program. Please see patterns and instructions on pages 131–138. See additional suggested titles on pages 129–130 to substitute for older or younger audiences.

## Music

Play "picnic" music as the audience is gathering in your storytime area. Possibilities include "Ladybugs' Picnic" on *Songs from the Street: 35 Years of Music* (Sony Wonder, 2003), "The Teddy Bears' Picnic" on *The Teddy Bears' Picnic* arranged and performed by Jerry Garcia and David Grisman (Acoustic, 1993), *There's a Hippo in My Tub* by Anne Murray (Capitol, 1977), *Unbearable Bears* by Kevin Roth (Marlboro, 1997), "Picnic of the World" on *Mother Earth* by Tom Chapin, "Watermelon" on *Family Garden* by John McCutcheon (Rounder, 1993), and many others.

# Sample Program

Please adjust content and length as needed.

## Introduction

*Say:* Today, we are having a pretend picnic—a Storytime Picnic! I brought a picnic basket we can use, but we will need to do some picnic packing! What are some of the things you might want to bring on a picnic? *(All guesses are good.)* Those are all great ideas! We can sing about what we should bring.

## Song with Props

Share Lynn Freeman Olson's song "Going on a Picnic" from Raffi's sound recording *The Corner Grocery Store* (MCA Records, 1979).

Before you begin, produce each picnic item one at a time from your picnic basket and identify it as a group. As you sing, place each item back in the basket.

Create cutouts of the food mentioned in the song from the patterns on pages 133–134, or package plastic play food items. If you prefer to branch out from the original version of the song, you may wish to share other creative picnic food options and sing about them, as well as toys and other supplies you might want to bring such as a Frisbee®, blankets, books, bug spray/lotion, and so forth.

## Segue

*Say:* In our first story, Mr. Pig is getting ready for a picnic as well. He already has his picnic lunch packed, but some of his animal friends try to help him get ready!

## Read Aloud

*(Produce book from picnic basket/cooler.)*

*The Pigs' Picnic* by Keiko Kasza. Putnam, 1988. PK–3. Nervous about inviting Miss Pig on a picnic, Mr. Pig allows his animal friends to persuade him to borrow and wear various handsome portions of their own bodies. The initial results are alarming, but when Mr. Pig returns to his own normal appearance, Miss Pig is delighted to accompany him.

Make sure you shriek with feeling when Miss Pig opens her door and sees the astonishing "monster" outside!

*Extension Idea: This story makes a wonderful flannel board.*

## Segue

*Say:* After you're ready to start out on your picnic, you may have some troubles along the way. Watch the pictures carefully as we read this story, and see if you can tell who is eating the picnic lunch that Hen, Duck, and Goose have packed.

## Read Aloud

*(Produce book from picnic basket/cooler.)*

*We're Going on a Picnic!* by Pat Hutchins. Greenwillow Books, 2002. PK–K. Hen, Duck, and Goose gather berries, apples, and pears to take on their picnic, but end up having several difficulties. First they have trouble deciding where to stop and eat their picnic, and then they discover that their food has mysteriously disappeared along the way!

## Segue

*(Produce plastic hot dog on bun OR paper/foamies version from picnic basket/cooler.)*

*Say:* I hope there's a little bit of picnic left for Hen, Duck, and Goose! Thankfully it looks like they packed enough for everyone. Here's one picnic food that they didn't pack: hot dogs!

## Action Rhyme (Sitting to Standing)

"Five Little Hot Dogs" (Adapted from "Five Fat Sausages" by Kimberly Faurot)

Five little hot dogs cooking on the grill.
*(Sit curled up, or lie on the floor.)*

At first they lie there very still.

Then they all go POP!
*(Leap to your feet, throwing your arms high in the air.)*

They must be done!
*(Jump in place.)*

Quick! Let's get them on some buns!
*(Put one hand in other hand like a sandwich, pretend to eat.)*

Write out the words on a piece of grid board so attending adults can follow along. Point out to the group that the poem is written on the poster. Repeat the rhyme several times, encouraging the audience to say it with you. For at least one of the repetitions, follow the printed text on the poster with your finger as you read from left to right to reinforce print directionality as well as the concept that print stands for spoken language.

## Read Aloud OR Creative Dramatics with Props

*(Produce book from picnic basket/cooler.)*

*Here Comes Henny* by Charlotte Pomerantz, pictures by Nancy Winslow Parker. Greenwillow Books, 1994. PK–1. Henny packs a snicky-snacky for her chicky children in her backpack picnic sacky, but they prove to be unbelievably picky and demand a snacky-snicky instead. Henny therefore eats the entire snicky-snacky, leaving nothing for the children, and they realize they may "have been too picky." The chicks subsequently work together to pack their own snacky-snicky for their picnic-nicky, to Henny's obvious pride.

If you wish to act the story out, be Henny yourself, wearing a straw hat, pearl necklace, and picnic backpack, and walking with chicken movements and clucking! Use two or three baby chick hand puppets or plush as your picky "chicky" children. Memorize the text (or print the words where you'll be able to read them easily) and tell the story with plastic play food. Print the word "CLUCK!" on a piece of card stock and mount it on a wooden paint stick. Each time Henny says "CLUCK!," hold up the sign and point to it, inviting audience participation. Make sure to chicken-snore (ZZZzzzzzz-bawk-bawk-bawk) as you gently fall asleep.

## Segue

*(Produce large plastic ant from picnic basket/cooler as they guess.)*

*Say:* Sometimes we end up with picnic visitors that we wish hadn't joined us. Can you guess what little creepy-crawly insect I'm thinking about? Ants!

## Clapping Game/Action Song (Standing)

"Ants at the Picnic"

*(Sung to the tune: "Skip To My Lou")*

*(Clapping chorus available on various teacher Web sites; additional action verses added by Kimberly Faurot.)*

CHORUS:
Ants at the picnic, what'll I do?

(Clap hands throughout.)
Ants at the picnic, what'll I do?
Ants at the picnic, what'll I do?
Guess I'll eat real quickly!
(Pretend to gobble food.)

Ants, ants, ants on my feet,
(Shake feet.)
Ants, ants, ants on my knees,
(Shake knees.)
Ants, ants, ants in my pants,
(Jump around wildly.)
Gotta' get rid of those ants!

Repeat CHORUS.

Ants, ants, ants on my hands,
(Shake hands.)
Ants, ants, ants on my arms,
(Shake arms over head.)
Ants, ants, ants down my shirt,
(Shake shirt.)
Gotta' get rid of those ants!

Repeat CHORUS.

Ants, ants, ants in my ears,
(Shake head, brush at ears.)
Ants, ants, ants on my tongue,
(Shake tongue.)
Ants, ants, ants in my hair,
(Shake hair.)
Gotta' get rid of those ants!

Repeat CHORUS twice, very fast the last time through.

*Fun Fact: Many ants can carry things much heavier than themselves. Some worker ants can even carry objects that are 50 times their own weight! (Source:* Ants *by Paul Fleisher. Benchmark Books, 2002.)*

## Sing Aloud Book OR Song with Props

*(Produce book OR single ant stick puppet from picnic basket/cooler.)*

### Book

*The Ants Go Marching* by Mary Luders, illustrated by Geoffrey Hayes. HarperFestival, 1999. PK–1. The ants go marching away from a picnic to get out of the rain, but the little one stops to do all sorts of things including making a s'more, picking up pretzel sticks,

and so forth, to subsequently share at an ant picnic down in the dry underground ant burrow.

OR

### Song with Props

Before storytime begins, affix your cutout or three-dimensional "The Ants Go Marching" props to the front of the Velcro or magnet board so the audience can see everything clearly. Add each stick puppet ant one at a time to the foam puppet base as you sing the song. Mounting the ants into the base will allow you to easily manipulate the group of puppets as a unit. As the "ants go marching," have each stick puppet grouping gradually appear over the top edge of the Velcro/magnetic board. Clip the ants' pilfered picnic item to an ant's clothespin so it looks like they are all carrying it together, and then have them disappear again behind the board. While the ants are hidden behind the board, remove the picnic item from the clip, and slide the next ant stick puppet into its slot in the foam base. At the very end of the song, talk about what the audience thinks the ants may be doing with all of that picnic food they carried away. Maybe having a party? Maybe having their own picnic? *(All guesses are good guesses!)*

Write out the words to the song ahead of time on a piece of grid board. Encourage everyone to sing along, and to pat their knees for the repeated "BOOM! BOOM! BOOM!" If you have very young children in your group, you may want to pause between verses to count the ants again each time you add one to the grouping.

## Participation Song with Props and Actions

"The Ants Go Marching
(Away with Our Picnic)"

*(Sung to the tune: "When Johnny Comes Marching Home" by Patrick S. Gilmore.)*

*(The original author and copyright date of "The Ants Go Marching" are unknown; the following picnic adaptations are by Kimberly Faurot.)*

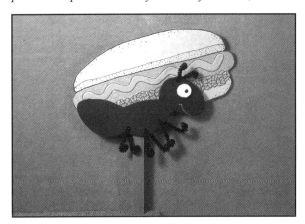

The ants go marching one by one,
hurrah, hurrah.
To come join in our picnic fun,
hurrah, hurrah.
The ants go marching one by one,
There goes my hot dog on its bun!
And they all go marching down
to the ground
With our food, BOOM! BOOM! BOOM!

The ants go marching two by two,
hurrah, hurrah.
The ants go marching two by two,
hurrah, hurrah.
The ants go marching two by two,
They're carrying my potato chips too!
And they all go marching down
to the ground
With our food, BOOM! BOOM! BOOM!

The ants go marching three by three,
hurrah, hurrah.
The ants go marching three by three,
hurrah, hurrah.
The ants go marching three by three,
They took the jug with Mom's iced tea!
And they all go marching down to the
ground
With our food, BOOM! BOOM! BOOM!

The ants go marching four by four,
hurrah, hurrah.

It looks like they've come back for more,
hurrah, hurrah.
The ants go marching four by four,
They carry off my apple core.
And they all go marching down
to the ground
With our food, BOOM! BOOM! BOOM!

The ants go marching five by five,
hurrah, hurrah.
The ants go marching five by five,
hurrah, hurrah.
The ants go marching five by five,
They take the mayo and mustard knives.
And they all go marching down
to the ground
With our food, BOOM! BOOM! BOOM!

The ants go marching six by six,
hurrah, hurrah.
The ants go marching six by six,
hurrah, hurrah.
The ants go marching six by six,
They carry away the Kool-aid mix.
And they all go marching down
to the ground
With our food, BOOM! BOOM! BOOM!

The ants go marching seven by seven,
hurrah, hurrah.
The ants go marching seven by seven,
hurrah, hurrah.
The ants go marching seven by seven,
With my choco-coconut cupcake heaven!
And they all go marching down to the
ground
With our food, BOOM! BOOM! BOOM!

The ants go marching eight by eight,
hurrah, hurrah.
The ants go marching eight by eight,
hurrah, hurrah.
The ants go marching eight by eight,
They took my entire picnic plate!
And they all go marching down to the
ground
With our food, BOOM! BOOM! BOOM!

The ants go marching nine by nine,
hurrah, hurrah.
They're leaving in a long straight line,
hurrah, hurrah.
The ants go marching nine by nine,
There's not much left on which to dine.
And they all go marching down to the
ground
With our food, BOOM! BOOM! BOOM!

The ants go marching ten by ten,
hurrah, hurrah.
I hope they won't come back again,
hurrah, hurrah.
The ants go marching ten by ten,
The last thing to go is our watermelon.
And they all go marching down
to the ground
With our food, THAT'S THE END!
*(Hold up sign that says "THE END.")*

*Extension Craft: Make individual stick puppet ants, with food for them to carry.*

## Conclusion

Sing the following "Our Picnic is Over" closing song to the same tune as "Going On a Picnic" from the beginning of storytime.

"Our Picnic is Over"

It's time to go home, we're leaving right away.
The picnic was great—we stayed all day!
Do we have our basket?
*Yes, we have our basket.*
Do we have our stories?
*Yes, we have our stories.*

Do we have our ants?
*Yes, we have our ants.*
Do we have our blankets?
*Yes, we have our blankets.*
And so forth ...
We have everything, so let's go home!

## Craft Idea

• Make miniature picnic baskets with picnic food. Make baskets from paper bowls or cups, paper punch holes in the rims and attach pipe cleaner handles. Have the children draw their own picnic food and

toys to bring along, or cut out pictures from old magazines. Sing "Going On A Picnic" with the children's selected items.

## Additional Resources

*Ants At the Picnic: Counting by Tens* by Michael Dahl, illustrated by Zachary Trover. Picture Window Books, 2006. PK–2. Go on a picnic with lots of ants and learn to count by tens. The ants carry away all of the picnic food, and even take Aunt Helen!

*The Ants Go Marching* by Berniece Freschet, illustrated by Stefan Martin. Scribner, 1973. PK–1. In numerically changing formations, the ants march out of the earth, up a hill, and across a meadow to a picnic.

*The Best Picnic Ever* by Clare Jarrett. Candlewick Press, 2004. Toddler–PK. When Jack and his mom take a picnic to the park, Jack plays with some jungle animal friends while his mother gets the picnic ready.

*Claude Has a Picnic* by Dick Gackenbach. Clarion Books, 1993. PK–1. Claude the dog solves his neighbors' problems, then gathers them all together for a neighborhood picnic.

*Mouse's First Summer* by Lauren Thompson, illustrated by Buket Erdogan. Simon & Schuster, 2004. Toddler–PK. Little Mouse and his sister Minka explore the many colorful aspects of a summer picnic.

*Mr. Bear's Picnic* by Debi Gliori. Western Publishing, 1995. PK–1. Mr. Bear plans to take the baby out for the day and have a picnic, but ends up with more than he bargained for when the three neighbor grizzly bear cubs tag along. Although they discover that Mr. Bear brought the wrong picnic basket (the one with the baby's toys in it instead of the one with the picnic food in it!), they end up with a delicious picnic anyway when Mr. Bear extricates a hunk of honeycomb for them all to share.

*Old Black Fly* by Jim Aylesworth, illustrations by Stephen Gammell. Henry Holt & Company, 1992. PK–4. A mischievous fly has a very busy bad day romping through the alphabet, landing many places where he shouldn't. He ultimately meets his match and his demise, however, when he has the audacity to buzz around Mama. (Available as a BIG Book.)

*Once Upon a Picnic* by John Prater. Candlewick Press, 1996. PK–1. A young boy who expects that his family's picnic will be boring is pleasantly surprised when a variety of familiar fairy tale characters appear on the scene.

*One Hundred Hungry Ants* by Elinor J. Pinczes. Houghton Mifflin, 1993. K–3. One hundred ants begin marching single file toward a picnic, but when their progress seems too slow the littlest ant suggests that they divide and travel in rows. Other creatures that move faster stream back past them with their own picnic plunder as the ants continue to head toward the hoped-for feast. By the time the ants finally arrive, the picnic has all been eaten or carried away, to their great dismay.

*Over in the Meadow: A Traditional Counting Rhyme* by Louise Voce. Candlewick Press, 1994. Toddler–Grade 1. What else might be going on in the meadow where you are planning to have your picnic? This is a delightfully illustrated version of the traditional song. (Available as a BIG Book.)

*Panda Foo and the New Friend* by Mary Murphy. Candlewick Press, 2007. PK–1. Three best animal friends include a new friend on a picnic outing.

*The Picnic* (Little Critter) by Mercer Mayer. Golden, 1988. Toddler–Grade 1. Little Critter and his family have a difficult time finding a good picnic location, but finally end up in the perfect place—on their own living room floor in front of the fireplace!

*Picnic Farm* by Christine Morton, illustrated by Sarah Barringer. Holiday House, 1998. Toddler–Grade 1. Some children visit a farm and enjoy a picnic made up of food grown and produced there.

*Picnic with Piggins* by Jane Yolen. Harcourt Brace, 1988. Grades 2–5. Piggins the butler is a wonderful detective, so his friends and employers surprise him with a birthday picnic mystery to solve.

*Pig Picnic* by Patricia Hubbell, illustrated by Nadine Bernard Westcott. Golden Books, 1999. (Road to Reading series.) PK–1. Pictures and very simple rhyming text describe the picnic of some pigs and their misunderstanding with a wolf. Although the pigs naturally assume he is skulking about in hopes of eating them, he really only wants some picnic pie and cake.

*Please DO Feed the Bears* by Phyllis Reynolds Naylor, illustrated by Ana López Escrivá. Atheneum Books for Young Readers, 2002. PK–2. Percy almost ruins the family picnic at the beach when he insists on bringing all his large teddy bears along (replacing the picnic food in the cooler with the bears), but in the end his ingenuity saves the day and the family has a picnic after all.

*The Rattlebang Picnic* by Margaret Mahy; pictures by Steven Kellogg. Dial, 1994. K–3. The McTavishes, their seven children, and Granny McTavish take their old rattlebang car on a picnic up Mt. Fogg and have an unexpected adventure when the mountain turns out to be an active, erupting volcano.

*The Stray Dog: From a True Story* by Reiko Sassa, retold and illustrated by Marc Simont. HarperCollins, 2001. PK–3. While on a picnic, a family befriends a stray dog and eventually adopts him.

*Sweet Dream Pie* by Audrey Wood; pictures by Mark Teague. Scholastic, 1998. K–4. The neighbors all feast together on Ma Brindle's incredible Sweet Dream Pie, but nobody heeds her warning that one piece each is enough.

*The Teddy Bears' Picnic* by Jimmy Kennedy, illustrated by Michael Hague. Holt, 1992.

OR

*The Teddy Bears' Picnic* by Jimmy Kennedy, illustrated by Bruce Whatley. HarperCollins, 1996. Illustrated versions of the classic song where teddy bears picnic merrily in the woods without their owners.

*This is the Bear and the Picnic Lunch* by Sarah Hayes, illustrated by Helen Craig. Little, Brown and Company, 1988. PK–1. A boy, his dog, and his teddy bear plan a picnic, then the bear unsuccessfully guards the lunch from the hungry dog while the boy gets ready to go. They eventually share the picnic indoors due to rain!

*Up the Ladder, Down the Slide* by Betsy Everitt. Harcourt Brace, 1998. Toddler–PK. Children make new friends as they play at the park and have a picnic lunch together.

# Story Prop Directions

## "Going On a Picnic" Food

(sandwiches, salad, melon, apples, lemonade, cookies)

Prepare these yourself ahead of time, or have your students make them. Copy the picnic food patterns on pages 133–134 at 100% on colored card stock, or mount them on poster board and color them with crayons, markers, or colored pencils.

## "The Ants Go Marching (Away with Our Picnic)"

### Tools and Supplies

- scissors
- card stock: white
- markers, colored pencils, or crayons
- puffy paint: black, red, green, brown, yellow, white, pink
- adhesive magnet mounting squares or Velcro® dots/squares
- black poster board OR black foamies
- black pipe cleaners/chenille stems (3 mm size): 27 three-inch lengths, each bent in half (legs); 12 two-inch lengths, each bent in half (nine antennae; three for Baby Ant's legs); one 1½" length, bent in half (Baby Ant's antennae)
- small hole punch (¹⁄₁₆")
- hot glue gun and hot glue sticks
- acrylic craft paint: lime green
- clear gloss acrylic varnish
- craft paintbrush
- ten wooden popsicle sticks
- ten miniature clip clothespins (1¾" long)
- piece of craft or floral Styrofoam 1¾" wide x 3" high x 24" long (or two 12" lengths glued together in the middle)

## Directions

### PICNIC ITEMS

1. Copy the patterns from pages 135–137 onto white card stock and cut out and color the picnic items. Embellish with puffy paint if desired: yellow mustard on the hot dog; brown apple core stem; white coconut on the cupcake; green watermelon rind.

   - hot dog and bun
   - potato chip wrapper
   - iced tea jug
   - apple core
   - choco-coconut cupcake heaven
   - watermelon
   - THE END sign

2. Gather real picnic items:

   - mayo and mustard knives (use plastic knives)
   - Kool-Aid® mix (use a paper packet of Kool-Aid mix)
   - paper plate (use a lightweight paper plate)

3. Affix adhesive magnet squares or Velcro® to the back of each picnic item.

### ANTS

1. Copy the ant patterns from page 138 onto card stock and cut them out. Trace nine copies of the large ant outline and one copy of Baby Ant onto black poster board OR black foamies and cut them out.

2. Punch three leg holes and one antennae hole in each ant as shown on the patterns.

3. Insert the bent leg and antennae pipe cleaners into the leg and antennae holes. Hot glue the legs and antennae in place on the back of the ants so they won't end up sliding around. Curl the pipe cleaner/leg ends to look like tiny feet, and club the antennae.

4. Cut out Baby Ant's bonnet from white foamies or card stock and glue it on. Highlight the edges with pink puffy paint, if desired.

5. Cut out nine large white eyeballs and one small white eyeball from white card stock OR white foamies and glue one on each ant. Dot a black puffy paint pupil on each eyeball. Draw red smiles on each ant as shown on the patterns. Allow the paint to dry completely.

6. Paint the ten popsicle sticks and the ten miniature clip clothespins lime green, and allow the paint to dry completely. Apply a coat of clear acrylic varnish if desired, and allow it to dry completely.

7. Hot glue each ant securely to one of the green popsicle sticks.

8. Hot glue one clip clothespin to the back of each green popsicle stick, with the clip or jaws pointing upward.

9. Make a 1¾" wide x 3" high x 24" long foam holder for your ten ant stick puppets. Glue together shorter pieces of foam if needed. Paint the entire holder lime green, and allow the paint to dry completely.

10. Make indentations in the foam base to hold the ant puppets' Popsicle® sticks. The indentations should be at least ½" deep so the sticks will be held securely and not slip out unintentionally. Beginning ¾" in from the edge, space the indentations approximately 2½" apart. The last ant in line (Baby Ant) should be the furthest forward, with the others gradually receding along the width of the base until the leader ant, who should be the furthest toward the back of the base. This alignment will allow each ant's face to show as it is added to the row during the song.

# Picnic Item Patterns

Prepare these ahead of time or have the children make them. Copy the picnic food patterns at 100% onto colored card stock, or mount them on poster board and color them with crayons, markers, or colored pencils. Make sure that you have enough picnic food for all the children in your group!

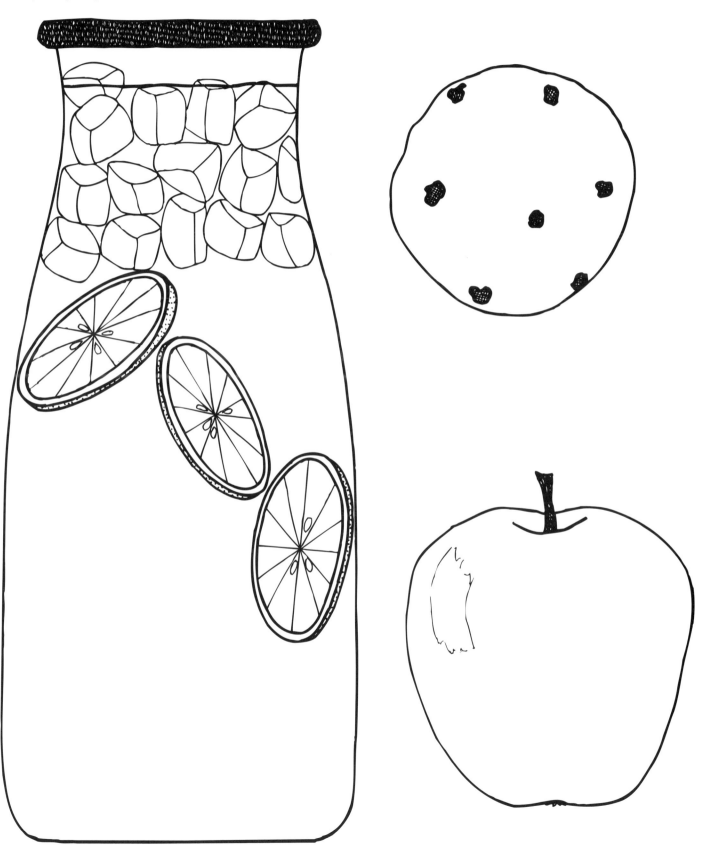

# Picnic Item Patterns

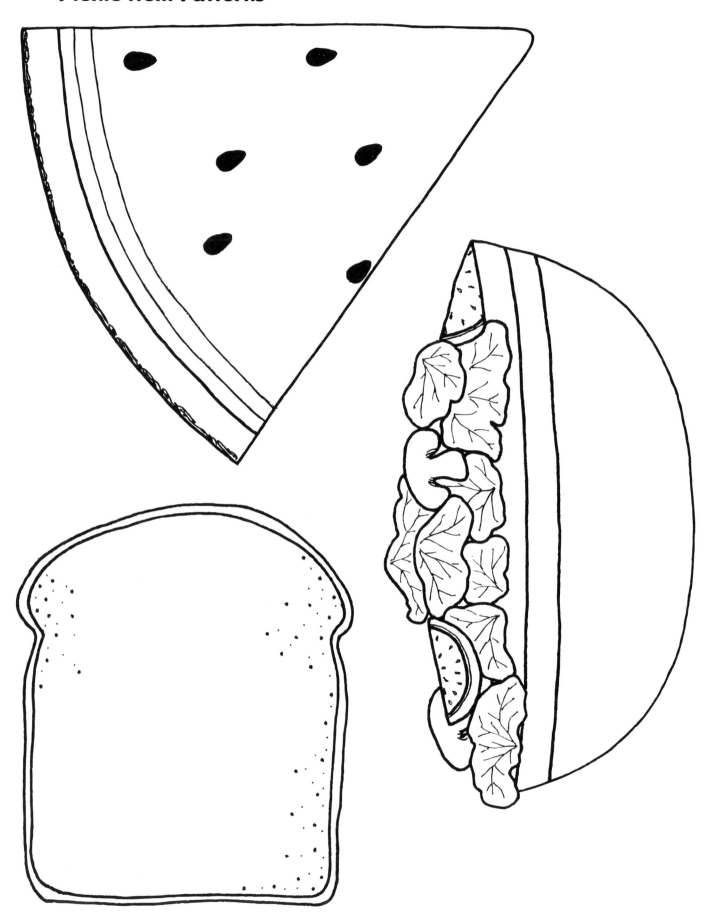

## "The Ants Go Marching" Patterns

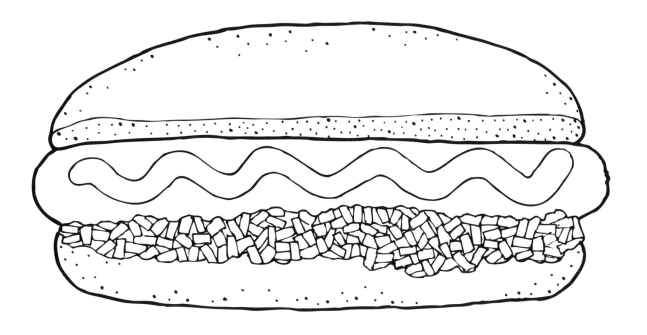

# "The Ants Go Marching" Patterns

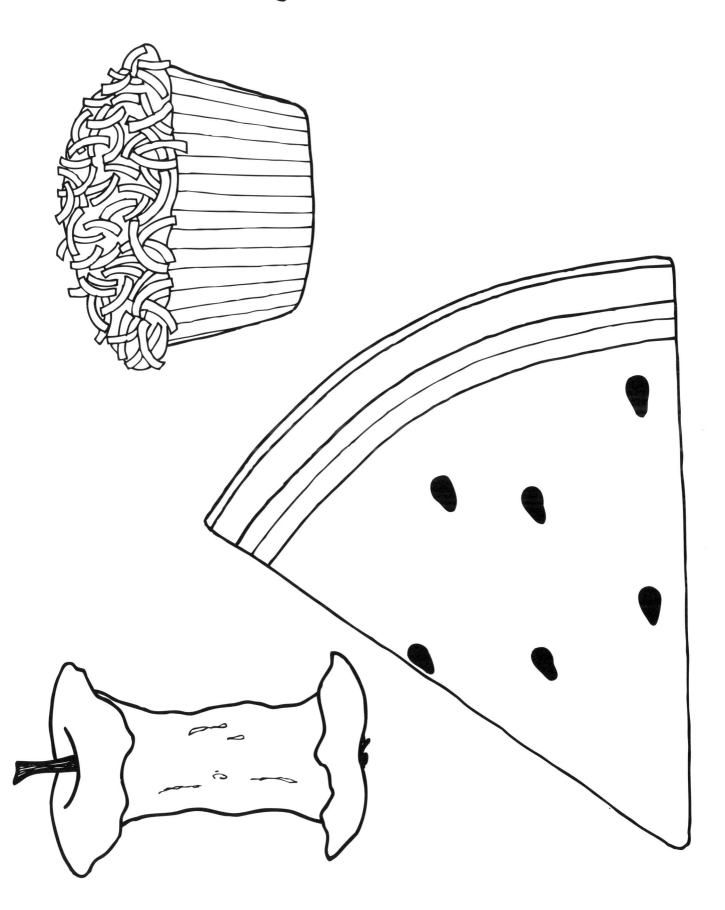

# "The Ants Go Marching" and Here Comes Henny Patterns

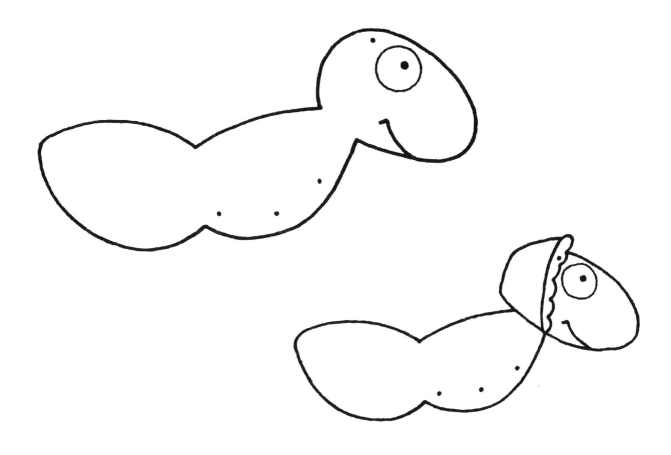

# Let's Take a Trip
## August

## Early Literacy Activities

### Name Tags

Suitcase or backpack stamp or sticker

### Clue(s)

Doll backpack or suitcase

### Mailbox "Letter" of the Day

"T" and "t"

Trip, Toast, Ten, Tummy, Toes, Tickle, Toys, Tape

### Mother Goose Rhyme Time

*There Was an Old Woman Tossed Up in a Basket*

*There was an old woman tossed up in a basket,*
*Seventeen times as high as the moon.*
*Where she was going I couldn't but ask it,*
*For in her hand she carried a broom.*

*"Old woman, old woman, old woman," said I,*
*"Where are you going to up so high?"*
*"To brush the cobwebs off the sky!"*
*"May I go with you?"*
*"Aye, by-and-by."*

### Rhyming Basket

Bag/Tag; Car/Star; Boat/Goat

### Early Literacy Skill: Print Awareness

Notice print and know how to handle books and follow the written word on a page.

- As you prepare to read one of the books aloud, hold it upside down as if you are going to begin reading it that way and see if the children detect the problem.

- When Pig exclaims "Stop!" three times near the end of *The Big Trip* by Valeri Gorbachev (Philomel Books, 2004), run your finger along under the word and have the audience "read" it with you.

- "Read" the map together: As you prepare for the next story or activity, affix the appropriate paper sign to the map that will require you to switch to a new mode of transportation. Read the sign aloud to the group as you point to it: *"This sign says: BUSES ONLY. We're going to need to ride on a BUS!"*

- Repeat the chant *"We're going on vacation, vacation, vacation. / We're going on vacation, how will we go?"* as a group throughout the program as you make each major transition. Write out the words ahead of time so attending adults can follow along, and point out that the rhyme is written on the poster.

- Write out the words ahead of time to Ralph Covert's action song "Drivin' In My Car" on a piece of grid board so attending adults can follow along, and point out to the group that the poem is written on the poster.

- As you read *Rattletrap Car* by Phyllis Root (Candlewick Press, 2001), have the audience help you say various interesting words such as "boomsssssssss" when the tire goes flat and "whumpety whomp!" as the floor falls off. Read the word or phrase first then invite participation "Can you say that with me?" as you run your finger along and "read" it together.

# Program Summary and Theme

August is often a time for family vacations. You can travel with your audience on a storytime trip, as well. Have several backpacks and bags or an old suitcase lined up next to you before you begin the program. Prepare a giant "road map" ahead of time, with your circular route clearly marked, that you can put up on a large magnet board next to you. Make sure to designate your starting/ending location and mark a route that will match your program outline. For example, if you will include a boat story your map route should cross a river or lake. Prepare small paper signs such as "buses only," or "pedestrians only" to affix to the route with tape as you progress through storytime. (This will give you maximum flexibility in case you need to change a book selection or activity at the last minute, or if the program is running long and you need to cut out material.)

As you progress on your journey, the audience can help you figure out where you are going next and what type of vehicle you will need to travel in (car, bus, or boat for the sample program outlined below, or whatever vehicles match the stories you have chosen). Gather small plastic or wooden toy vehicles ahead of time and glue strong magnets to the bottom of each so you can change vehicles as you move along the route. As you switch to each new vehicle, pretend as a group to unbuckle seat belts, get out of the old vehicle, climb into the new one, buckle seatbelts again, make the correct noises, and start the next leg of the vacation. Don't forget to return "home" to the library at the end of your storytime trip!

Prepare the props and puppets ahead of time so you can use them throughout the program. See additional suggested titles on pages 144–146 to substitute for older or younger audiences.

*Storytime Vacation Map*

## Music

Play "traveling" music as the audience is gathering in your storytime area. Possibilities include *Travelin' Magic* by Joanie Bartels (Discovery Music, 1988), *Sing-Along Travel Songs* by Sesame Street (Sony Wonder, 1996), "Riding in My Car" on *Woody's 20 Grow Big Songs* by Woody Guthrie (Warner Brothers, 1992), "Choo Choo Boogaloo" on *Choo Choo Boogaloo* by Buckwheat Zydeco (Music for Little People, 1994), "The Airplane Song" on *Whaddaya Think of That?* by Laurie Berkner (Two Tomatoes, 2000), "I've Been Working on the Railroad" on *Playing Favorites* by Greg & Steve (Youngheart, 1991), and many others.

## Sample Program

Please adjust content and length as needed.

### Introduction

*(Launch right in singing.)*
"We're Leaving on Vacation"
Adapted by Kimberly Faurot

*(Sung to the tune "Down By the Station" by Lee Ricks and Slim Gaillard.)*

Listen to the tune on the sound recording *Great Big Hits* by Sharon Lois and Bram (Elephant, 1992), *Wee Sing Children's Songs and Fingerplays* by Pamela Beall and Susan Nipp (Price Stern Sloan, 1977), *Wee Sing Sing-Alongs* by Pamela Beall and Susan Nipp (Price Stern Sloan, 1982), and many others if you don't know it. Also see the musical notation in *This Little Piggy: Lap Songs, Finger Plays, Clapping Games, and Pantomime Rhymes* edited by Jane Yolen (Candlewick Press, 2005); *Treasury of Folk Songs* compiled by Tom Glazer (Grosset & Dunlap, 1964); and *Wee Sing Children's Songs and Fingerplays* by Pamela Conn Beal and Susan Hagen Nipp (Price Stern Sloan, 2002).

We're leaving on vacation
*(Pat lap while swaying rhythmically.)*
Early in the morning
See our bags and backpacks
*(Gesture to row of bags.)*
All in a row.

Don't forget the map
*(Hold it up or point to it.)*
And don't forget the stories
*(Hold up books.)*
Vroom, vroom, beep, beep
Off we go!

## Segue

*Say:* In our first story, Pig is planning to go on a trip. He definitely has his map. *(Point to map Pig is holding on the book cover.)* But he is trying to decide how he wants to travel.

## Read Aloud

*The Big Trip* by Valeri Gorbachev. Philomel Books, 2004. PK–1. When Pig plans a trip, his friend Goat thinks of how dangerous it could be. Pig decides that he had better not travel at all, but Goat suggests they take the trip together.

When Pig exclaims "Stop!" three times near the end of the book, run your finger along under the word and have the audience "read" it with you.

## Segue

*Say:* Do you think all of those accidents would have happened to Pig? I think that Goat just wanted to go along too! When things like that happen when you are traveling with a friend, they don't even seem like problems—they are adventures! Pig and Goat will need to plan ahead for a successful trip. We need to plan ahead too. If we're going on a trip, we need to make sure our bags are packed! What do you think we should bring? We've already remembered the map and our stories. *(Hold them up.)* What else might we need? *(All guesses are good guesses.)* Sometimes we get carried away and pack some silly things we don't really need. Are you ready?

## Song with Props

"This Is the Way I Pack My Bags"
Adapted by Kimberly Faurot

*(Sung to the tune: "Here We Go 'Round the Mulberry Bush.")*

Produce each item from the box/toybox as you sing about it, then pack it into the large traveling bag.

Prop pieces needed (these items are all readily available at second-hand stores, discount stores, or craft stores):

- large bag big enough to hold everything listed below, that will look very full when packed
- large box/toybox containing the following in reverse order
- pair of child's shoes
- pair of child's socks
- child's underwear
- toothbrush
- comb
- child's sweater
- child's shirt
- child's pants
- plastic car
- sparkly plastic star
- pickle jar
- candy bar
- frog (plastic, puppet, or plush)
- wooden log (Lincoln Logs™ or stick)
- china dog
- jogging book
- doll chair
- plastic pear
- purple costume wig (or can use purple yarn)
- miscellaneous child's shirts and sweaters
- teddy bear plush

This is the way I pack my bags,
pack my bags, pack my bags.
This is the way I pack my bags,
when I take a trip.

First I put in shoes and socks,
shoes and socks, shoes and socks.
First I put in shoes and socks,
when I take a trip.

Then I put in underwear,
underwear, underwear.
Then I put in underwear,
when I take a trip.

Now my toothbrush and my comb,
and my comb, and my comb.
Now my toothbrush and my comb,
when I take a trip.

A sweater, shirt, and pair of pants,
pair of pants, pair of pants.
A sweater, shirt, and pair of pants,
when I take a trip.

*(Quickly, speeding up as you go.)*

Don't forget my plastic car,
a sparkly star, the pickle jar,
And my favorite candy bar,
when we take a trip.

Now I need my jumping frog,
a wooden log, my china dog,
And a book on how to jog,
when we take a trip.

I think I'll bring a comfy chair,
a golden pear, some purple hair,
And some extra stuff to wear!
When we take a trip.

*(Begin to slow down.)*

Now I think my bag is full,
bag is full, bag is full.
Now I think my bag is full ...
But wait!
There's one more VERY important thing:

*(Slowly.)*

I can't forget my teddy bear,
teddy bear, teddy bear.
I can't forget my teddy bear,
when I take a trip!

That is the way I pack my bags,
pack my bags, pack my bags.
That is the way I pack my bags,
when I take a trip.

## Segue

*Say:* Well, surely we have everything that we need and I think a lot that we don't need too! *(Hold up purple hair or other extraneous item and look at it dubiously. Return it to the bag, and add bag to the row of others.)* We're ready to go on vacation! Let's see, here's our road map *(gesture toward it)* so we know where we're going. Now we just need to figure out how we will get there!

*(Keep rhythm with clapping or patting lap; encourage the audience to chant with you.)*

We're going on vacation, vacation, vacation.
We're going on vacation, how will we go?

*(Write out the words ahead of time on a piece of grid board so attending adults can follow along, and point out to the group that the rhyme is written on the poster.)*

Oh! I see a road! *(Point to road on the map.)* How will we travel on that road? In a *(hold up small toy car, affix it to the magnet board map)* CAR! Buckle your seatbelts! *(Pretend to do so.)* Ready? *(Pretend to drive steering wheel; move magnetic car forward.)*

Zippety-zast, zippety-zast,
this car is going very fast!
Zippety-zast, zippety-zast,
this car is going very fast!

Our car is going very fast, but the car in our first story is having some problems. It's a "rattletrap" car, which means it's really old and worn out. Thank goodness the family packed some supplies for their trip, too!

## Read Aloud

*Rattletrap Car* by Phyllis Root. Candlewick Press, 2001. PK–2. On a very hot day, Junie and Jakie and Poppa and the baby pack a picnic of razzleberry dazzleberry snazzleberry fizz and some chocolate marshmallow fudge delight and head for the lake in their old rattletrap car to swim and cool off. The rattletrap car gradually falls apart on the way, but is successfully patched together again through the children's ingenuity.

Have the audience help you say various interesting words such as "boomsssssssss" when the tire goes flat and "whumpety whomp!" as the floor falls off. Read the word or phrase first then invite participation "Can you say that with me?" as you run your finger along and "read" it together.

## Segue

*Say:* Since we've been driving in a car, we really should sing a song about it.

## Action Song (Standing)

Share "Drivin' In My Car" by Ralph Covert on *Ralph's World* (Mini Fresh, 2001) with enthusiastic actions.

Write out the words ahead of time on a piece of grid board so attending adults can follow along, and point out to the group that the song lyrics are written on the poster.

## Segue

*(Keep rhythm by patting your lap or clapping; move the toy car forward. Affix the BUSES ONLY sign directly in front of it.)*

*Say:* We're going on vacation, vacation, vacation. We're going on vacation, how will we go?

Oh! I see a sign. It says: "BUSES ONLY." *(Point to the sign on the map.)* We're going to need to ride on a BUS!

*Switch to the magnetic bus, pretend to take off your seatbelts and climb out of the car, get on the bus climbing big steps, sit back down, and buckle up again. Chant the following while moving the bus forward on the map:*

Zippety-zound, zippety-zound,
these wheels are going round and round.
Zippety-zound, zippety-zound,
these wheels are going round and round.

## Read Aloud

*The Wheels On the Bus* adapted and illustrated by Paul O. Zelinsky, paper engineering by Rodger Smith. Dutton's Children's Books, 2006, 1990. PK–2. The wheels on the bus go around, the wipers go swish, the doors open and close, and the people go in and out in this movable book version of the classic song.

OR

*Don't Let the Pigeon Drive the Bus* by Mo Willems. Hyperion Books for Children, 2003. PK–2. A pigeon tries to convince the reader to let it drive the bus.

## Segue

*Say:* Since we're riding on a bus now *(gesture to the map with the magnetic bus)*, do any of you know a song about a bus?

## Action Song (Standing)

Sing "The Wheels On the Bus" on the sound recording *Rise and Shine* by Raffi (MCA Records, 1996).

## Segue

*Say:* We're going on vacation, vacation, vacation. We're going on vacation, how will we go?

*(Move the magnetic bus to the edge of the lake/ river.)*

Oh! I see a lake/river! *(Point to it on the map.)* I don't see a bridge, so how will we get over that lake/river? In a BOAT!

*(Pretend to climb into the boat as a group, put on sunglasses, flip your hair, buckle up, and so forth.)*

Swishety-swish, swishety-swish,
our boat can go just like a fish.
Swishety-swish, swishety-swish,
our boat can go just like a fish.

## Read Aloud OR Storytelling with Props OR Creative Dramatics

*Mr. Gumpy's Outing* by John Burningham. Holt, Rinehart and Winston, 1970. Toddler–Grade 1. Mr. Gumpy accepts more and more riders on his boat until the inevitable occurs and they tip over into the river. (Available as a BIG Book.)

Explain the title—that an "outing" is like a short pleasure trip.

To share with puppets, cut the top off a long, shallow box. Cut a long, shallow boat shape from cardboard or paper and glue/tape it to the front of the box. Cover a long narrow table with blue "water" fabric, or tape poster-board "waves" to the front of the table. (A half card table works well, since they are long enough but not too deep.) Place the box on the table in the middle of the water. You will be Mr. Gumpy, standing behind the table with the boat pretending to pole it through the water. Use dolls, puppets, or plush for the characters as you tell the story.

If your group is small enough, consider acting out the story with creative dramatics. Be Mr. Gumpy yourself with a hat and cardboard tubing pole (such as the tube inside a roll of wrapping paper or bulletin board paper. Cut out a large boat shape from fabric (an old sheet would work)—a size that will enable your entire storytime group to join you on it. Make animal headbands for each character and act out the story. Make sure there are enough roles for everyone to participate, and allow the children to choose who or what they would like to be. It's fine if you end up with multiples of some characters and none of some others.

## Segue (Sing)

"Row Row Row Your Boat"

Row, row, row your boat,
Gently down the stream.
Merrily, merrily, merrily, merrily,
Life is but a dream.

Row, row, row your boat,
Time to go ashore.
*(Pretend to climb over the side of the boat.)*
Merrily, merrily, merrily, merrily,
We're finally home once more.
*(Move the boat to your starting/ending location on the map.)*

## Conclusion (Sing)

"We're Home From Vacation"
Adapted by Kimberly Faurot

*(Sung to the tune: "Down By the Station" by Lee Ricks and Slim Gaillard—sing and sway slowly, as if you are very tired.)*

We're home from vacation
It's late in the evening
See the tired children
*(Gesture to audience.)*
All in a row.

We had a lovely journey
We're happy to be home, now
It's time for bed, so
*(Pull teddy from bag and snuggle up with it.)*
Off we go!

## Craft Ideas

- Make and fill some storytime suitcases! Use brown or brightly colored file folders for suitcases, and punch two holes along each side (opposite the fold) to affix pipe cleaner handles so the suitcases will stay closed when they are carried. Decorate the outside of the folder suitcases with stickers or stamps to look like travel stickers. Have the children cut out pictures from old magazines of items they would like to bring on their trip, or draw pictures of the items. Glue the pictures inside the folder suitcases. Sing the opening chorus of "This Is the Way I Pack My Bags" and have each child show what they have packed.

- Cut up old road maps into manageable sized sections, and make paper cars, buses, boats, and so forth to drive on them.

# Additional Resources

***All Aboard! A True Train Story*** by Susan Kuklin. Orchard Books, 2003. Toddler–Grade 1. A photographic journey through part of the Colorado Rockies aboard a steam locomotive of the Durango & Silverton Narrow Gauge Railroad. Includes historical and descriptive notes on the Durango & Silverton trains.

***The Bag I'm Taking to Grandma's*** by Shirley Neitzel, illustrated by Nancy Winslow Parker. Greenwillow Books, 1995. PK–1. In cumulative verses and rebuses, a young boy and his mother have different views on how to pack a bag for a trip to Grandma's.

***Big Brown Bear Goes to Town*** by David McPhail. Harcourt, 2006. PK–1. Rat's car fills up with water when it rains, but his friend Big Brown Bear comes to the rescue.

**"Bumping Up and Down"** on the sound recording *Singable Songs for the Very Young* by Raffi (MCA Records, 1976); musical notation is in *The Raffi Singable Songbook: A Collection of 51 Songs From Raffi's First Three Records for Young Children.* (Crown Publishers, 1987.)

**Extension Idea:** Make up additional verses with other modes of transportation.

*Cars! Cars! Cars!* by Grace Maccarone, illustrated by David A. Carter. Scholastic, 1995. Toddler–K. Simple rhymes and pictures portray many different kinds of cars.

*Chugga-Chugga Choo-Choo* by Kevin Lewis, illustrated by Daniel Kirk. Hyperion Books for Children, 1999. Toddler–K. A rhyming story about a toy freight train's day, from loading freight in the morning to retiring to the roundhouse after the day's work is done.

*Clickety Clack* by Rob and Amy Spence, illustrated by Margaret Spengler. Viking, 1999. PK–1. A train gets noisier and more crowded as quacking ducks, dancing acrobats, talking yaks, and packs of elephants board.

*Cosmo Zooms* by Arthur Howard. Voyager Books, 2003. PK–2. Cosmo the dog discovers a special talent when he accidentally takes a nap on a skateboard.

*Down By the Station* by Will Hillenbrand. Harcourt Brace, 1999. PK–1. In this version of a familiar song, baby animals ride to the children's zoo on the zoo train. Printed music on last page. (Available as a BIG Book.)

*Duck On a Bike* by David Shannon. Blue Sky Press, 2002. PK–3. A duck decides to ride a bike and soon influences all the other animals on the farm to ride bikes too.

*Emma's Vacation* by David McPhail. Dutton, 1991. PK–1. Emma's idea of a good vacation is quite different from that of her parents.

*Freight Train* by Donald Crews. Greenwillow Books, 1978. Toddler–Grade 1. Brief text and illustrations trace the journey of a colorful train as it goes through tunnels, by cities, and over trestles. (Available as a BIG Book.)

*Go! Poetry in Motion* by Dee Lillegard, illustrated by Valeri Gorbachev. Knopf, 2006. PK–1. Short, snappy poems capture the unique personalities of things that go, including bikes, skateboards, airplanes, sleds, skates, wagons, and many more.

*Henry and Mudge and the Bedtime Thumps: The Ninth Book of Their Adventures* by Cynthia Rylant, illustrated by Suçie Stevenson. Macmillan, 1991. Easy Reader. PK–1. Henry worries about what will happen to his big dog Mudge during their visit to his grandmother's house in the country.

*Maisy Drives the Bus* by Lucy Cousins. Candlewick Press, 2000. Toddler–K. Maisy the mouse picks up an assortment of passengers as she drives her bus.

*Mr. Gumpy's Motor Car* by John Burningham. Crowell, 1976. Toddler–Grade 1. Mr. Gumpy's human and animal friends squash into his old car and go for a drive. When it starts to rain, however, the car gets stuck in the mud and everyone must get out to help push.

*My Car* by Byron Barton. Greenwillow Books, 2001. Toddler–Grade 1. Sam lovingly describes his car and how he drives it.

*Now We Can Go* by Ann Jonas. Greenwillow Books, 1986. Toddler–K. A child must take all the toys from her toy box and put them in her bag before she is ready to go.

*Oh No, Gotta Go!* by Susan Middleton Elya, illustrated by G. Brian Karas. Putnam, 2003. PK–1. As soon as she goes out for a drive with her parents, a young girl needs to find a bathroom quickly. Text includes Spanish words and phrases; there is a Spanish glossary and pronunciation guide at the end of the book.

*On the Go* by Ann Morris; photographs by Ken Heyman. Lothrop, Lee & Shepard Books, 1990. PK–1. Discusses the ways in which people all over the world move from place to place, including walking, riding on animals, and traveling on wheels and water.

*A Pet for Mrs. Arbuckle* by Gwenda Smyth, illustrated by Ann James. Crown Publishers, 1984. PK–2. Mrs. Arbuckle, who longs for a pet, travels the world with a helpful ginger cat to interview exotic animals for the position.

*The Relatives Came* by Cynthia Rylant, illustrated by Stephen Gammell. Bradbury Press, 1985. K–3. The relatives come to visit from Virginia and everyone has a wonderful time.

*Rooster's Off to See the World* by Eric Carle. Picture Book Studio, 1987. PK–1. A simple introduction to the meaning of numbers and sets as a rooster, on his way to see the world, is joined by fourteen animals along the way. (Available as a BIG Book.)

**Sheep Take A Hike** by Nancy Shaw, illustrated by Margot Apple. Houghton Mifflin, 1994. PK–1. Having gotten lost on a chaotic hike in the great outdoors, the sheep find their way back by following the trail of wool they have left.

**Silly Sally** by Audrey Wood. Harcourt Brace Jovanovich, 1992. Toddler–Grade 1. A rhyming story of Silly Sally, who makes many friends as she travels to town—walking backward, upside down. (Available in Spanish and as a BIG Book.)

**Extension Idea:** Read the story rhythmically, inviting participation with the repeated refrain "Silly Sally went to town, walking backward, upside down." Make animal noises for each creature she meets, enhancing their ensuing interactions as desired. For example, bark "Woof, woof-leapfrog!" for the dog; sing a wacky operatic well-known tune for the loon; fall asleep snoring with the sheep, "Zzzzzz-baaaaa, zzzzzzz-baaaaa;" and so forth. When the tickling begins, encourage the audience to giggle and laugh like each animal might ("oink-ha-ha" and so forth).

**Tooth-Gnasher Superflash** by Daniel Pinkwater. Macmillan, 1990. PK–3. The Popsnorkle family test drives the Tooth-Gnasher Superflash, pleased with the car's ability to turn into several different animals.

**Extension Idea:** Make a magnet board story with colored flexible magnetic sheeting!

**"Traffic Light"** (author unknown)

*Red on top; Green below.*
*Red means stop; Green means go.*
*Yellow means wait, Even if you're late!*

**Extension Idea:** Make a flannel board, magnet board, or cardboard traffic light and practice "Red means stop; green means go; and yellow means wait!"

**Truck Driver Tom** by Monica Wellington. Dutton Children's Books, 2007. Toddler–Grade 1. The driver of a tractor-trailer picks up a load of fresh fruits and vegetables, then drives through the countryside, past small towns, and into the big city, passing farms, construction sites, and many other vehicles. After delivering the produce, he relaxes with other drivers.

**Truck Jam** by Paul Stickland. Ragged Bears, 2005. Toddler–Grade 1. Large pop-up illustrations feature various trucks engaged in activities such as pouring sand, getting stuck in traffic, and being towed.

**Vroomaloom Zoom** by John Coy, illustrated by Joe Cepeda. Crown Publishers, 2000. PK–1. Daddy takes Carmela on an imaginary car ride, lulling her to sleep with various sounds, from the wurgle lurgle of swamps to the hoopty doopty swoopty loopty of driving in circles.

**We're Going On a Bear Hunt** retold by Michael Rosen, illustrated by Helen Oxenbury. Margaret K. McElderry Books, 1989. K–1. Brave bear hunters go through grass, a river, mud, and other obstacles before the inevitable encounter with the bear forces a headlong retreat. (Available in Spanish.)

**The Wheels On the Race Car** by Alexander Zane, illustrated by James Warhola. Orchard Books, 2005. PK–1. Animal racecar drivers roar around the track. Text based on the popular song "The Wheels on the Bus."

# Picking Apples
## September

## Early Literacy Activities

### Name Tags

Apple stamp or sticker

### Clue(s)

Miniature apple

### Mailbox "Letter" of the Day

"A" and "a"

Apple, Alligator, Astronaut, Animals, Alphabet, Abracadabra, Ant, Anteater

### Mother Goose Rhyme Time

*There Was an Old Woman Lived Under a Hill*

*There was an old woman*
*Lived under a hill,*
*And if she's not gone*
*She lives there still.*

*Baked apples she sold,*
*And cranberry pies,*
*And she's the old woman*
*That never told lies.*

### Rhyming Basket

Pie/Fly; Tree/Three; Dog/Frog

## Early Literacy Skill: Letter Knowledge

Learn to recognize and identify letters, knowing that they have different names and sounds and that the same letter can look different.

- Mailbox "letter" of the day.

- Identify the A-P-P-L-E letters as you put them up, and "read" the word several times as a group. Draw each letter in the air. Know that letters have names and sounds. Dramatically identify each letter again as you remove it from the board and replace it with a "clapping apple."

- Comparing the differences in Valeri Gorbachev's wonderful front and back endpaper illustrations in *All for Pie, Pie for All* by David Martin (Candlewick Press, 2006) helps develop children's abilities to notice what is alike and what is different—one of the beginning steps toward letter knowledge. Consider having two copies of the book so you can hold both of them up next to each other at the same time to more easily compare the two illustrations.

# Program Summary and Theme

Celebrate Johnny Appleseed's birthday (September 26) during the month of September with a storytime about APPLES! Cover your storytime table with a bright red or apple-patterned cloth, and intersperse your books and props with a few real or plastic apples and inexpensive bushel baskets.

Prepare the props and puppets ahead of time so you can use them throughout the program. Please see patterns and directions on pages 154–162. See suggested titles on pages 152–154 to substitute for older or younger audiences.

## Music

Play "apple" music as the audience is gathering in your storytime area. Possibilities include "I Like Picking Apples" on *All of the Seasons* by Ken Whiteley (Pyramid, 1993); "Apple Picker's Reel" on *Daydreamer* by Priscilla Herdman (Music for Little People, 1993) and *One, Two, Three, Four, Live!* by Sharon, Lois and Bram (Elephant Records, 1982); "Five Green Apples" on *One Light One Sun* by Raffi (Troubadour, 1987) and *Mainly Mother Goose: Songs and Rhymes For Merry Young Souls* by Sharon, Lois & Bram (Elephant Records, 1984); "Apples and Bananas" on *Raffi in Concert with the Rise and Shine Band* (MCA Records, 1989); "Apple Pickin' Time" on *I'm Gonna Reach!* by Tom Pease (Tomorrow River, 1989); "The Pie Song" on *Reaching for the Stars!* by Kathy Reid-Naiman (Merriweather Records, 2005); and many others.

# Sample Program

Please adjust content and length as needed.

## Introduction

*(Show the audience a real apple with a birthday candle sticking up out of it.) Say:* Today, we are going to celebrate the birthday of a person who was born a very long time ago, in the year 1774, in the month of September. His real name was John Chapman, but most people know him by the name of "Johnny Appleseed."

## Read Aloud

*Johnny Appleseed* by Patricia Demuth, illustrated by Michael Montgomery. (All Aboard Reading, Level 1.) Grosset & Dunlap, 1996. PK–2. Recounts the story of the man who traveled west planting apple seeds to make the country a better place to live.

OR

*Johnny Appleseed* by Madeline Olsen and Madeline Boskey, illustrated by Steven James Petruccio. (Hello Reader!, Level 1.) Scholastic, 2001.

## Segue

*Say:* I think that many of us are very thankful to Johnny Appleseed for planting so many apple trees, so we could have delicious apples to eat. It makes me so happy, I want to sing about it!

## Action Song (Standing)

Sing "A-P-P-L-E" as a group with your cutout letters and clapping apples. (see patterns and instructions on pages 154–155 and 158.) Identify the letters together as you put them up, and "read" what it says several times as a group. Explain how the song, the A-P-P-L-E letters, and clapping apple letter replacements work before you begin. As you take each letter away, make sure to identify it again as a group, and name the color of each replacement clapping apple.

"A-P-P-L-E" Song and Clapping Game

*(Sung to the tune: "B-I-N-G-O.")*

*(Sing out the letters A-P-P-L-E on the first verse, then begin removing letters one at a time. Replace each letter as you remove it with a "clapping apple" as a signal to the children that they should clap at that point in the song. Clap your hands below the clapping apples and point to the letters as you go across the word each time. Gradually substitute claps for letters until you clap out Apple's whole name, keeping the rhythm of the song as you go.)*

*I know a fruit that grows on trees,
and APPLE is its name-o.*

*A-P-P-L-E, A-P-P-L-E, A-P-P-L-E,
and APPLE is its name-o.*

Note: If you wish to incorporate other verses into this song, see options on Victoria Smith's wonderful Web site at www.kinderkorner.com/apple.html ("A is for Apple" unit).

## Segue

*Say:* In our story about Johnny Appleseed we learned a little bit about how many apple trees were planted, but how do apples actually grow on the trees?

## Read Aloud

*I Am An Apple* by Jean Marzollo, illustrated by Judith Moffat. Scholastic, 1997. (Hello Reader! Level 1.) Toddler–Grade 1. A bud on an apple tree grows into an apple, ripens, is harvested, and provides seeds as a promise for the future. (Available as a BIG Book.)

Sing the text of this book's first few pages, making up a majestic tune as you go and encouraging the audience to join you as you identify parts of the pictures such as the "rain" and "sun." Count the apple blossom's five petals together. Pre-cut a real apple in half (horizontally around its middle) and preserve the flesh from browning with lemon juice so that you can show its star pattern at the point where the book describes it. Together, count the seed star's five parts.

Note: If you have a very young audience, consider reading only the first half of the book—stopping at "We are ready to be picked!"

OR

*The Apple Pie Tree* by Zoe Hall, illustrated by Shari Halpern. Scholastic, 1996. PK–1. Describes an apple tree as it grows leaves and flowers and then produces its fruit, while in its branches robins make a nest, lay eggs, and raise a family. Includes a recipe for apple pie.

## Segue

*Say:* Here is a little song about the book we just read *(it works with either of the two suggested books, above).* This is called an ECHO SONG—which means I'll sing something to you, and then you will sing the same thing back to me, as my "echo." When we get to the very last line, we get to sing it all together!

## Echo Song

Using your flannel board pieces (see instructions and patterns on pages 155–156 and 159–161) to illustrate, share the echo song: "I Am An Apple" (words by Kimberly Faurot) to the tune: "I Am A Pizza" by Peter Alsop. "I Am a Pizza" is on the sound recording *10 Carrot Diamond* by Charlotte Diamond (Hug Bug Records, 1985), *Wha'd'ya Wanna Do?* by Peter Alsop (Moose School Records, 1983), and *Peppermint Wings* by Linda Arnold (A & M Records, 1990).

### "I Am An Apple"

I am an apple. *I am an apple.*
I grew on a tree. *I grew on a tree.*

I used to be a flower— *I used to be a flower—*

Had a visit from a bee. *Had a visit from a bee.*

I started out little, *I started out little,*

And then I grew! *And then I grew!*

*Together:* Now I am ready to be picked by you!

Write out the words ahead of time on a piece of grid board so attending adults can follow along, and point out to the group that the song is written on the poster. Write the echo part in red to cue the audience on which part to sing, although it's great if they already know the tune and want to sing both parts with you.

## Segue

*Say:* Sometimes when apples are really ripe, they fall right out of their trees and we can pick them up off the ground! We're going to shake the tree a little bit to help them fall in this poem.

## Action Rhyme (Standing)

"Apple Tree"

Way up high in the apple tree, *(Fling arms exuberantly over head, reaching as high as possible.)*

Two little eyes looking down at me. *(Peer downward through hands cupped in circles over eyes.)*

I shook that tree as hard as I could, *(Pretend to shake tree enthusiastically.)*

And DOWN came the apples— *(Slap hands dramatically down onto your thighs.)*

Mmmm good! *(Rub stomach.)*

*(Repeat with other fruits and foods, including some silly ones. For example, BANANA, PEAR, CHERRY, PIZZA, MARSHMALLOW, PICKLE, and so forth. Invite the children to suggest ideas.)*

Write out the words ahead of time on a piece of grid board so attending adults can follow along, and point out to the group that the rhyme is written on the poster.

## Segue

*Say:* Now that we have some apples and other things down from the trees, what do you think we should do with them? *(All guesses are good guesses!)* Maybe they would taste good in some PIE!

## Read Aloud

*All for Pie, Pie for All* by David Martin, illustrated by Valeri Gorbachev. Candlewick Press, 2006. PK–1. Grandma Cat bakes an apple pie that is heartily enjoyed by her family as well as by the Mouse and Ant families that live nearby.

Snore appropriately as the Cat family (ZZzzzz-meow, ZZzzzz-meow) and the Mouse family (ZZzzzz-squeak, ZZzzzz-squeak) take naps. When Grandma Cat asks if she should bake another pie, show the children the word "Yes" on the page as meowed by the cats. Meow "Yes. Yes. Yes. Yes." together as you underline each word with your finger, then repeat the process in squeaky mouse voices, and then in tiny ant voices. Don't forget to linger a bit over the endpapers at the book's beginning and end. Ask the children what they notice that is different about the kitchen in the two pictures! (Consider having two copies of the book so you can hold both of them up next to each other at the same time to more easily compare the two illustrations.)

## Segue

*Say:* We're going to make some pretend apple pie of our own right here, with some very silly apples.

## Poem with Props and Actions (Sitting or Standing)

Share "Apple Happy" with your Apple Faces and Pie props. (See instructions and pattern on page 156 and 162.) Please note that this is an adaptation of the well-known "Jack-o-Happy" pumpkin rhyme.

*Say:* This is Apple HAPPY.
*(Smile broadly.)*

This is Apple SAD.
*(Sad face.)*

Now you see him SLEEPY.
*(Yawn and pretend to sleep with droopy eyes.)*

Now you see him MAD.
*(Mad frowning face.)*

Now Apple is in pieces small,
*(Hold out cupped hands to show "small.")*

'Cause in apple pie he's best of all!

Yum, yum!
*(Rub stomach.)*

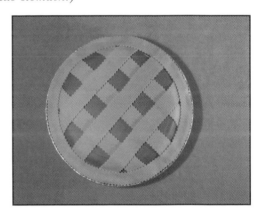

## Segue

*Say:* In this next story, someone wants to make a pie, too, but there may not be any apples left!

## Read Aloud

*Ten Red Apples* by Pat Hutchins. Greenwillow Books, 2000. Toddler–Grade 1. In rhyming verses, one animal after another neighs, moos, oinks, quacks, and makes other appropriate sounds as each eats an apple from the farmer's tree.

Read rhythmically (or sing!—try adapting a well-known tune), patting your lap with your free hand for rhythm if desired. Repeat the refrain "Save some for me!" together with your audience, underlining each word with your finger to promote print awareness as you collectively say the phrase.

## Segue

*Say:* Let's sing a song about those ten apples on the farmer's tree.

## Counting Song

Share "Ten Little Apples" with your flannel board tree and apples (see instructions and patterns on pages 156–157 and 160–161). Lead the audience in hand motions, holding up your fingers for counting and then pretending to take a big bite of an apple as you say "CRUNCH!"

"Ten Little Apples" *(Sung to the tune: "Ten Little Indians")*

1 little, 2 little,
3 little apples,
4 little, 5 little,
6 little apples,
7 little, 8 little,
9 little apples,
10 little
apples to eat–
CRUNCH!

*(Reverse from 10 to 1, removing the apples one by one as you sing.)*

## Conclusion

*Say:* Well, it looks like we have eaten up all of our apples *(point to your empty flannel apple tree)*, and all of our stories for today, too. They were sure tasty!

## Craft Ideas

• Make construction paper or card stock apple trees (or use a green paper plate for the foliage). Decorate each with ten red apples, using paper, sponge paint, or apple stickers.

• Make small-size "Apple Happy" props with small red paper plates, pipe cleaners, tan foamies or felt, and foil patty pans.

## Additional Extension Ideas

• Make a second flannel board apple tree with another set of apples, and act out *Ten Red Apples* by Pat Hutchins as a group

using both flannel board trees. Consider making representative hats or headbands for the farmer, horse, cow, donkey, goat, pig, sheep, goose, duck, hen, and farmer's wife. Make sure everyone gets to play a part, and to choose who or what they want to be. It is fine to have several children play each character at once if they want to!

# Additional Resources

*The Apple Doll* by Elisa Kleven. Farrar, Straus and Giroux, 2007. K–2. Lizzy is scared to start school, so she makes a doll out of an apple from her favorite tree to take with her on the first day and keep her company. Includes instructions for making an apple doll.

*Apple Farmer Annie* by Monica Wellington. Dutton Children's Books, 2001. Toddler–Grade 1. Annie the apple farmer saves her most beautiful apples to sell fresh at the farmers market.

*The Apple Pie That Papa Baked* by Lauren Thompson, illustrated by Jonathan Bean. Simon & Schuster Books for Young Readers, 2007. PK–1. These are the apples, juicy and red, that went in the pie, warm and sweet, that Papa baked!

"**The Apple Story.**" Please see citations below for "The Little Red House With No Doors and No Windows and a Star Inside."

*An Apple Tree Through the Year* by Claudia Schnieper; photographs by Othmar Baumli. Carolrhoda Books, 1987. Translation of: Der Apfelbaum im Jahreslauf. PK–1. Follows an apple tree through the four seasons, detailing the yearly growth cycle and examining the ecosystem of the entire apple orchard.

"**Apples and Bananas**" on the sound recording *Raffi in Concert with the Rise and Shine Band.* Rounder Records, 1989.

*Apples* by Gail Gibbons. Holiday House, 2000. K–2. Explains how apples were brought to America, how they grow, their traditional uses and cultural significance, and some of the varieties grown.

*Apples* by Rhoda Nottridge, illustrated by John Yates. Carolrhoda Books, 1991. K–4. Surveys the history of apples from the wild crab apple to modern-day cultivation, production, and role in nutrition. Includes recipes for desserts and salad.

*Apples* text and pictures by Ken Robbins. Atheneum Books for Young Readers, 2002. PK–4. Describes how apples are grown, harvested, and used, and details facts about apples in history, literature, and our daily lives.

*Apples, Apples, Apples* by Nancy Elizabeth Wallace. Winslow Press, 2000. PK–1. Members of the Rabbit family visit an apple orchard, where they have fun picking apples and discovering their many uses. Includes a recipe for applesauce, directions for a craft activity, and sayings about apples.

**"5 Green Apples"** on the sound recording *Mainly Mother Goose: Songs and Rhymes* For Merry Young Souls by Sharon, Lois & Bram. Elephant Records, 1984.
**Extension Idea:** Make five green apples for your flannel board tree, and act out the song with the props. Dress up a puppet in overalls and a straw hat to play the role of "Farmer Brown."

**"Growing Apples"**

Eat an apple
*(Pretend to eat apple.)*
Save the core
*(Cup hands.)*
Plant the seeds
*(Bend down and pretend to plant seeds.)*
And grow some more!
*(Stretch arms up like an apple tree.)*

*How Do Apples Grow?* by Betsy Maestro, illustrated by Giulio Maestro. HarperCollins, 1992. PK–2. Describes the life cycle of an apple from its initial appearance as a spring bud to that point in time when it becomes a fully ripe fruit.

*How to Make An Apple Pie and See the World* by Marjorie Priceman. Knopf, 1994. PK–3. Since the market is closed, the reader is led around the world to gather the ingredients for making an apple pie.
**Extension Idea:** As you read the story, locate all of the places you are traveling on a large wall map.

*Johnny Appleseed, A Tall Tale* retold and illustrated by Steven Kellogg. Morrow

Junior Books, 1988. K–3. Presents the life of John Chapman, better known as Johnny Appleseed, describing his love of nature, his kindness to animals, and his physical fortitude. (Available as a BIG Book.)

*The Life and Times of the Apple* by Charles Micucci. Orchard Books, 1992. PK–4 (selected informational pages). Presents a variety of facts about apples, including how they grow, crossbreeding and grafting techniques, harvesting practices, and the uses, varieties, and history of this popular fruit.

*Little Apple: A Book of Thanks* by Brigitte Weninger, illustrated by Anne Möller. North-South Books, 2001. PK–1. A little girl describes the outside and inside of apples, then explains their life cycle in simple language. She ends with the observation, "I am so thankful for this little apple" as she bites into the fruit.

*Little Apple Goat* by Caroline Jayne Church. Oxford University Press, 2007. PK–1. Fruit-loving Little Apple Goat loves to eat in the orchard, and always spits the pips and stones over the hedge on her way home to her own meadow. When an autumn storm topples all of the orchard's fruit trees, the animals fear that there will be no more fruit. Spring reveals, however, that Little Apple Goat has inadvertently planted a new orchard on the other side of the hedge!

**"The Little Red House With No Doors and No Windows and a Star Inside"** by Carolyn Sherwin Bailey in *A World of Children's Stories* edited by Anne Pellowski, illustrated by Gloria C. Ortiz. Friendship Press, 1993. Also known as "The Apple Story." When a little boy is bored and wants to have an adventure, his mother tells him to search for a "little red house with no doors and no windows but with a star inside." After questioning several people as well as the wind, the little boy finds a red apple that turns out to be the "house" for which he is looking. See an adapted version online at: www.agr.state.nc.us/agscool/commodities/redhouse.htm.
**Additional versions are included in the following resources:**

- *Early Childhood Experiences in Language Arts: Early Literacy by Jeanne Machado, 8th Ed.* Cengage Delmar Learning, 2006.

- *Easy-to-Tell Stories for Young Children* by Annette Harrison. National Storytelling Network, 1992.
- *Is Your Storytale Dragging?* by Jean Stangl. Fearon Teacher Aids, 1989. (This version uses a pear instead of an apple, and is called "A Special Yellow House.")

**Extension Idea:** Tell this story with puppets and props. Shorten it as necessary for telling to a very young audience. Cut a real apple horizontally to reveal its "star" of seeds as you reach that point in the story. (Use a folding jackknife and keep it in your pocket, or secure the knife in another very safe place!)

*Lunch* by Denise Fleming. Henry Holt & Company, 1992. Toddler–Grade 1. A very hungry mouse eats a large lunch comprised of colorful foods, including an enormous apple.

*The Mouse and the Apple* by Stephen Butler. Tambourine Books, 1994. Toddler–K. Mouse waits patiently for a ripe red apple to fall from the tree, but his friends aren't as patient.

*My Apple* by Kay Davies and Wendy Oldfield; photographs by Fiona Pragoff. Gareth Stevens, 1994. PK–1. Clear photographs and simple text reveal facts about apples.

*A New House For Mouse* by Petr Horácek. Candlewick Press, 2004. PK–1. Mouse finds a nice juicy apple that is too big to fit inside her tiny home, so she goes in search of a new house.

*Orange Pear Apple Bear* by Emily Gravett. Simon & Schuster Books for Young Readers, 2007, 2005. Toddler–K. Explores concepts of color, shape, and food using only five simple words, as a bear juggles and plays.

*Ouch!* by Ragnhild Scamell, illustrated by Michael Terry. Good Books, 2006. PK–1. Just as Hedgehog is entering her winter nest for a long nap, a falling apple gets stuck on her spiny back. Her friends' suggested solutions only lead to more trouble, with more and more debris getting stuck to Hedgehog's back. Finally she sees Goat, who knows just what to do—he eats everything!

**Extension Idea:** This makes a fun puppet or flannel board story, as Hedgehog gets more and more things stuck to her back.

*The Prince's Tooth is Loose* by Harriet Ziefert, illustrated by R.W. Alley. Sterling, 2005. (Reissue of *The Prince's Tooth is Loose* by Harriet Ziefert, illustrated by R. W. Alley. Random House, 1990.) K–1. When the prince complains that he cannot eat because he has a loose tooth, everyone rallies to help him make it come out. The king finally recommends finding the nearest apple, and when the prince bites into it his tooth does indeed come out. The prince then requests that someone locate the nearest tooth fairy!

*The Seasons of Arnold's Apple Tree* by Gail Gibbons. Harcourt Brace Jovanovich, 1984. PK–1. As the seasons pass, Arnold enjoys a variety of activities as a result of his apple tree. Includes a recipe for apple pie and a description of how an apple cider press works.

*Ten Apples Up On Top!* by Theo LeSieg (Dr. Seuss), illustrated by Roy McKie. Beginner Books, 1961. (Beginner Books series.) PK–1. A lion, a dog, and a tiger balance an increasing number of apples on their heads.

*"Ten Brown Bears"* in *The Frogs Wore Red Suspenders* rhymes by Jack Prelutsky; pictures by Petra Mathers. Greenwillow Books, 2002. PK–3. A short poem about ten brown bears that gobble plates of apple pies!

*Ten Red Apples: A Bartholomew Bear Counting Book* by Virginia Miller. Candlewick Press, 2002. Toddler–K. Bartholomew and George, two bears, and Little Black Kitten enjoy the apple tree in the garden and count its shiny red apples.

*Where Is the Apple Pie?* by Valeri Gorbachev. Philomel Books, 1999. PK–1. A simple question about the location of an apple pie leads to an outlandish yet seemingly verified explanation.

# Story Prop and Craft Directions

## "A-P-P-L-E" Letters and Clapping Apples

### Tools and Supplies

- felt, foamies, or card stock: red, yellow, apple green

- three brown pipe cleaners/chenille stems (3 mm size), each cut in half
- scissors
- small-size (¹⁄₁₆") hole punch
- hot glue gun and glue sticks
- puffy paint: red, yellow, green
- small flexible magnets or Velcro® pieces (if using foamies or card stock)

### Directions

1. Photocopy the letter and apple patterns on page 158. Cut the pieces from colored felt or foamies:

    Red: A and L, two apples

    Yellow: P and E, two apples

    Green: P, one apple

2. Punch a hole near the center top of each apple and twist a piece of pipe cleaner through it for a stem.

3. With matching puffy paint, draw a small swoosh beneath each stem as shown on the pattern. Allow the paint to dry completely.

4. If letters and apples are made from foamies or card stock, hot glue small pieces of flexible magnet or Velcro to the back of each cutout.

## "I Am An Apple" Flannel / Velcro® Board Pieces

(pink flower with yellow center, yellow and black bee, small green apple, large red apple, tree)

### Tools and Supplies

- bolt felt or other Velcro-compatible fabric for the tree: brown, bright green
- polyester fiberfill
- tan Velcro® strips
- foamies, card stock, or felt squares: light pink, yellow, black, apple green, red, bright green
- one brown pipe cleaner/chenille stem (3 mm size)
- one apple green pipe cleaner/chenille stem (3 mm size)

- one black pipe cleaner/chenille stem (3 mm size)
- small-size (¹⁄₁₆") paper punch
- bright yellow pom poms (5 mm size)
- scissors
- Tacky Glue® craft glue
- hot glue gun and hot glue sticks
- puffy paint: pink, white, black, red, apple green, bright green
- small piece of white netting or translucent plastic fruit/vegetable bag (for bee's wings)
- wooden craft stick
- acrylic craft paint: black
- clear gloss acrylic varnish
- Velcro® dots (if using foamies or card stock)

### Directions

1. Photocopy the TREE, FLOWER, BEE, SMALL GREEN APPLE, and LARGE RED APPLE patterns on pages 159–161, and cut the pieces from colored foamies, felt, or Velcro-compatible fabric.

2. To make the double-layered slightly stuffed tree, see directions on pages 156–157.

3. Glue Velcro to the back of the tree near the top to affix it to a Velcro board, or you can T-pin it to a flannel board.

4. Hot glue the yellow flower center to the flower, and the bee's yellow stripes onto the bee.

5. Punch a hole near the center top of each apple and twist a piece of pipe cleaner through it for a stem (apple green stem for the green apple, and a brown stem for the red apple). Twist the bright green leaf onto the stem of the large red apple.

6. Punch leg and antennae holes for the bee as shown on the pattern, and twist black pipe cleaners through the holes. Bend the ends for feet and clubbed antennae.

7. Highlight the pieces with puffy paint as desired for added interest, and paint the

eyes and mouth on the bee. Allow the paint to dry completely.

8. Hot glue the yellow pompoms to the flower center. Hot glue the netting or plastic baggie wings to the back of the bee.

9. Paint the craft stick black and allow the paint to dry completely. Apply clear varnish, if desired, and allow to dry. Hot glue the black stick to the back of the bee to make it a stick puppet.

10. If the flower, bee, and apple pieces are made from foamies or card stock, hot glue Velcro dots to the back of each cutout.

## "APPLE HAPPY" Story Prop

### Tools and Supplies

- seven red paper plates, 9" size
- four brown pipe cleaner / chenille stems (5 mm size)
- small-size (1/16") paper punch
- scissors
- one sheet bright green foamies
- puffy paint: bright green
- black Sharpie® marking pen
- one large size sheet (12" x 18") of tan foamies
- pinking shears
- 9" foil pie plate
- hot glue gun and glue sticks
- acrylic craft paint: red (needed only if the red paper plates aren't red on the bottom side)
- foam paintbrush (needed only if the red paper plates aren't red on the bottom side)

### Directions

1. Punch one hole near the center top of four of the paper plates. Twist a pipe cleaner through each hole for an apple stem. Cut green leaves and glue or twist to attach to the stems. Highlight the leaves with green puffy paint "veins."

2. Draw one face on each plate: happy, sad, sleepy, and mad.

3. Trace the outer rim of the foil pie tin onto the tan foamies and cut out the circle with your pinking shears. Measure in 3/4" all the way around the circle, and cut out the inner circle with the pinking shears as well.

4. With your pinking shears, cut six 1" wide by approximately 12" long straight strips from the sheet of tan foamies.

5. Hot glue the three remaining paper plates (directly on top of each other) upside down along the rim of the foil pie plate. Layering three together is for sturdiness—if you have heavy duty plates, you could likely get by with one or two layers. If the top plate is not red on the bottom, paint it red and allow the paint to dry completely.

6. Hot glue three of the tan foamies strips one direction across the upside down paper plates, and glue the other three strips the other direction so they form a latticework. Trim the extra ends of the strips so they match the edges of the upside-down paper plates.

7. Hot glue the piecrust circle firmly around the edge of the pie tin, making sure it covers the paper plate edges all the way around.

## "Ten Red Apples" Flannel Board Pieces

### Supplies

- bolt felt or other Velcro-compatible fabric for the tree: brown, bright green
- polyester fiberfill
- foamies or felt squares: red (you may alternatively wish to use ten small red craft apples)
- five brown pipe cleaners/chenille stems (3 mm size), each cut in half
- puffy paint: red
- scissors
- small-size (1/16") paper punch
- ten red Velcro® dots
- tan Velcro® strips

## Directions

1. Photocopy the TREE TRUNK, TREE FOLIAGE, and GRASS AROUND TREE patterns on pages 160–161 at 250%. Tape the enlarged paper pattern pieces together as necessary.

2. Cut out one large brown backing piece for the entire tree trunk/tree foliage/ grass around tree combined. Cut one green TREE FOLIAGE piece, one brown TREE TRUNK piece, and one green GRASS AROUND TREE piece.

3. To make the double-layered slightly stuffed tree, first stitch or glue the green grass to the brown backing. Next, stitch or glue the edges of the tree trunk front layer to the brown backing layer. It will overlap the green grass as shown by the dotted line on the pattern. Allow the glue to dry completely and then lightly stuff the tree trunk with polyester fiberfill.

4. Stitch or glue the green tree foliage to the brown backing, covering the top edges of the tree trunk branches as shown by the dotted lines on the patterns. Allow glue to dry completely.

5. Photocopy the APPLE pattern on page 160 at 100% and cut 10 apples from red foamies or felt.

6. Punch a hole near the center top of each apple and twist a piece of pipe cleaner through it for a stem.

7. Highlight the pieces with puffy paint as desired. (A small swoop under the stem adds definition.)

8. Glue a red Velcro dot to the back of each apple.

9. Glue Velcro to the back of the tree near the top to affix it to a Velcro board, or you can T-pin it to a flannel board.

# A-P-P-L-E Letter and Clapping Apple Patterns

Enlarge as desired.

"Clapping Apple"

# "I Am An Apple" Patterns

**"I Am An Apple"**
Flower, Bee, Small Green
Apple, and Large Red Apple

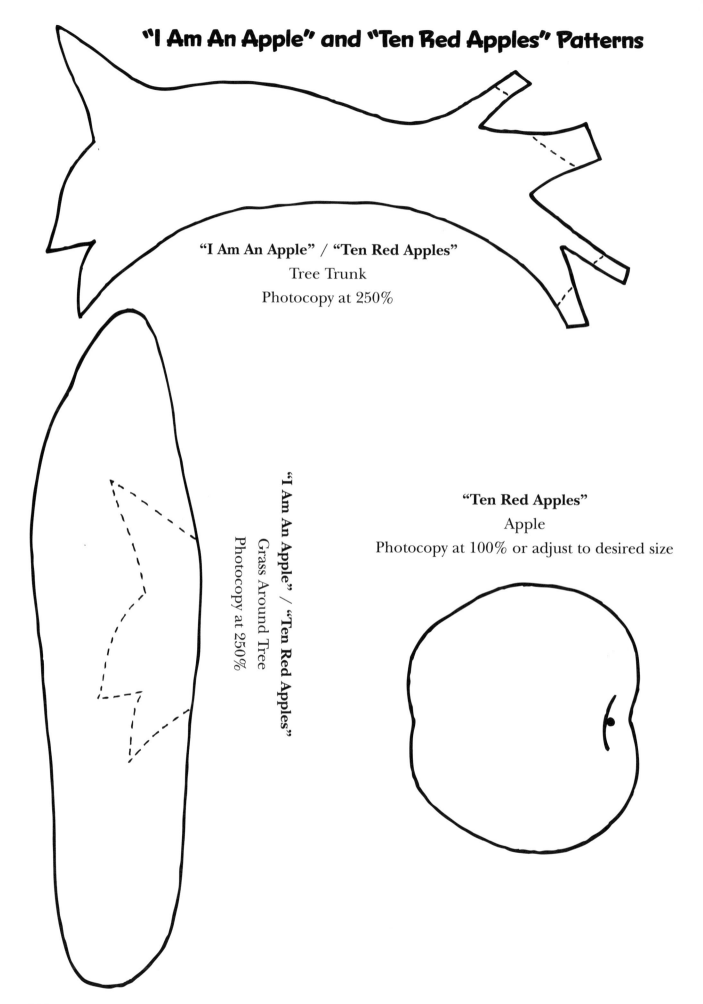

**"I Am An Apple" / "Ten Red Apples"**
Tree Trunk
Photocopy at 250%

**"I Am An Apple" / "Ten Red Apples"**
Grass Around Tree
Photocopy at 250%

**"Ten Red Apples"**
Apple
Photocopy at 100% or adjust to desired size

# "I Am An Apple" and
# "Ten Red Apples" Patterns

"I Am An Apple" / "Ten Red Apples"
Tree Foliage
Photocopy at 250%

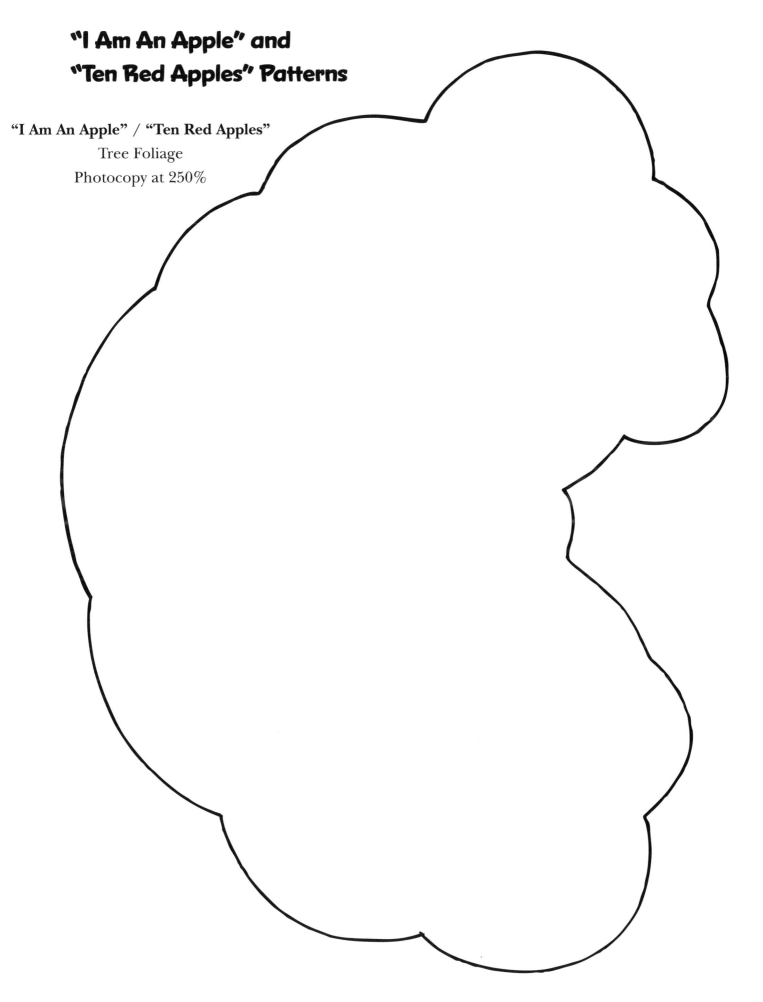

# "Apple Happy" Patterns

**"Apple Happy"**
Leaf

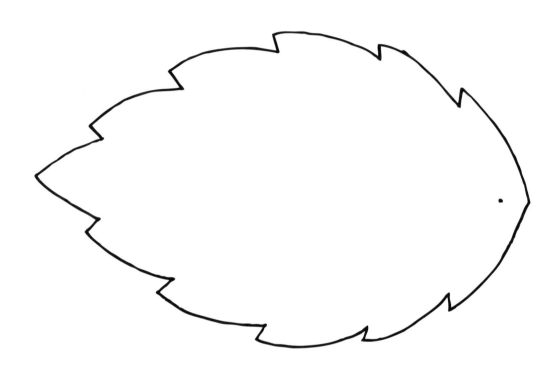

# Ten Little Apples

1 little, 2 little, 3 little apples,

4 little, 5 little, 6 little apples,

7 little, 8 little, 9 little apples,

10 little apples to eat–CRUNCH!

# Sing a Song of Scarecrows
## October

## Early Literacy Activities

### Name Tags

Scarecrow or crow stamp or sticker

### Clue(s)

Miniature scarecrow finger puppet or doll; blackbird finger puppet

### Mailbox "Letter" of the Day

"S" and "s"

Scarecrow, Sing, Sister, Socks, Sick, Sun, Soap, Silly

### Mother Goose Rhyme Time

*Little Boy Blue*

*Little Boy Blue,*
*Come blow your horn.*
*The sheep's in the meadow,*
*The cow's in the corn.*
*Where is the boy*
*Who looks after the sheep?*
*He's under a haystack,*
*Fast asleep.*

### Rhyming Basket

Horn/Corn; Bat/Cat; Block/Clock

## Early Literacy Skill: Language and Vocabulary

Introduce and explain new words or new meanings to familiar words.

- Use informational books and realia throughout storytime to illustrate and elaborate new words or concepts as you are learning about scarecrows and so forth.

- Talk about the words "Dingle," "Dangle," and "Floppy," and demonstrate what they mean with body movements and with your scarecrow puppet.

- Before you share the Mother Goose song "Sing a Song of Sixpence," define the words "sixpence" and "rye." Show photographs or realia to visually clarify if possible. Talk about "four-and-twenty blackbirds" being the same as twenty-four, and consider counting to twenty-four as a group! Explain what it means if something is a "nonsense" rhyme like "Sing a Song of Sixpence"—it is really silly!

- Demonstrate that the words "high" and "low" have multiple meanings by holding one blackbird "high" in the air while trilling the word "high" in a lofty high voice, and holding the other blackbird "low" while intoning the word "low" in a low voice.

# Program Summary and Theme

Celebrate the harvest with a scarecrow and blackbird storytime! If possible, arrange your storytime area with thematic decorations such as scarecrows and pumpkins. Buy real pumpkins/jack-'o-lanterns or purchase a few of the very realistic looking foam models from a craft store, which you can use again and again each year. Many of these foam pumpkins can even be carved!

Prepare the props and puppets ahead of time so you can use them throughout the program. Please see patterns and directions on pages 171–184. See suggested titles on pages 169–171 to substitute for older or younger audiences.

## Music

Play "scarecrow," "harvest," "seasons," or "farm" music as the audience is gathering in your storytime area. Possibilities include "Hard Scrabble Harvest" on *Daydreamer* by Priscilla Herdman (Music for Little People, 1993); "It's Fall" and "Colors" on *Autumnsongs* by John McCutcheon (Rounder, 1998); "Jumping in the Leaves" on *Improvise with Eric Nagler* by Eric Nagler (Rounder, 1989); "All of the Seasons" on *All of the Seasons* by Ken Whiteley (Pyramid, 1993); "What Falls in the Fall?" on *Whaddaya Think of That?* by Laurie Berkner (Two Tomatoes, 2000); "I Like the Fall" on *Sing A Song of Seasons* by Rachel Buchman (Rounder, 1997); "Gray Squirrel" on *Where Is Thumbkin?* (Kimbo Educational, 1998); "Down on Grandpa's Farm" on *One Light One Sun* by Raffi (Troubadour, 1987); "Grandpa's Farm" on *Great Big Hits* (Elephant, 1992) and *Sing A to Z* (Elephant, 1990) by Sharon, Lois, and Bram; "Crow Song" on *Wee Sing in the Car* by Pamela Conn Beall and Susan Hagen Nipp (Price Stern Sloan, 2002); and many more.

## Sample Program

Please adjust content and length as needed.

## Introduction

*Say:* Our stories and poems today are about scarecrows *(hold up your Dingle Dangle/Floppy Scarecrow puppet (see page 171) and gesture to any display scarecrows in the storytime area)* and crows or blackbirds. *(Ask the audience what they think scarecrows are supposed to do—all guesses are good guesses.)* Those are good guesses. Scarecrows are supposed to frighten away birds and other animals that are trying to eat the seeds we plant in our gardens, or eat the plants that are already growing there! When the wind blows, a scarecrow's arms and legs flop around *(wave your Dingle Dangle scarecrow back and forth so that his arms and legs move)*, which makes birds and animals think that something alive and big and scary is already in the garden. They think it is a person, since a scarecrow is usually made with a head and arms and legs like a person. Here are some pictures of a few real scarecrows that people have made.

Show the audience photographs of several real scarecrows from the book *Scarecrows: Making Harvest Figures and Other Yard Folks* by Felder Rushing (Storey Books, 1998) or from another nonfiction title.

## Segue

*Say:* Scarecrows often get to wear some very interesting clothes and hats, don't they? In this next story, Chicken would really like to have the hat that Scarecrow is wearing.

## Read Aloud

*The Scarecrow's Hat* by Ken Brown. Peachtree Publishers, 2001. PK–2. Chicken orchestrates an elaborate, progressive swap of items among the various farmyard creatures until she is finally able to procure Scarecrow's hat for herself.

## Segue

*Say:* The scarecrow in that story seemed pretty tired out, but the scarecrows in the next poem and story have a lot more energy!

## Action Rhyme (Standing)

Share "Dingle Dangle Scarecrow" OR "Floppy Scarecrow" with actions as well as with your scarecrow puppet. (See pages 171–172 for instructions.)

"Dingle Dangle Scarecrow"

When all the cows are sleeping
*(Head on arms, pretend to snore moo-zzz, moo-zzz.)*
And the sun has gone to bed
Up jumps the scarecrow
*(Jump UP, flinging arms high over your head.)*
And this is what he says:

CHORUS:

"I'm a dingle, dangle scarecrow
With a flippy floppy hat. *(Shake head.)*
I can shake my hands like this; *(Shake hands.)*
I can shake my feet like that!" *(Shake feet.)*

When all the hens are roosting
*(Tuck head under arm "wing," pretend to snore bawk bawk-zzz.)*
And the moon's behind a cloud
*(Hands hide face.)*
Up jumps the scarecrow
*(Jump UP, flinging arms high over your head.)*
And shouts out very LOUD:

(CHORUS)

When the dogs are in the kennels
*(Head on arms, pretend to snore arf-zzz, arf-zzz.)*
And the doves are in the loft
Up jumps the scarecrow
*(Jump UP, flinging arms high over your head.)*
And whispers very soft:
*(Whisper the word "soft" and the ensuing chorus as well.)*

(CHORUS 2x)

OR

"Floppy Scarecrow"

This great action rhyme is included on many scarecrow curriculum Web sites. I've been unable to determine the original adaptor. Be creative and try many different motions! Before you begin, talk about what the word "floppy" means.

The floppy, floppy scarecrow
*(Move your body as if it was made of rubber!)*
Guards his fields all day.

He waves his floppy, floppy HANDS
*(Flop hands.)*
To scare the crows away!
*(Repeat rhyme with ARMS, LEGS, SHOULDERS, ELBOWS, TOES, KNEES, and so forth.)*

Write out the words ahead of time on a piece of grid board so attending adults can follow along, and point out to the group that the rhyme is written on the poster.

## Segue

*Say:* In our next story, the scarecrow ends up doing a lot more than just shaking his hands and feet like our Dingle Dangle/Floppy Scarecrow! Listen and find out what happens and why.

## Read Aloud

*Nothing At All* by Denys Cazet. Orchard Books, 1994. PK–1. As the farm animals gradually awaken, each greets the new day with some distinctive behaviors and remarks. The scarecrow, however, says nothing at all until he is startled by a little mouse who takes refuge from the cat in the scarecrow's pants!

## Segue

*Say:* I imagine that any hungry birds who saw that scarecrow dancing and flipping around would stay far away from that farmer's field. I think they would have flown away in a hurry! Here is a little rhyme that many of you may know called "Two Little Blackbirds," where the blackbirds fly away.

## Action Rhyme
## (Standing or Sitting)

Do the following rhyme together with the audience using your thumbs. Once they understand how to do it, you can put your blackbird finger puppets (see instructions and patterns on pages 173 and 178 OR purchase ready-made puppets) on your thumbs or wear two crow hand puppets (see instructions and patterns on pages 174 and 182–184) to lead the group through the rhyme again. Make sure the puppets bow to the audience when they are through performing!

"Two Little Blackbirds"

Two little blackbirds sitting on a hill.
*(Make fists, thumbs up.)*
One named Jack, one named Jill.
*(Raise one thumb and shake it, then the other.)*
Fly away Jack! Fly away Jill!
*(Fly first thumb behind your back, then the other.)*
Come back Jack! Come back Jill!
*(Fly first thumb forward again, then the other.)*

Try extending the rhyme by changing the blackbirds' names and accompanying actions such as:

Fly away HIGH, fly away LOW; Fly away FAST, fly away SLOW; fly away QUIET, fly away LOUD; and so forth. See Rob Reid's engaging and original adaptations of this rhyme in his book *Family Storytime: Twenty-Four Creative Programs for All Ages* (ALA Editions, 1999).

## Segue

*Say:* I have another little rhyme about blackbirds that some of you may have heard before. It is called "Sing a Song of Sixpence," and it has a pie in it!

## Mother Goose Rhyme with Props

Hold up your paper pie as you say or sing the first two lines of the poem, then pop the blackbirds up out of the center of the pie as you get to: "Four-and-twenty blackbirds ..."

Alternately, make a paper plate/foil pie pan pie as described in the "Apple Happy" directions for September's "Picking Apples" chapter (see page 156), and leave an opening in one side into which you can reach. Pull out a string of fold-and-cut blackbirds or felt blackbirds glued to a length of fishing line or yarn (see patterns on page 181).

Pretend to be amazed that there were birds in the pie!

"Sing a Song of Sixpence"

Sing a song of sixpence,
A pocket full of rye;
Four-and-twenty blackbirds
baked in a pie!
When the pie was opened,
the birds began to sing.

*(You may wish to caw one or two lines of "Twinkle Twinkle Little Star" or another well-known children's song before finishing the rhyme.)*

Wasn't that a dainty dish to set before the king?

Write out the words ahead of time on a piece of grid board so attending adults can follow along, and point out to the group that the rhyme/song is written on the poster. Repeat the rhyme several times, encouraging the audience to say it with you. For at least one of the repetitions, follow the printed text on the poster with your finger as you read from left to right to reinforce print directionality as well as the concept that print stands for spoken language (encouraging the children's print awareness, another of the six early literacy skills).

## Segue

*Say:* Well, that was sure a surprise—blackbirds popping out of a pie! Here is another surprise story for you, but all this one needs is a piece of orange paper *(flutter a folded-in-half sheet of orange paper in front of you as it was blowing along with the wind)* and a pair of scissors.

## Cut-and-Tell Story

"The Little Orange House" cut-and-tell story in *Paper Stories* by Jean Stangl. Lake Publishing Co., 1984. Also available online at: www.dcrafts.com/orangehouse.htm. Toddler–Grade 3. In the original, a little witch with a pointy hat engineers a cozy house for herself and a tiny homeless ghost by strategically cutting a roof, windows, and doors from a piece of orange paper. When the paper is opened at the end of the story so the audience can "see inside their little orange house," it reveals a smiling jack-'o-lantern!

Truly one of my favorite stories to tell in October, "The Little Orange House" is endlessly adaptable, and the surprise ending delights every time. In the public library where I typically need to avoid witches and ghosts, I often tell the story with a bunny rabbit finger puppet (with tall pointed ears necessitating the special pointed door) in the lead role making the house, and a homeless little mouse (with a pointed nose) finger puppet instead of the ghost. Tell it with a tiny scarecrow as the main protagonist to complement your "Sing a Song of Scarecrows" storytime!

## Segue

*Say:* I have one last story for you. It is a very, very old story, and was first told by a wise man named Aesop, who lived many, many, many years ago!

## Storytelling with Puppet and Props

Tell Aesop's fable "The Crow and the Pitcher" using props. A full script and patterns are provided on pages 168–169 and 182–184.

Also see an illustrated version of the story in *Professor Aesop's The Crow and the Pitcher* by Stephanie Gwynne Brown (Tricycle Press, 2003). PK–5. A thirsty crow learns that "little by little does the trick!"

## Conclusion

*Say:* The crow in that story really used his head to solve his problem, even though it took him awhile to figure things out. That's why I called him a "clever crow." I saw all of you thinking about what was happening as the crow was putting stones in the water, and I could tell you were all using your heads, too. I can call you a "clever class." Just like the crow, you can work on things a little bit at a time until you solve a problem. Remember what the crow told us: *(encourage the audience to join you in saying this)* "Little by little does the trick!"

## Prop Story

### *"The Crow and the Pitcher" by Aesop*

Aesop's fable adapted by Kimberly Faurot and Crosby Coghill; prop originated by Marcia Tyriver.

### Story Pieces

- one crow puppet (use a purchased hand puppet, see Resources—OR make a paper bag puppet using the patterns on pages 182–184)

- one green towel

- clear pitcher or water carafe with a narrow neck (often available at second-hand stores)

- medium- to large-size stones (they must still fit easily through the neck of the pitcher/carafe)

### Set-up

1. Spread out the green towel on a table or desk.

2. Fill the pitcher approximately ⅔ full of water before you start. The water level should be low enough so the crow will be unable to reach it with his beak, but high enough so that adding your stones will raise the water level quickly and

sufficiently to get it to the top of the pitcher. Place the pitcher of water on the green towel.

3. Arrange the stones on the towel around the pitcher of water.

4. Hide the crow puppet in a box or basket nearby until it is time to begin the story.

### Presentation

- Story narration is in regular type; movement notes and miscellaneous directions are shown within the script in *italics*.

- Learn the story and tell it to your audience from memory, using the puppet and props. Practice in front of a mirror to work on your puppet's believability.

- Look at your puppet while it is talking so that you are not competing with it for the audience's attention. Manipulate the puppet's mouth carefully to make him talk believably. Open the puppet's mouth to let a word or syllable out, then gently close it again. Avoid the common mistake of making the puppet "bite" or "eat" his words.

### Introduction

Aesop usually told stories that helped his listeners learn things about themselves and about the world around them. These were called the morals of the stories. See if you can figure out what the moral to this story might be before the end.

To tell the story, I am going to use this. *(Hold up the pitcher/carafe of water.)* What is it? Do you think this is real water? Yes, it is. *(Set pitcher down again.)* I'm also going to use these. *(Hold up two of the stones, then clink them together so they make noise.)* What do you think they are? Yes, they are stones—real ones. *(Replace stones around pitcher.)* I'm also going to use this puppet. *(Pull out your crow puppet from its hiding place.)* Can anyone guess what kind of a bird it is supposed to be? *(Take a few guesses—all are good guesses.)* It is actually a crow puppet, because the story I am going to tell you is called: "The Crow and the Pitcher" by Aesop.

**Script**

Standing a short distance away from the pitcher and stones, hold up your crow puppet and begin narrating.

*Narrator:* There once was a crow who was very thirsty. He was so thirsty that he was afraid he might die if he didn't find some water.

*Crow:* "Thirsty, thirsty!" *(Cough, cough.)*

*Narrator:* As he was dragging himself along, he amazingly discovered a pitcher of water, right in the very heart of the forest!

*Crow:* "Water! Water! I'm saved!"

*Narrator:* The crow rushed to the pitcher, but as he tried to drink *(fly crow to rim of pitcher/ carafe and have him try to drink—his beak is clearly too wide, and he bounces back each time; take care that you don't allow the pointed beak end to poke down into the pitcher—make it clear that there is no way he can reach the water)*, he found he could not reach the water! The poor crow couldn't believe it—he was right in front of a pitcher of water, but he might die of thirst anyway!

*Crow:* "This is ridiculous!"

*Narrator:* This crow was not the kind of fellow to give up easily, however. He looked at the pitcher and thought about his problem. *(Hold crow on one side of the pitcher and have him look at it, then move him to the other side and have him look at it from that angle.)* He thought some more, and thought some more, and at last that clever crow had an idea! He picked up one of the stones in his beak that was lying near the pitcher *(help the crow pick up one of the larger stones)*, and flew up and dropped it into the pitcher *(help crow drop stone in pitcher)*. He added another *(add another stone)*, and another *(add another stone)*, and another *(add another stone)*. Something was happening! *(The audience may call out what they see happening.)* With each stone that the crow dropped, the water was rising closer and closer to the top of the pitcher! *(Add enough stones so that the water level is up near the top of the pitcher.)* At last, the water had risen far enough, and the clever crow was able to drink.

*Crow:* "I'm saved!" *(Crow pretends to drink, dipping his beak near the water, then raising his head back to swallow like birds do. If you have a crow*

*with a water-resistant beak, you can lightly dip the beak into the water, then have him flick it out on the audience as he tips his head back to drink!)*

*Narrator:* Because of his quick thinking, the crow was able to get a drink and save his life. And the moral of this story is:

*Crow:* "Little by little does the trick!" *(Crow bows to the audience.)*

# Additional Resources

*Autumn Leaves* by Ken Robbins. Scholastic, 1998. K–2. Examines the characteristics of different types of leaves and explains how and why they change colors in the autumn.

*Barn Dance!* by Bill Martin, Jr. and John Archambault, illustrated by Ted Rand. Henry Holt & Company, 1986. PK–2. Unable to sleep on the night of a full moon, a young boy follows the sound of music across the fields and finds an unusual barn dance in progress.

*The Bears' Autumn* by Keizaburo Tejima, translated from the Japanese by Susan Matsui. Green Tiger Press, 1986. PK–1. In the mountains of Hokkaido, the northern island of Japan, a little bear and his mother get ready for their long winter sleep by gathering food and catching salmon.

*Beautiful Blackbird* by Ashley Bryan. Atheneum, 2003. K–3. In a story of the Ila people, the colorful birds of Africa ask Blackbird, whom they think is the most beautiful of birds, to decorate them with some of his "blackening brew."

*Black Crow, Black Crow* by Ginger Foglesong Guy. Greenwillow Books, 1991. Toddler–Grade 1. High up in a tree, a mother crow tends her young.

*The Busy Little Squirrel* by Nancy Tafuri. Simon & Schuster Books for Young Readers, 2007. Toddler–K. Squirrel is too busy getting ready for winter to nibble a pumpkin with Mouse, run in the field with Dog, or otherwise play with any of the other animals. Encourage the audience to join in on the repeated refrain: "But Squirrel couldn't … He was so busy!" The pictures reveal the details of Squirrel's busy activities, leaving ample opportunity to discuss as a group what he is doing.

***Days of the Blackbird*** by Tomie de Paola. Putnam, 1997. 1–4. At the request of a kind duke's loving daughter, La Colomba, a pure white bird, braves the bitter winter of the northern Italian mountains to sing for the gravely ill man.

***Every Autumn Comes the Bear*** by Jim Arnosky. Putnam, 1993. K–1. Every autumn a bear shows up behind the farm, and goes through a series of routines before finding a den among the hilltop boulders where he sleeps all winter long.

***Fall Is Not Easy*** by Marty Kelley. Zino Press, 1998. PK–2. With rhyming text and illustrations that humorously extend the story, a tree tells why, out of all four seasons, Autumn is the most difficult.

***Fall Leaves Fall!*** by Zoe Hall, illustrated by Shari Halpern. Scholastic, 2000. PK–1. When fall comes, two children enjoy catching the falling leaves, stomping on them, kicking them, jumping in piles of them, and using them to make pictures. Includes a description of how leaves change through the year.

***Felt Board Stories*** by Liz & Dick Wilmes. Building Blocks, 2001. PK–1. Includes four short seasonal felt board stories about Flip-Flop Scarecrow, along with patterns and directions for making the pieces.

**"Five Little Leaves"** in *Mitt Magic: Fingerplays for Finger Puppets* by Lynda Roberts. Gryphon House, 1985. Toddler–K. Five little leaves, each one a different color, blow around town. Patterns are included for colored felt or paper leaves to affix to a glove or Velcro mitt.

**"Four Autumn Leaves"** in *Cut & Tell: Scissor Stories for Fall* by Jean Warren. Warren Publishing House, 1984. PK–K. Four leaves blow from a tree one at a time, until none are left. Paper plate cut-and-tell.

**"Gray Squirrel"** traditional rhyme/song on the sound recording *Where is Thumbkin?; Action Songs for Every Month* (Kimbo Educational, 1996). Toddler–K.

***Leaf Man*** by Lois Ehlert. Harcourt, 2005. PK–2. A man made of leaves blows away, traveling wherever the wind may take him. On die-cut pages.

***Leaves*** by David Ezra Stein. G.P. Putnam's Sons, 2007. PK–1. A curious bear observes how leaves change throughout the seasons.

**"Like Leaves in Windy Weather"** in *Listen! And Help Tell the Story* by Bernice Wells Carlson. Abingdon Press, 1965. Toddler–K. Dance together like leaves with this action rhyme.

***The Little Old Lady Who Was Not Afraid of Anything*** by Linda Williams, illustrated by Megan Lloyd. Crowell, 1986. PK–2. A little old lady who is not afraid of anything must deal with a pumpkin head, a tall black hat, and other spooky items of clothing that follow her through the dark woods trying to scare her. In the end, the little old lady suggests that the disappointed clothes and head arrange themselves into a scarecrow and use their special skills to frighten the crows away from her garden.

**Extension Idea:** Share this story with enthusiastic audience participation actions and with gathered props. Purchase a child-size, white, long-sleeved shirt; green pants; and heavy shoes at a second hand store. White gloves are readily available at discount stores, and inexpensive black foam or felt hats and foam pumpkins/jack-'o-lanterns can be found at many craft stores. Cut a hole in the bottom of the pumpkin. Set a 24" x 36" standard size flannel board on an easel, with a small table just underneath it. At the very end of the story when the little old lady whispers in the pumpkin's ear, pin the clothing to the board to form the scarecrow, placing the shoes on the small table and balancing the pumpkin head and the hat atop the easel. (See photo.) If you have a crow puppet, fly it by the scarecrow. When the scarecrow clomps, wiggles, and shakes through its actions at the end of the story, hurriedly squawk the cawing frightened crow away.

***The Little Scarecrow Boy*** by Margaret Wise Brown, illustrated by David Diaz. HarperCollins, 1998. PK–1. Early one morning, a little scarecrow whose father warns him that he is not fierce enough to frighten a crow goes out into the cornfield alone.

*Nuts to You!* by Lois Ehlert. Harcourt Brace Jovanovich, 1993. PK–1. A rascally squirrel has an indoor adventure in a city apartment.

*Red Leaf, Yellow Leaf* by Lois Ehlert. Harcourt Brace Jovanovich, 1991. PK–2. A child describes the growth of a maple tree from seed to sapling. (Available as a BIG Book.)

*The Scarebird* by Sid Fleischman, illustrated by Peter Sis. Greenwillow Books, 1987. 1–4. A lonely old farmer realizes the value of human friendship when a young man comes to help him and his scarecrow with their farm.

*Scarecrow* by Cynthia Rylant, illustrated by Lauren Stringer. Harcourt, 1998. PK–2. Although made of straw and borrowed clothes, a scarecrow appreciates his peaceful, gentle life and the privilege of watching nature at work.

*Scaredy Squirrel* by Melanie Watts. Kids Can Press, 2006. PK–2. Scaredy Squirrel never leaves his nut tree because he's afraid of the unknown "out there."

*Scaredy Squirrel Makes A Friend* by Melanie Watts. Kids Can Press, 2007. PK–2. Scaredy Squirrel sets out to make the perfect friend— preferably one with no teeth and who is germ-free and predictable.

*Six Crows* by Leo Lionni. Knopf, 1988. PK–2. An owl helps a farmer and some crows reach a compromise over the rights to the wheat crop.

*The Surprise* by George Shannon, illustrated by Jose Aruego and Ariane Dewey. Greenwillow Books, 1983. PK–2. Squirrel gives his mother a special surprise on her birthday.

**Extension Idea:** Share the story with puppets and props. Purchase or make two identical small squirrel hand puppets. Purchase or make a large squirrel (mother) hand puppet, or be the mother squirrel yourself. Hide one of the small puppets inside a small box tied with ribbon, and nest the box in a series of other variously shaped, decorated, and beribboned boxes with removable lids. Introduce the story with your other small squirrel puppet, and have him "call" his mother with a miniature cell phone to tell her about the birthday package before you hide him away. As Squirrel's mother opens each box, discuss its shape with the audience and speculate together what could be inside: A cake? A bike? A stop sign? At the end, Squirrel jumps out of the innermost box and gives his mother a big hug and kiss!

*Time to Sleep* by Denise Fleming. Henry Holt & Company, 1997. PK–2. When Bear notices that winter is nearly here he hurries to tell Snail, after which each animal tells another until finally the already sleeping Bear is awakened in his den with the news.

**"Today Is a Day to Crow About"** in *The New Kid On the Block: Poems* by Jack Prelutsky, illustrated by James Stevenson. Greenwillow Books, 1984. PK–4. In a turnabout, the crows are chasing the scarecrow away!

*Waltz of the Scarecrows* by Constance W. McGeorge, illustrated by Mary Whyte. Chronicle Books, 1998. K–3. While staying with her grandparents on their farm, Sarah discovers the secret behind the local tradition of dressing the scarecrows in formal gowns and fancy coats.

# Story Prop and Craft Directions

## Dingle Dangle/Floppy Scarecrow Stick Puppet Story Prop and/or Student Craft

### Tools and Supplies

- white or colored card stock
- scissors
- crayons, markers, or colored pencils
- paper punch
- six metal brad fasteners OR yarn
- bendable plastic drinking straw
- heavy duty clear tape

### Directions

1. Copy the scarecrow patterns from pages 175–177 onto white or colored card stock and cut them out. Color the pieces with crayons, markers, or colored pencils as desired.

2. Punch holes at the scarecrow's joints with a paper punch, as shown by the black circles on the patterns. Connect the scarecrow with the metal brad fasteners, or knot yarn through the holes.

3. Tape the short end of a bendable drinking straw on the back of the scarecrow's head so it may be manipulated as a stick puppet.

## "Sing a Song of Sixpence" Pie Story Prop and/or Student Craft

### Tools and Supplies

- white or colored card stock paper
- scissors
- crayons, markers or colored pencils
- Tacky glue® craft glue
- wooden paint stick

### Directions

1. Copy the pie and blackbird patterns from pages 179–180 onto white or colored card stock. Cut them out. Color the pieces with crayons, markers, or colored pencils as desired.

2. Apply a line of glue around the bottom edge of the pie plate backing along the dotted lines, leaving an opening in the middle for the paint stick as shown on the pattern. Glue the front and back pie plate pieces together. Allow the glue to dry completely.

3. Glue the paint stick securely to the center back of the blackbirds. The stick should extend as high as possible on the blackbird piece to give it the maximum amount of support. Allow the glue to dry completely.

4. Insert the paint stick into the slot at the bottom of the pie plate so that you will be able to pop the blackbirds up out of the pie.

## Alternate "Sing a Song of Sixpence" Pie Story Prop

### Pie and Fold-and-Cut Blackbirds OR Felt Blackbirds on a String

- three red paper plates, 9" size
- one large size sheet (12" x 18") of tan foamies
- scissors
- pinking shears
- 9" foil pie pan
- hot glue gun and glue sticks
- acrylic craft paint: red (needed only if the red paper plates aren't red on the bottom side)
- foam paintbrush (needed only if the red paper plates aren't red on the bottom side)
- four strips of black paper, each 24" long x 3¼" wide OR four squares of plain black felt, four squares of sparkly black felt, and a three-yard length of fishing line or black string
- embellishments such as: googly eyes; black feathers; crayons, acrylic paints, or gel pens OR puffy paints

### Pie

1. Make a paper plate/foil pie pan pie as described in the "Apple Happy" directions for September's "Picking Apples" chapter (see page 151). Cut an opening in one side of the pie into which you will be able to reach to remove the blackbirds.

### Fold-and-Cut Blackbirds

1. Cut four strips of black paper 24" long x 3¼" wide. (You can glue several strips together if you can't find paper long enough.) Accordion-fold the strip at four-inch-wide intervals so that you have four sets of six folded panels.

2. Photocopy the fold-and-cut blackbird template on page 181 and cut it out. Trace the blackbird outline on the front and back panels of each folded strip.

3. Cutting through half of the folded layers, cut out the blackbird shape; then cut the other half. Make sure to leave the sides attached at the wings!

4. Tape the four sets of blackbirds together so you have one long strip with 24 birds.

5. Decorate the blackbirds as desired with crayons, paints, or gel pens.

6. Accordion-fold the finished blackbirds and hide them in the pie.

### Felt Blackbirds on a String

1. Photocopy the felt blackbird pattern on page 181 and cut it out. Cut 24 blackbirds from plain black felt and 24 from sparkly black felt.

2. Lay the 24 plain black felt blackbirds in a row, beak to tail but with about 1½" of space between them. Glue a solid three-yard length of fishing line or black string down the center of the line of birds so they are all connected. Allow the glue to dry completely.

3. Glue each blackbird's top layer over the bottom layer, sparkle side up, so the fishing line/string is glued between the layers.

4. Decorate and embellish as desired with googly eyes, painted beaks, black feathers, and so forth. Allow the paint and glue to dry completely.

5. Fold the 24 blackbirds back and forth, end to end so they don't become tangled, and hide them inside the pie.

## "Two Little Blackbirds" Storytime Finger Puppets

### Tools and Supplies

- black felt
- dressmaker's pins
- scissors
- contrasting fabric for kerchief and necktie
- Fray Check™
- acrylic craft paint: silver gray, white
- small-size craft paintbrush

- black feathers
- four googly eyes, 7 mm size
- Tacky Glue® craft glue

### Directions

1. Copy the "Two Little Blackbirds" finger/stick puppet patterns from page 178 and cut them out along the solid line (not along the dotted line, which is intended for the student craft stick puppet option).

2. Pin the patterns to the felt and cut, so you will have two cutouts for each bird.

3. Squeeze a thin line of craft glue around the edge of the bottom layer, taking care to leave an opening along the bird's stomach for your thumb. Glue layers together.

4. Cut the patterns apart so you can cut the kerchief and necktie from contrasting fabric and the wings from more black felt. Make two of each piece for each bird so you can make the finger puppets double-sided. Fray Check the fabric cutouts around the edges if needed and allow them to dry, then glue the fabric pieces and wings in place on the bird.

4. Paint the birds' beaks with the silver gray paint, then outline the entire bird and its wings with white paint.

5. Glue the birds' eyes in place, and decorate the wings and tails with feathers if desired. Allow the glue to dry completely.

*Extension Activity: Use a Dingle Dangle/Floppy Scarecrow Stick Puppet and Blackbird Finger/Stick Puppet to share the following rhyme/song (Sung to the tune: "I'm a Little Teapot").*

"Conversation" by Kimberly Faurot

*Scarecrow: "I'm a little scarecrow stuffed with straw."*
*Crow: "I am a crow who says Caw! Caw!"*
*Scarecrow: "I will wave my hands and feet all day."*
*Crow: "And when I see you, I'll fly away!"*

## "Two Little Blackbirds" Student Craft

### Tools and Supplies

- white card stock
- safety scissors

- crayons, colored pencils, or washable markers
- colored feathers
- stickers
- wooden craft sticks
- Tacky Glue® craft glue or double-stick tape

**Directions**

1. Copy the "Two Little Blackbirds" finger/stick puppet patterns from page 178 onto white card stock and cut out along the dotted lines.

2. Color the birds as desired. If children prefer to make their birds other colors, repeat the poem with that color such as "Two little red birds ... "

3. Decorate the birds with feathers and so forth.

4. Affix each bird to a craft stick with glue or double-stick tape.

## Crow Hand Puppet Story Prop or Student Craft

(*Note: Craft difficulty level most appropriate for older children, in primary grades. If making the hand puppet as a student craft, you may wish to use black, gray, and yellow construction paper instead of foamies sheets.)*

**Tools and Supplies (for one crow puppet)**

- small paper lunch bag
- scissors
- ballpoint pen
- Tacky Glue® craft glue or hot glue gun and glue sticks

- two black foamies sheets
- one gray foamies sheet
- one yellow foamies sheet
- two googly eyes, 24 mm size
- black craft feathers (optional)
- hair ribbon (optional—if making an additional "Jill" crow for the "Two Little Blackbirds" rhyme)

**Directions**

1. Cut out the crow puppet patterns from pages 182–184 and trace them onto the foamies with a ballpoint pen. Cut out the foamies pieces.

2. Glue the foamies pieces onto the paper bag as shown in the photo on page 167. Affix the googly eyes and feathers. Allow the glue to dry completely.

3. Your crow puppet is ready to perform his fable!

# Scarecrow Patterns

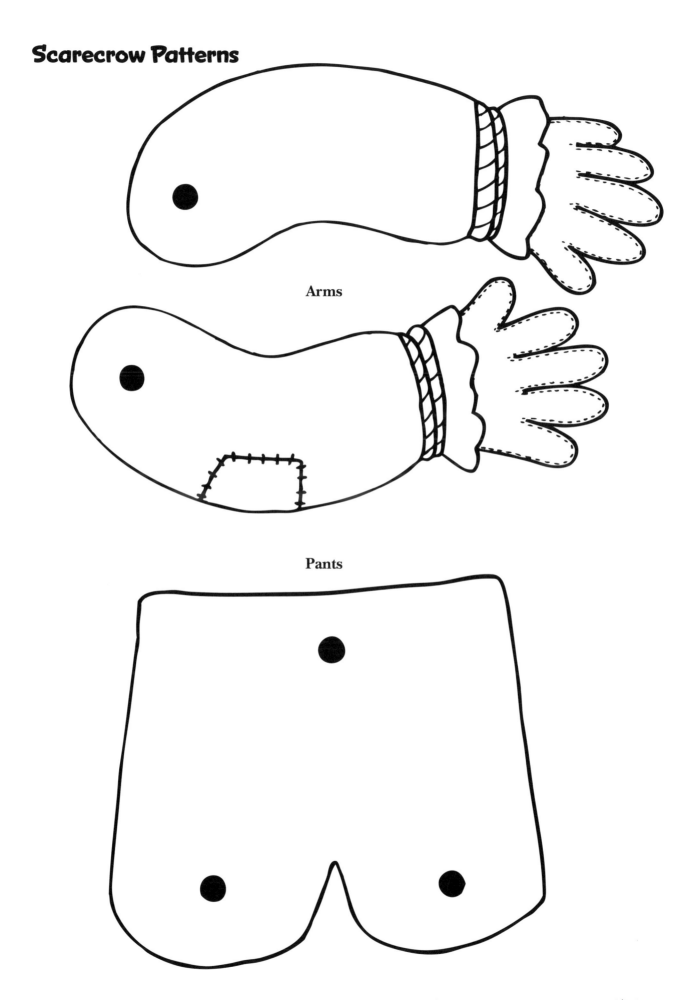

Arms

Pants

# Scarecrow Patterns

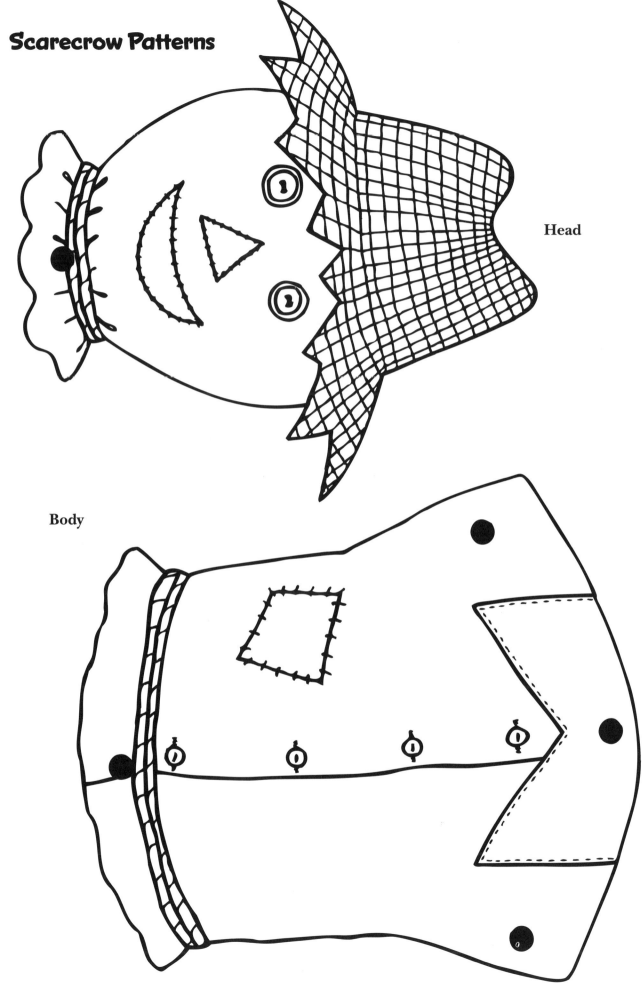

Head

Body

# Scarecrow Patterns

Legs

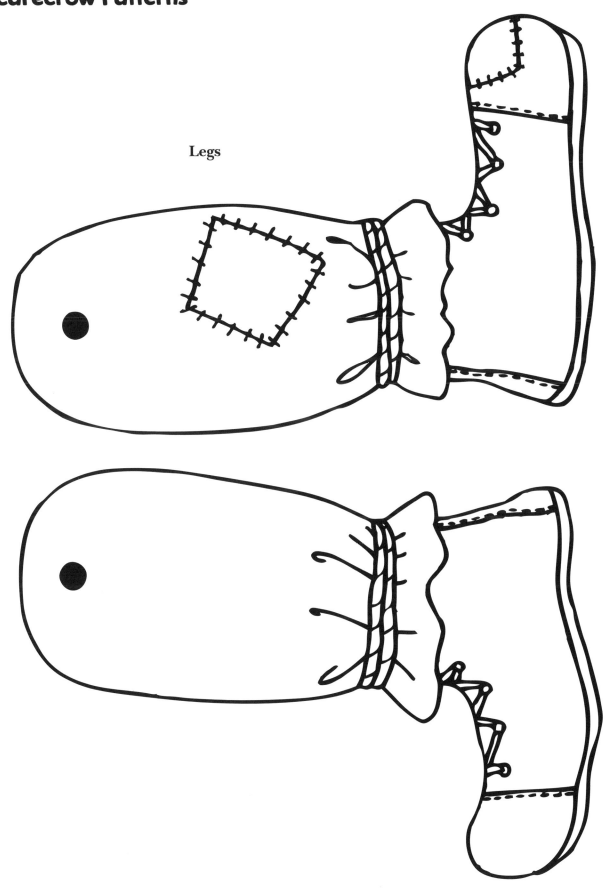

# "Two Little Blackbirds" Patterns

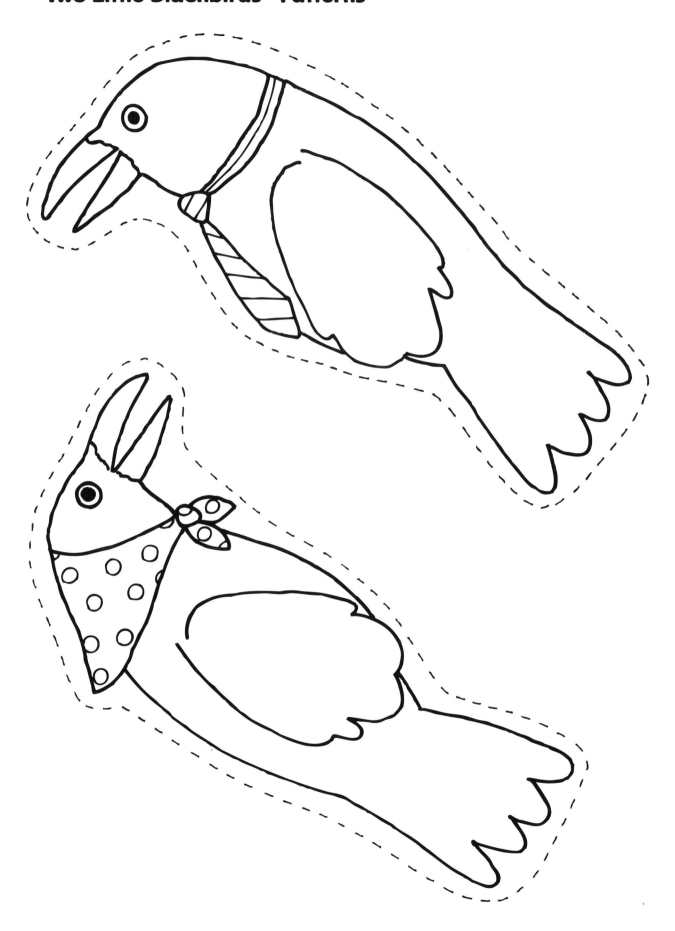

# "Sing a Song of Sixpence" Pie and Blackbirds Patterns

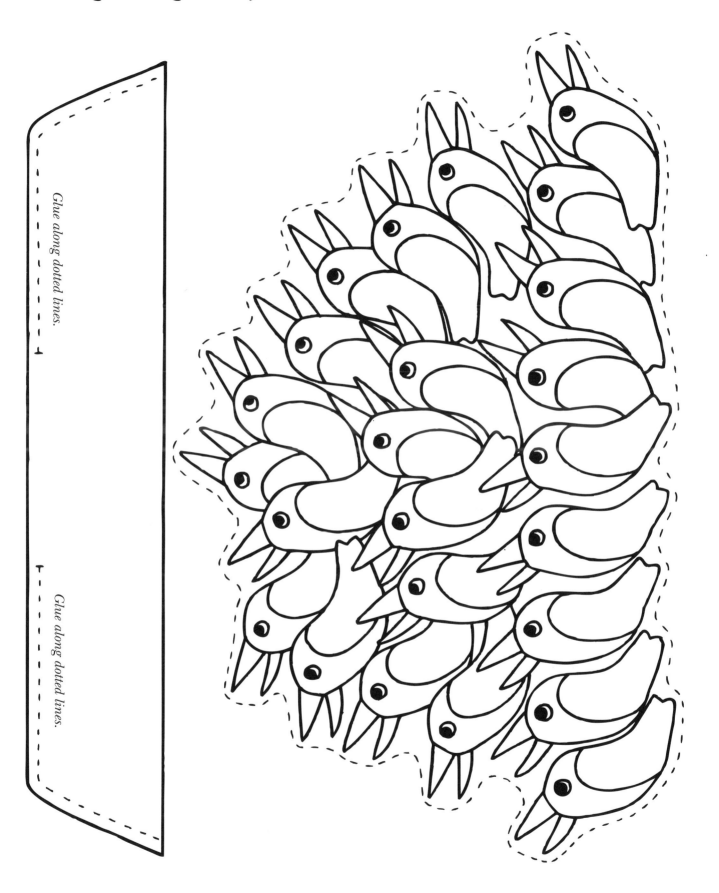

Glue along dotted lines.

Glue along dotted lines.

# "Sing a Song of Sixpence" Pie Pattern

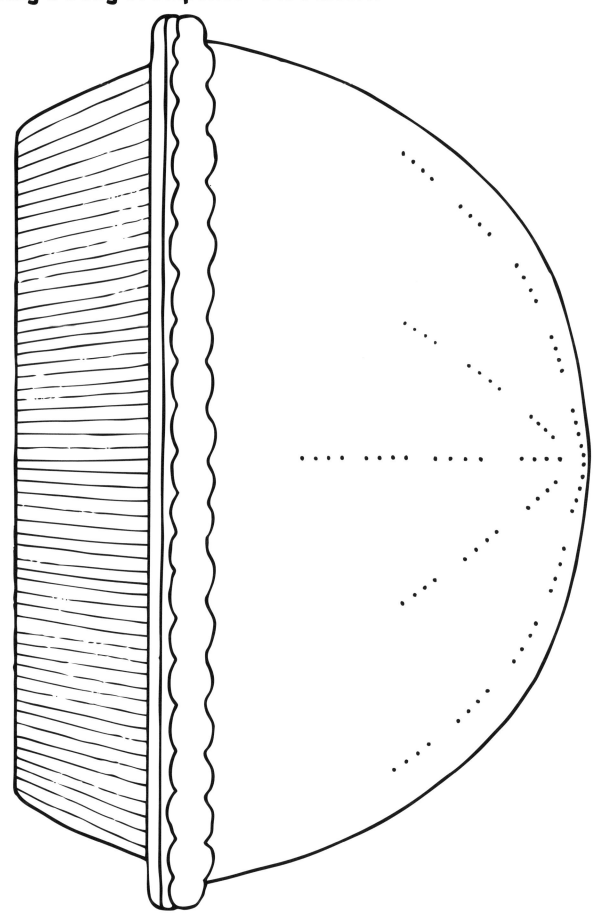

# "Sing a Song of Sixpence" Blackbird Patterns

*Place on folds.*

*Place on folds.*

**Fold-And-Cut Blackbirds**

**Blackbirds On a String**

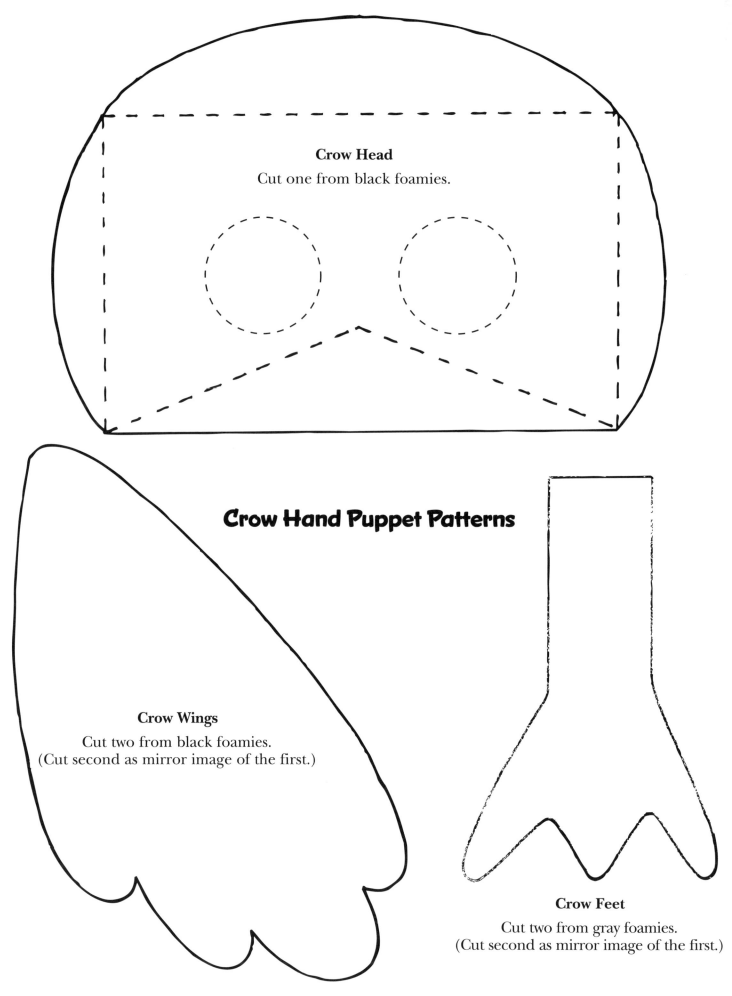

**Crow Head**

Cut one from black foamies.

## Crow Hand Puppet Patterns

**Crow Wings**

Cut two from black foamies.
(Cut second as mirror image of the first.)

**Crow Feet**

Cut two from gray foamies.
(Cut second as mirror image of the first.)

**Crow Body**

Cut one from black foamies.

# Crow Hand Puppet Patterns

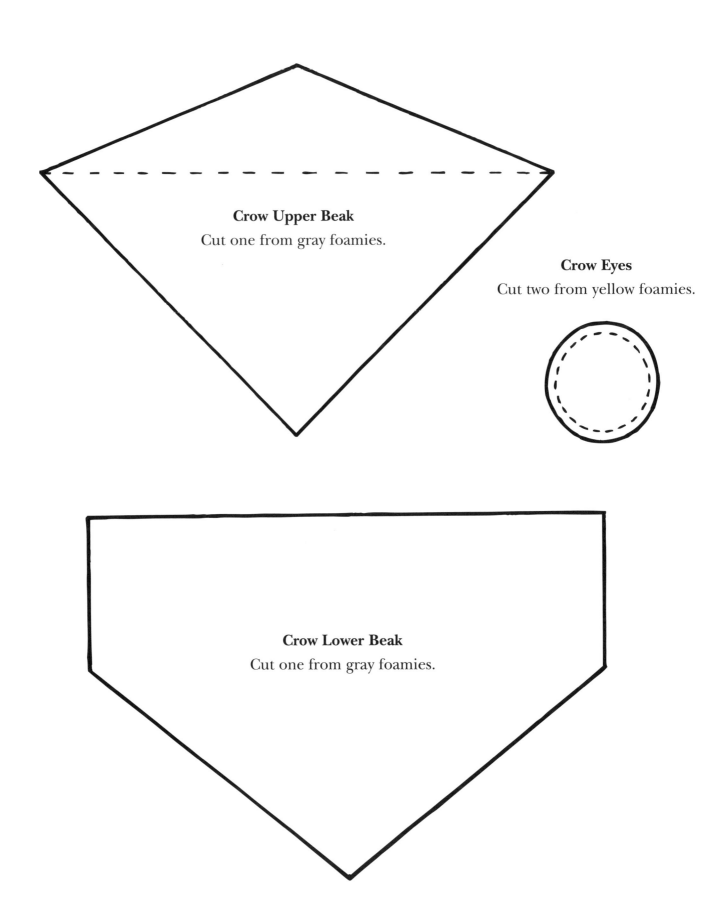

**Crow Upper Beak**

Cut one from gray foamies.

**Crow Eyes**

Cut two from yellow foamies.

**Crow Lower Beak**

Cut one from gray foamies.

# Fabulous Food
## November

## Early Literacy Activities

### Name Tags

Vegetables stamp or stickers

### Clue(s)

Miniature plastic vegetables or other plastic play food

### Mailbox "Letter" of the Day

"F" and "f"

Food, Fabulous, Fancy, Funny, Face, Fingers, Fox, Fork

### Mother Goose Rhyme Time

*Blow, Wind, Blow!*

*Blow, wind, blow!*
*And go, mill, go!*
*That the miller may grind his corn;*
*That the baker may take it,*
*And into bread make it,*
*And bring us a loaf in the morn.*
*Blow, wind, blow!*
*And go, mill, go!*

### Rhyming Basket

Carrot/Parrot; Pot/Dot; Bat/Hat

### Early Literacy Skill: Print Motivation

Encourage interest in and excitement about reading and books.

- Be delighted by the stories and activities that you share. Your enthusiasm will be infectious.

- Read *The Beastly Feast* by Bruce Goldstone (Henry Holt & Company, 1998) and *Peanut Butter & Jelly: A Play Rhyme* illustrated by Nadine Bernard Westcott (Dutton, 1987) with practiced rhythm and rhyme.

- Repeat "Oodles of Noodles" by Lucia & James L. Hymes, Jr. and the Mother Goose Rhyme "Bat, Bat, Come Under My Hat" several times together with the children, encouraging their own enjoyment and internalization of the poems' lively rhythms.

- Lead the group in Laurie Berkner's action song "I Feel Crazy So I Jump in the Soup" with joy and jumping.

## Program Summary and Theme

One of my favorite storytime activities is making "Story Soup." This "recipe" calls for ingredients such as vegetables and seasoning, but also requires letters, paper, pictures and imagination. After "cooking" awhile, the soup produces a book or an item representing the first storytime activity. Check the soup between each story or activity to see what has bubbled to the surface to be shared next. The variety and options are truly endless, so have fun cooking!

Prepare the props ahead of time so you can use them throughout the program. Please see patterns and directions on pages 192–196. See suggested titles on pages 190–192 to substitute for older or younger audiences.

## Music

Play "food" or "soup" music as the audience is gathering in your storytime area. Possibilities include "Soup" on the sound recording *Wintersongs* by John McCutcheon (Rounder, 1995), "All Around the Kitchen" on *Family Dance* by Dan Zanes (Festival Five, 2001), "Aikendrum" on *Singable Songs for the Very Young* by Raffi (Troubadour, 1976), "The Corner Grocery Store" on *Corner Grocery Store* by Raffi (Troubadour, 1979), "Let's Go to the Market" on *We All Live Together*, vol. 5 by Greg & Steve (Youngheart, 1994), "(I'm Gonna Eat) On Thanksgiving Day" on *Whaddaya Think of That?* by Laurie Berkner (Two Tomatoes, 2000), "Animal Crackers in My Soup" on *Animal Crackers in My Soup* by Maria Muldaur (Music for Little People, 2002) and *Farkle and Friends* by John Lithgow (Kid Rhino, 2002), and many more.

## Sample Program

Please adjust content and length as needed.

### Introduction

See page 189–190 for "Story Soup" set-up directions.

*(Dramatically put on your apron and chef hat. Place the large cauldron/soup pot on top of your box stove or Kik-Step® stool, where you can sit or stand behind it. Make sure that the pot is positioned low enough so the children can see into it when they come forward to add their items. This will convince them that it is empty to begin with.) Say:* Today we are going to make "Story Soup!" I will need help from all of you. One of the most important parts of making the soup is this song that I will teach you—it helps the soup to cook properly.

Teach the following chorus to the group:

"Story Soup Song"

*(Sung to the tune: "The Farmer in the Dell.")*

(CHORUS)

We're making Story Soup,
we're making Story Soup.
Stir slow—around we go—
we're making Story Soup!

adapted from the "Vegetable Soup Song" on the sound recording *Piggyback Songs: Singable Poems Set to Favorite Tunes* (Kimbo, 1995).

*(Hold up the "Story Soup" recipe card or your recipe book.)* Here is our recipe that tells us how to make "Story Soup." The first section is for the soup part. What do we sometimes put in soup? *(Take guesses—all guesses are good guesses.)* This seems to be a vegetable soup, so it looks like we'll need a lot of vegetables. *(Distribute vegetables to each child if you have a small enough group. Otherwise you can add them yourself as the group names each food item.)* Listen carefully as we sing about this soup—when I say your vegetable, you can bring it up and add it to the pot. I already have some blue pretend water in the bottom of the pot for the vegetables to cook in.

*(Sing the "Story Soup Song" chorus again as a group while pretending to stir with your spoon or ladle, then add vegetables as detailed below.)*

First we add some CARROTS,
*(Children bring up carrots and drop them into the pot, then sit back down.)*
Then we add POTATOES.
*(Children bring up potatoes and drop them into the pot, then sit back down.)*
Stir slow—around we go—we're making Story Soup!

*(Continue through all of the vegetables, singing as you go. Repeat the chorus in between verses if you like. Shake the salt and pepper shakers over the pot and stir. When all of the vegetables and the salt and pepper have been added, lift up your ladle or wooden spoon and sniff as if smelling a spoonful of soup.)* This is smelling pretty good for ordinary soup, but we've been planning to make STORY SOUP today! We have a lot of vegetables in our pot to make soup, and we put in some salt and pepper to season it, but what things go into a story? *(Hold up a picture book to get them thinking.)*

*(Hopefully the audience will suggest letters or words, paper, pictures, etc. If not, lead them in that direction by pointing out parts of the book you are holding up. If your group is small enough and you have sufficient time, distribute letter cutouts, pictures, and paper for the audience to bring up like they did the vegetables. Otherwise, you can add the items yourself while the audience sings along.)*

First we add some PAPER,
then we add some PICTURES;
Stir slow—around we go,
we're making Story Soup!

*(Continue the song, adding things that go into stories such as letters, ideas, music, and so forth. Make sure to name the alphabet letters as you add them. You can draw this whole process out as long as you want!)*

There is one more ingredient that is the most important thing of all to make "Story Soup" turn out just right. We need IMAGINATION, the secret ingredient in all good stories. I need some from everyone who would like to give me some: you can just pull a tiny bit out of your head like this *(mime pulling a tiny bit of something from your forehead)*, and put it in the measuring spoon when I bring it around. I'll stir all of the imagination bits together in the measuring cup, and then we'll add it to the soup! *(Go around and gather "imagination" from each child and adult. If you have a very large group and individual imagination-gathering is impossible, have them pull a little out and place it on their outstretched palms and blow it to you at the front of the room. Pretend to catch it in an animated way in the measuring spoon and cup—some almost escapes you! Stir all of the collected imagination in the measuring cup with your measuring spoon, then add it to the soup while singing— scraping the edges of the cup to make sure you get every last drop.)*

*(Hold up the recipe card/book and peer at it.)* I think our soup is ready! Let's sing the Story Soup Song one more time and see what happens. *(Stir the pot and maneuver your first pre-planted item that was previously hidden under the blue fabric water into your ladle—The Beastly Feast book by Bruce Goldstone. Act surprised and excited, and as if it's a little bit difficult to ladle up whatever it is.)* It looks like it worked! The soup cooked something up to show us what our first story will be today! Oh my goodness—it's a book! Did somebody put a book

in our pot? I thought there were just vegetables and paper! Wow—all of that imagination stirred together in there must really be working …

*(Make sure that you hold the book and other ensuing items up high so the audience can see them clearly and the children don't feel an urge to rush forward. Take the item from your ladle with your oven mitt to make sure it is "cool enough," and then hold it up so they can all see. If it is a representative item, ask the children if they can tell which of the displayed books you're going to read next from the clue that cooked up from the soup.)*

## Read Aloud

*The Beastly Feast* by Bruce Goldstone, illustrated by Blair Lent. Henry Holt & Company, 1998. Toddler–Grade 2. The beasts are having a feast, and animals from everywhere bring their favorite rhyming foods to share: bears bring pears, parrots bring carrots, and so forth. At the end of the wonderful feast, everyone claps. Then armadillos bring some pillows, and everybody naps.

## Segue

*Say:* There were a lot of rhymes in that story, weren't there? Words that sounded the same at the end, like "Bears" and *(pause and encourage the children to supply the rhyme if they remember)* "Pears." "Flies" and "Pies." That's right! I wonder if we'll have any pears or pies, or bears or flies in our soup! We'd better check and see how it's doing. *(Sing the "Story Soup Song" chorus while stirring the pot; ladle up some loops of yarn "spaghetti noodles.")* I'll bet this spaghetti is from this pot over here, for our poem about NOODLES.

## Poem with Props

Share "Oodles of Noodles" by Lucia & James L. Hymes, Jr. with your story props. See instructions on page 192. The poem is included in *Tasty Poems* collected by Jill Bennett, illustrated by Nick Sharratt (Oxford University Press, 1998).

> **"Oodles of Noodles"**
>
> *I love noodles.*
> *Give me oodles.*
> *Make a mound up to the sun.*

*Noodles are my favorite foodles.*
*I eat noodles by the ton.*

*—Lucia & James L. Hymes, Jr.*

*Say:* Our poem had even more rhyming words, didn't it? "Ton" and *(hold up the sun)* "Sun." And the poet made up a word to rhyme with "Noodles"—"Foodles!"

## Segue

*(Hold up your hand to your ear and look quizzical.) Say:* I think I hear some bubbling noises. This soup must be really cooking now! *(Listen carefully again; look uncertain.)* Maybe it's actually music! We'd better find out—and there's only one way to do that! *(Repeat the "Story Soup Song" chorus; ladle up the sound recording* Victor Vito *by Laurie Berkner.)* Oh my goodness, I did hear music! We cooked up Laurie Berkner's CD *Victor Vito,* with the song "I Feel Crazy So I Jump in the Soup!" That is crazy. We definitely get to stand up for this one!

Write out the words to the song on grid board ahead of time so attending adults can follow along and help you sing.

## Action (Standing and Moving)

"I Feel Crazy So I Jump in the Soup" on *Victor Vito* by Laurie Berkner. (Two Tomatoes, 1999). Be enthusiastic as you jump, swim, gallop, splash, and finally sit down again.

*(Reminder: Encourage everyone to participate, but be understanding if some prefer not to do so. Just make sure they are in a safe place so they won't get stomped or jumped upon!)*

## Segue

*Say:* Wow, that song really was crazy. I don't think I want to jump in this soup pot, but maybe something else will be ready if we stir it up! *(Stir soup while singing the "Story Soup Song." Ladle up your next book or a representational item such as purple cat-eye glasses for* To Market, To Market *by Anne Miranda or a small chicken plush for* The Wolf's Chicken Stew *by Keiko Kasza. Encourage the children to help you match the item to its accompanying book; this will help them notice details and make connections.)*

## Read Aloud

*To Market, To Market* by Anne Miranda. Harcourt Brace, 1997. Toddler–Grade 1. Starting with the nursery rhyme about buying a fat pig at market, this tale goes on to describe a series of unruly animals that run amok, evading capture and preventing the narrator from cooking lunch.

OR

*The Wolf's Chicken Stew* by Keiko Kasza. Putnam, 1987. PK–2. A hungry wolf's attempts to fatten a chicken for his stewpot have unexpected results.

## Segue

*Say:* Do you think anything else has cooked up yet? *(Stir soup while singing the "Story Soup Song." Ladle up the tiny bat finger puppet.)*

## Poem with Props

Share the Mother Goose rhyme "Bat, Bat, Come Under My Hat" with props. Use your chef hat *(any hat or even a cooking pot on your head will work just fine)*, a bat finger puppet or plush, and a piece of plastic bacon and cake. A pattern for a paper bat finger puppet is included in *A Pocketful of Puppets: Mother Goose* by Nancy Renfro and Tamara Hunt (Nancy Renfro Studios, 1982).

*Bat, bat, come under my hat,*
*And I will give you some bacon!*
*And when I bake, I'll give you some cake*
*If I am not mistaken.*

Write out the words ahead of time on a piece of grid board so attending adults can follow along, and point out to the group that the rhyme is written on the poster. Repeat the rhyme several times, encouraging the audience to say it with you. For at least one of the repetitions, follow the printed text on the poster with your finger.

## Segue

Sing the "Story Soup Song" chorus again and ladle up a plastic peanut butter sandwich. Don't bring a real one, in case any of the children have peanut allergies!

## Read Aloud with Actions

Read *Peanut Butter & Jelly: A Play Rhyme* illustrated by Nadine Bernard Westcott. Dutton Children's Books, 1993, 1987. PK–1. Rhyming text and illustrations explain how to make a peanut butter and jelly sandwich. (Available as a BIG Book.)

Share the "Peanut Butter and Jelly" action rhyme as a group (standing or sitting).

REFRAIN:

Peanut butter, peanut butter, jelly, jelly.
*(clap, slap knees, clap, slap knees, clap, slap knees, clap, slap knees)*

First you take the dough and knead it, knead it. *(Push with heels of hands.)*

REFRAIN

Pop it in the oven and bake it, bake it. *(Extend arms towards "oven.")*

REFRAIN

Then you take a knife and slice it, slice it. *("Saw" back and forth with the side of your hand.)*

REFRAIN

Then you take the peanuts and crack them, crack them. *(Pound fists together.)*

REFRAIN

Put them on the floor and mash them, mash them. *(Push fist into palm of other hand.)*

REFRAIN

Then you take a knife and spread it, spread it. *(Move hand back and forth as if spreading the peanut butter.)*

REFRAIN

Next you take some grapes and squash them, squash them. *(Stamp feet.)*

REFRAIN

Glop it on the bread and smear it, smear it. *(Spreading motion again.)*

REFRAIN

Then you take the sandwich and eat it, eat it. *(Open and close mouth as if biting a sandwich.)*

REFRAIN

## Conclusion

*Say:* Storytime is almost over, so I wonder if there are any unusual things left in our soup? Let's try singing one last time, and see if any more special storytime ideas have bubbled up. *(Stir while singing the "Story Soup Song." Ladle up the laminated card stock "The End" sign from page 193, and read it aloud to the audience.)*

## Story Soup Preliminary Set-up Directions

**Tools you'll need**

- very large plastic cauldron or cooking pot (approximately 12" deep and 16" wide)

- long wooden spoon or ladle

- blue fabric "water" for the bottom of the pot (to cover your hidden books and representative story items)

- apron

- chef's hat

- oven mitt

- cookbook or "Story Soup" recipe card (see pattern on page 193.)

- pretend box stove or library Kik-Step® stool with colored red, orange, and yellow tissue paper between the layers for your "fire" to heat the "soup"

- measuring spoon and measuring cup to gather imagination from the audience

**Ingredients to be added with the help of your audience chefs**

- Plastic vegetables or card stock vegetables (see patterns on pages 193–194). Make sure you have enough so that everyone in your group can participate!

- Pretend salt and pepper (either use opaque shakers or else put white and gray seed beads in real transparent salt and pepper shakers; the beads are big enough so they won't go through the holes, but they look and sound real for the audience).

- S-T-O-R-Y S-O-U-P Letters (plastic, foamies, or card stock—see patterns on page 196); may also use other letters instead.

- Paper (8½" x 11" pages cut in half work well).

- Pictures (cut out pictures from old book jackets or publishers' catalog covers, or from an old magazine or coloring sheet).

- Imagination (use measuring spoon and measuring cup to collect it).

**Preliminary set-up**

- Hide your representative story items and/or the books you plan to use in your program beneath the blue fabric "water" at the bottom of the pot. Arrange the water fabric carefully, tucking it down and around the hidden items so they will not be visible as other things are added to the pot.

- Place your long-handled spoon or ladle into the pot so that the handle is sticking up.

- Arrange your vegetables in a basket or container for easy distribution; make sure that you have enough for all of the children in your group.

- Hide your salt and pepper shakers, letters, paper, pictures, measuring spoon, and measuring cup nearby in a basket or container.

# Additional Resources

*Cook-a-Doodle-Doo!* by Janet Stevens and Susan Stevens Crummel. Harcourt, 1999. PK–2. With the questionable help of his friends, Big Brown Rooster manages to bake a strawberry shortcake which would have pleased his great-grandmother, Little Red Hen.

*Feast For 10* by Cathryn Falwell. Clarion Books, 1993. Toddler–K. A loving family shops for their meal's ingredients, then prepares a feast to share together and with their grandparents.

*Feeling Thankful* by Shelley Rotner and Sheila Kelly, photographs by Shelley Rotner. Millbrook Press, 2000. PK–2. Colorful photographs and short, easily understandable sentences encourage young children to explore the things they are thankful for in their lives.

*Growing Vegetable Soup* by Lois Ehlert. Harcourt, 1987. PK–1. A father and child grow vegetables in a garden and then make the vegetables into a soup. (Available as a BIG Book.)

*I Know An Old Lady Who Swallowed A Pie* by Alison Jackson. Dutton, 1997. PK–3. In this Thanksgiving twist on the familiar cumulative song "I Know An Old Lady Who Swallowed A Fly," an old lady gobbles down an entire Thanksgiving meal. Full at last, she has nevertheless swollen up to enormous proportions from her feast, and she joins the Thanksgiving Day parade as one of its airborne balloons.

*If You Give A Moose a Muffin* by Laura Joffe Numeroff, illustrated by Felicia Bond. HarperCollins, 1991. PK–2. Chaos can ensue if you give a moose a muffin and start him on a cycle of urgent requests. (Available as a BIG Book.)

*If You Give A Pig a Pancake* by Laura Numeroff, illustrated by Felicia Bond. Laura Geringer Book, 1998. PK–2. One thing leads to another when you give a pig a pancake. (Available as a BIG Book.)

*The Little Mouse, the Red Ripe Strawberry, and the Big Hungry Bear* by Don and Audrey Wood, illustrated by Don Wood. Child's Play, 1990. PK–1. Little Mouse worries that his freshly picked, ripe, red strawberry will be taken by the big hungry bear. (Available as a BIG Book.)

*The Little Red Hen Makes A Pizza* by Philemon Sturges. Dutton, 1999. PK–3. In this version of the traditional tale, the Little Red Hen's friends all refuse to help her make a pizza. She nevertheless generously allows them to help eat it, however, and they gratefully do the cleaning up afterward.

*Lunch* by Denise Fleming. Henry Holt & Company, 1992. Toddler–Grade 1. A very hungry mouse eats a large lunch comprised of colorful foods.

**Extension Idea:** Make a Lunch mouse puppet and props from patterns and directions in *Books in Books in Bloom* by Kimberly Faurot (ALA Editions, 2003).

*Maisy Goes Shopping* by Lucy Cousins. Candlewick Press, 2001. Toddler–PK. When it's time for lunch, Maisy and Charley find that the refrigerator is empty! They go to the grocery store and find all kinds of healthy foods to eat, then come home and have lunch.

**"Mix A Pancake"** by Christina Georgina Rossetti in *A New Treasury of Children's Poetry* selected by Joanna Cole. Doubleday, 1984. Toddler–Grade 1.

**Extension Idea:** Share this poem as an action rhyme, using props.

*Mrs. Biddlebox: Her Bad Day … and What She Did About It!* by Linda Smith, illustrated by Marla Frazee. Harcourt, 2007. 1–4. With baking magic, Mrs. Biddlebox uses fog, dirt, sky, and other ingredients of a rotten day to transform it into a sweet cake.

*Mudluscious: Stories and Activities Featuring Food For Preschool Children* by Jan Irving and Rob Currie. Libraries Unlimited, 1986.

*The Muppets' Big Book of Crafts* by The Muppet Workshop and Stephanie St. Pierre. Workman Publishing, 1999. Make a talking sandwich puppet to use in storytime!

*Never Let Your Cat Make Lunch for You* by Lee Harris, illustrated by Debbie Tilley. Tricycle Press, 1999. K–2. Although Pebbles the cat is great at cooking breakfast, she is a disaster when it comes to fixing lunch: the narrator ends up with an anchovy in her peanut butter and jelly sandwich, as well as a mouse and mustard!

*Over the River and Through the Wood* by Lydia Maria Francis Child, illustrated by David Catrow. Henry Holt & Company, 1996. PK–3. The familiar Thanksgiving poem, first published in 1844, is the backdrop for a modern family's struggle to get their minivan through a snowstorm, traffic jam, and Thanksgiving day parade to finally arrive at their grandparents' house.

*Pancakes, Pancakes!* by Eric Carle. Knopf, 1970. PK–1. By cutting and grinding the wheat for flour, Jack starts from scratch to help make his breakfast pancake.

*Pancakes for Supper!* by Anne Isaacs, illustrated by Mark Teague. Scholastic, 2006. K–4. In the backwoods of New England, a young girl cleverly fends off the threats of wild animals by trading her clothes for her safety.

*Sitting Down to Eat* by Bill Harley, illustrated by Kitty Harvill. August House Little Folk, 1996. K–2. In this cumulative story, a young boy agrees to share his snack with an ever-growing menagerie of animals, each insisting that there is room for one more! A slightly different version with a wonderful tune can be found on the recording *Play It Again* by Bill Harley (Round River, 1999).

*Stone Soup* retold by Ann McGovern, pictures by Winslow Pinney Pels. Scholastic, 1986. When a little old lady claims she has no food to give him, a hungry young man proceeds to make soup with a stone and water.

*Thank You, Thanksgiving* by David Milgrim. Clarion Books, 2003. Toddler–K. While on a Thanksgiving Day errand for her mother, a girl says thank you to all the things around her.

*Thanks for Thanksgiving* by Julie Markes, illustrated by Doris Barrette. HarperCollins Publishers, 2004. Toddler–Grade 1. At Thanksgiving time, children express their gratitude for the people and things in their lives.

*Today Is Monday* illustrated by Eric Carle. Philomel Books, 1993. PK–1. Each day of the week brings a new food, until on Sunday all the world's children can come and eat it up. Musical notation for the traditional tune is included at the back of the book, or listen to a version on the following sound recordings: *Wee Sing Sing-Alongs* by Pamela Conn Beall and Susan Hagen Nipp (Price Stern Sloan, 2002) and *Shake, Rattle & Rock* by Greg & Steve (Greg & Steve Productions, 2006). (Available as a BIG Book.)

*Turkey Riddles* by Katy Hall and Lisa Eisenberg. Dial Books for Young Readers, 2002. PK–4. Clever turkey riddles include both general and Thanksgiving themes. For example, "What is Superturkey's real name? Cluck Kent!" and "What do you get if you cross a turkey with an octopus? A Thanksgiving dinner with drumsticks for everyone!"

**"Turkey Tale"** in *Twenty Tellable Tales: Audience Participation Folktales for the Beginning Storyteller* by Margaret Read MacDonald. H. W. Wilson

Company, 1986. PK–2. In this draw-and-tell story about an elderly couple who live by a lake, the wife discovers a turkey at the end.

*'Twas the Night Before Thanksgiving* by Dav Pilkey. Orchard Books, 1990. K–3. When a group of school children on a field trip to Mack Nugget's farm discover that the resident turkeys will be slaughtered for the next day's Thanksgiving meals, they surreptitiously rescue the birds.

*Uncle Willie and the Soup Kitchen* by DyAnne DiSalvo-Ryan. Morrow Junior Books, 1991. 2–5. A boy spends the day with his uncle in the soup kitchen, where he works preparing and serving food for people who are hungry.

*Veggie Soup* by Dorothy Donohue. Winslow Press, 2000. PK–1. Miss Bun, a rabbit who loves to cook, gets help from Bird, Cat, Frog, and Cow in making a very unusual veggie soup that ends up too disgusting to eat.

*What A Good Lunch! Eating* by Shigeo Watanabe, illustrated by Yasuo Ohtomo. W. Collins Publishers, 1980. Toddler–PK. Despite difficulties, a young bear eats his lunch all by himself.

# Story Prop and Craft Directions

## Story Soup

### Vegetables

*(Carrots, corn, green peppers, onions, potatoes, and tomatoes.)*

Prepare these yourself ahead of time, or have your students make them! Copy the vegetable patterns onto colored card stock, or mount them on poster board and color them with crayons, markers, or colored pencils. Make sure that you have enough vegetables for all of the children in your group!

### Cauldron or Soup Pot

If you can't find a large plastic cauldron or soup pot, you can make your own for storytime cooking! Use a large, fairly deep (12" or more) cardboard box, bucket, or basket as the base for your pot. Enlarge the cauldron pattern (page 195) so it is an appropriate size for your container, and cut the cauldron shape from black poster board. Affix the black cauldron cutout to the front of the container so that it faces the audience.

### Letters

Copy "STORY SOUP" onto card stock, or mount the letters on poster board. Cut the words apart so the letters may be added individually. You may also wish to affix small magnets to the back side of the letters so you can display them as a "Today's Menu: STORY SOUP" advertisement.

### Recipe Card

Copy the Story Soup recipe card onto white card stock and cut it out. Place it in a cookbook or in a recipe card box in preparation for your storytime cooking extravaganza.

## Student Craft

Distribute small-size "soup pot" bowls or cups along with plastic spoons. Copy miniature card stock vegetables to cut out and color, and provide blank card stock circles on which students may draw their own story items. Go around the room and encourage each child to explain what story(ies) cooked up in their personal pot of "Story Soup."

## "Oodles of Noodles" Props and Preliminary Set-up

- large spaghetti pot
- ivory-colored yarn to look like spaghetti (multiple skeins)
- giant sun stick puppet (see May— "Growing Gardens" chapter "Giant Sun Stick Puppet")
- chef hat
- spaghetti server
- giant bowl (optional)

Pack the yarn tightly down into the spaghetti pot. When you start to gradually pull it out as you say the poem, the "noodles" will seem to expand almost like magic!

# Story Soup Patterns

Enlarge as desired.

### SOUPS

**Recipe for:** STORY SOUP
**Ingredients:** vegetables--carrots, corn, green peppers, onions, potatoes, tomatoes
salt and pepper
letters (S-T-O-R-Y S-O-U-P)
paper
pictures
imagination

**Directions:**
            "Story Soup Song"
      (sung to the tune of "The Farmer in the Dell")
(CHORUS)
*We're making Story Soup, we're making Story Soup.*
*Stir slow--around we go, we're making Story Soup!*

      adapted from the "Vegetable Soup Song" on the sound recording
      *Piggyback Songs; Singable Poems Set to Favorite Tunes* (Kimbo, 1995)

Add the vegetables first, one type at a time, singing as you go:
      *First we add some CARROTS*
      *Then we add POTATOES*
      *Stir slow--around we go, we're making Story Soup!*
Repeat the chorus in between verses if you like.

Continue the song, adding things that go into stories such as letters, paper, pictures, ideas, music, imagination, and so on!

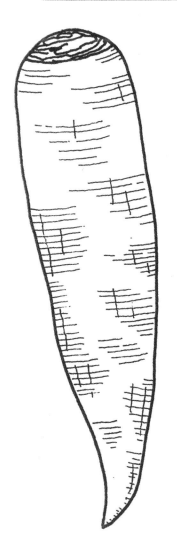

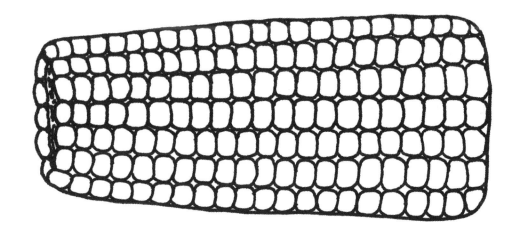

# THE END.

Please visit our storytime kitchen again soon for more exciting recipes!

# Story Soup Patterns
Enlarge as desired.

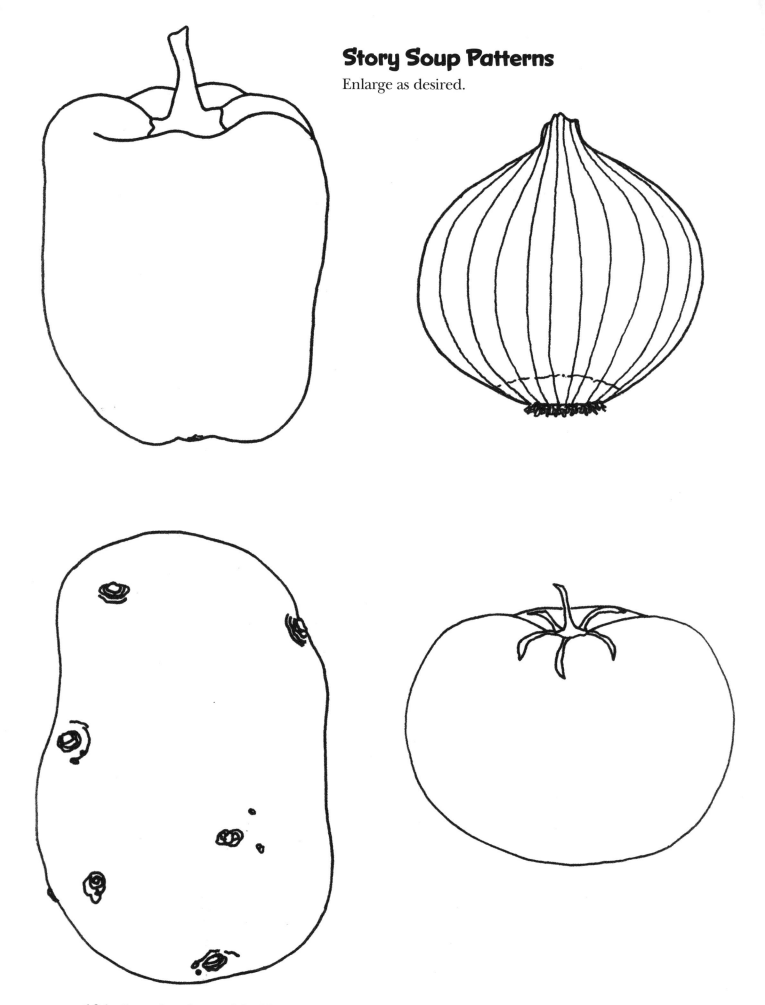

# Story Soup Patterns

Enlarge as desired.

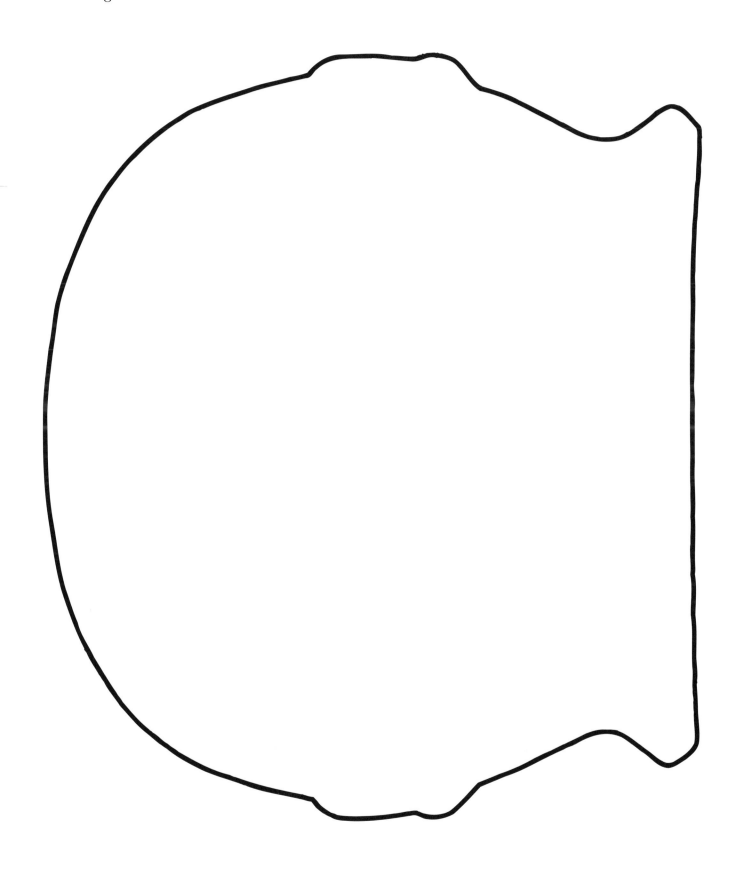

# Story Soup Patterns

Enlarge as desired.

# "C" is for Cookie
## December

## Early Literacy Activities

### Name Tags

Cookie stamp or sticker

### Clue(s)

Plastic cookie

### Mailbox "Letter" of the Day

"C" and "c"

Cookie, Cat, Cake, Carrot, Candy, Color, Cow, Car

### Mother Goose Rhyme Time

*Little Jack Horner*

*Little Jack Horner*
*Sat in a corner,*
*Eating a great big pie.*
*He stuck in his thumb,*
*And pulled out a plum,*
*And said, "What a good child am I!"*

### Rhyming Basket

Pie/Fly; Cake/Snake; House/Mouse

### Early Literacy Skill: Narrative Skills

Practice retelling stories or events, sequencing the order in which events happened, and adding descriptions.

- Talk and ask two or three open-ended questions about *The Doorbell Rang* by Pat Hutchins or "The Gingerbread Man" story.

- If you have a small enough group and adequate time, act out "The Gingerbread Man" with creative dramatics.

- Make miniature "Running Gingerbread Man" student crafts and retell the story together as a group.

- Make up a story with the audience about the adventures of your runaway storytime cookies. Encourage families to make up stories together about what cookies from their own homes might do if they ran away.

## Program Summary and Theme

Roll out a delicious batch of gingerbread and cookie stories! Cover your storytime display table with gingerbread-themed or solid bright red fabric. Arrange miscellaneous child-safe baking utensils such as a lightweight rolling pin, large plastic bowl, mixing spoon, oven mitt, measuring cups, and so

forth among the books and props that you plan to use. If your bowl is big enough, place some of your storytime books and/or props inside it!

Prepare the props and puppets ahead of time so you can use them throughout the program. Please see patterns and directions on pages 204–211. See additional suggested titles on pages 202–204 to substitute for older or younger audiences.

## Music

Play "cookie" music as the audience is gathering in your storytime area. Possibilities include "'C' is for Cookie" on *Songs from the Street: 35 Years of Music* (Sony Wonder, 2003) and *"C" is for Cookie: Cookie's Favorite Songs* by Sesame Street (Sony Wonder, 1995), "The Cookie Bakers of the Night" on *Buzz Buzz* by Laurie Berkner (Two Tomatoes, 1998), "I'm A Little Cookie" on *Mail Myself to You* by John McCutcheon (Rounder, 1988), and many others.

# Sample Program

Please adjust content and length as needed.

## Introduction

*Say:* The stories that I brought for you today are making me very hungry! They are about cookies, one of my favorite desserts. In this first story, Sam and Victoria are about to eat the delicious cookies that their mom just made, but the doorbell keeps ringing! That part happens over and over again throughout the story. It goes like this: *(Push your index finger forward as if ringing a doorbell, then pull it back.)* DING-DONG! Do you think you can do that with me? Let's practice it together so we'll be ready when it happens in the story. DING-DONG! Again! DING-DONG! That sounds great! I believe you're ready for our first delicious story ...

## Read Aloud

*The Doorbell Rang* by Pat Hutchins. Greenwillow Books, 1986. PK–2. Each time the doorbell rings, there are more people who have come to share Ma's wonderful cookies. (Available as a BIG Book.)

Each time the text says "... and the doorbell rang," lead the audience in saying "DING-DONG!"

## Segue

*Say:* Those cookies that Ma and Grandma made looked like they were chocolate chip cookies. That is one of my favorite kind of cookies, but when I read this next story, there are many other kinds of cookies that look good too!

## Read Aloud

*Cookie Count: A Tasty Pop-Up* by Robert Sabuda. Simon & Schuster, 1997. Toddler–Grade 4. A team of mouse chefs carefully prepare a feast of remarkable cookies—coconut kisses, peanut butter cookies, Linzer hearts, and more—in a truly magical concoction. Each page features remarkable and intricate pop-up actions, with an entire gingerbread house springing up in the final two-page spread.

## Segue

*Say:* In that book, the little mouse bakers and chefs are inside the gingerbread house. Who else do you think might live in a gingerbread house? *(Take guesses—all are good guesses.)* I think that gingerbread kid cookies might live in a gingerbread house like the one in that book. I brought two gingerbread kid puppets to teach you this gingerbread poem.

## Action Rhyme (Standing)

Share "Gingerbread Kids" with actions as well as with your gingerbread boy and girl stick puppets.

"Gingerbread Kids"

I'm a little gingerbread boy.
*(Boys bow.)*
I'm a little gingerbread girl.
*(Girls bow.)*
I can jump,
*(All jump.)*
And I can twirl.
*(All turn around.)*

I have raisins for my eyes, *(Point to eyes.)*
And bright red buttons just this size.
*(Point to imaginary buttons on chest.)*
I have a mouth—it looks like this.
*(Point to smiling mouth.)*
I can even blow a kiss! *(Blow a kiss.)*

I'm warm and tasty, *(Rub stomach.)*
But don't eat me! *(Shake head.)*
Hang me up for all to see!
*(Lift up arms in a "V.")*

Write out the words ahead of time on a piece of grid board so attending adults can follow along, and point out to the group that the poem is written on the poster. Repeat the rhyme several times, encouraging the audience to say it with you.

## Segue

*Say:* Those gingerbread kids seemed pretty well-behaved, but that isn't always the case with gingerbread people and animals! Do some of you know the story of the gingerbread man who ran away? In this next poem, the ginger cookies run away just like that gingerbread man!

## Action Poem (Sitting)

Share "Runaway Cookie Countdown" with five ginger cookie magnet pieces on a metal tray and as a hand clapping game. Make up clapping rhythms to suit the age of your group—simple hand clapping if they are very young, more complex rhythms and combinations if they are slightly older.

"Runaway Cookie Countdown"

Five ginger cookies, lying on a tray.
One jumped up and ran away!

Four ginger cookies, lying on a tray.
One jumped up and ran away!

Three ginger cookies, lying on a tray.
One jumped up and ran away!

Two ginger cookies, lying on a tray.
One jumped up and ran away!

One ginger cookie, lying on a tray.
He jumped up and ran away!

No ginger cookies, lying on a tray.
Next time I'll eat them right away!

## Segue

*Say:* Since we've been talking about runaway gingerbread cookies, I would like to share the story of the most famous runaway cookie—"The Gingerbread Man." In this version, the Gingerbread Man thinks he's Super-Cookie! I will need a lot of help telling this story. The gingerbread man says: "Run, run, run, just as fast as you can, you can't catch me—I'm the gingerbread man!" Everyone chasing him says: "You're a COOKIE! Cookies are for eating!" We'll say those parts again and again.

## Prop Story

Tell the folktale "The Gingerbread Man" using props. (Older PK–2.) A full script and patterns are provided on pages 200–202, 208, and 210. Also see various illustrated versions of the story listed on pages 203–204. A gingerbread man runs away from a little old man and a little old woman, some cows and pigs and chickens, but at last he is tricked and eaten by a wily fox.

At the end of the story, bring the gingerbread man puppet back out to bow to the audience like an actor so the children can see that the story was simply pretend! If you are concerned that the drama of the fox eating the gingerbread man may be too intense for your particular group, please substitute a different book or activity from the Additional Resources bibliography on pages 202–204. Also consider reassuring everyone before you begin that the story is just for pretend.

## Conclusion

*Say:* We had a lot of cookies running around in this storytime today! If you help make cookies at home, you might need to keep an eye on them. They could decide to run away and have some Super-Cookie adventures too! That's pretty silly, but maybe you can make up a story about what your cookies would do if they really could run away—just like the Gingerbread Man.

### Cookies Are For Eating! The Tale of Super-Cookie a.k.a. "The Gingerbread Man"

Folktale adapted by Kimberly Faurot

### Story Pieces

- gingerbread man hand puppet
- large unbreakable mixing bowl
- mixing spoon
- lightweight rolling pin
- gingerbread "dough" with man shape cut out
- dull table knife
- cookie sheet (or cardboard covered with aluminum foil)
- pretend oven (or a cardboard box, metal bread box, desk, etc.)
- oven mitt
- fox headband
- cloth or paper napkin

### Before You Begin

1. Hide your props in a nearby box or basket until it is time to begin the story.

2. Lay the gingerbread man hand puppet face down on the cookie sheet inside his dough outline.

3. Tuck the napkin into your pocket or in your sleeve.

4. Divide the audience into thirds and assign each group an animal: cows, pigs, and chickens.

### Presentation

- Story narration is in regular type; movement notes and miscellaneous directions are in *italics*.

- Learn the story and tell it to your audience from memory, using the puppet and props. Practice in front of a mirror to work on your puppet's believability.

- Look at your puppet while it is talking so that you are not competing with it for the audience's attention.

- Although it is not essential to use different character voices when presenting the story, it can truly help maintain the audience's interest. Try out different voices to figure out which sounds the best for the different characters. All voices must feel natural for you after practice so that you will be able to use and maintain them successfully during an actual performance.

- Animal sounds and the following phrases lend themselves well to verbal audience participation:

  "I'm Super-Cookie!"

  "You're a COOKIE! Cookies are for eating!"

  "Run, run, run, just as fast as you can, you can't catch me—I'm the gingerbread man!" *(Encourage the audience to clap or pat their laps to mirror the gingerbread man's running feet.)*

- Bring the gingerbread man puppet back out to bow to the audience with you at the end of the story so they can see that the story was "just pretend!"

### Script

Once upon a time there was a little old man and a little old woman who loved to eat cookies.

One day for a special treat, they decided to make a gingerbread man cookie. They stirred up the ingredients in a big bowl—flour, butter, sugar, and molasses *(stir wooden spoon around in large mixing bowl)*—then they rolled out the dough *(pretend to roll foamies dough out on cookie sheet with rolling pin)* and cut out a big fat gingerbread man *(move table knife around foamies gingerbread man shape, then lift away the foamies dough outline—hold it up so audience can see the outlined shape; set it aside)*.

They gave him raisin eyes, and red hot buttons (poke at gingerbread man), and put him in the oven to bake. (Place cookie sheet with face-down gingerbread man into your "oven.") They baked him until he was a beautiful golden brown, and then took him out of the oven to cool. (Put on oven mitt and remove cookie sheet from "oven.")

The little old woman made some icing and decorated him with little icing clothes and hair. (Dab at gingerbread man with knife.) She liked to eat icing. (Pretend to furtively lick at the knife.)

She had just finished decorating his second little shoe, however, when the gingerbread man suddenly leapt to his feet (quickly flip gingerbread man hand puppet over and hold him up so the audience can clearly see his decorated front side) and sang out: "Look at me! Look at me! I'm Super-Cookie! I'll run away from you today and you'll never catch me! You can run, run, run just as fast as you can, but you can't catch me 'cause I'm the gingerbread man!"

The little old man and the little old woman were astonished. And they were hungry! They said, "You're a COOKIE! Cookies are for eating!"

But the golden brown gingerbread man jumped down off the counter, wearing his beautiful icing clothes (gingerbread man hand puppet bobs back and forth as he "runs"), and ran right out the door!

The little old man and the little old woman chased after him, but he could run faster than they. He ran down the road singing (gesture to entire audience to say this with you): "Run, run, run, just as fast as you can, you can't catch me—I'm the gingerbread man!"

He ran past some cows (point to the cows), swishing their tails in the meadow. "Mooo!" called the cows. "Who are you and where are you going? We would like to eat you!"

"I'm Super-Cookie! I ran away from a little old man and a little old woman, and now I'll run away from you!"

The cows said (gesture to cows to say this with you): "You're a COOKIE! Cookies are for eating!" and they began to run after him, too.

But the gingerbread man sang (gesture to entire audience to say this with you): "Run, run, run, just as fast as you can, you can't catch me—I'm the gingerbread man!"

He ran past some pigs (point to the pigs), wallowing in the mud. "Oink, oink!" called the pigs. "Who are you and where are you going? We would like to eat you!"

"I'm Super-Cookie! I ran away from a little old man and a little old woman and some cows, and now I'll run away from you!"

The pigs grunted (gesture to pigs to say this with you): "You're a COOKIE! Cookies are for eating!" and they began to run after him, too.

But the gingerbread man sang (gesture to entire audience to say this with you): "Run, run, run, just as fast as you can, you can't catch me—I'm the gingerbread man!"

He ran past some chickens (point to the chickens), pecking for grain in the road. "Cluck, cluck!" called the chickens. "Who are you and where are you going? We would like to eat you!"

"I'm Super-Cookie! I ran away from a little old man and a little old woman and some cows and some pigs, and now I'll run away from you!"

The chickens squawked (gesture to chickens to say this with you): "You're a COOKIE! Cookies are for eating!" and they began to flap and run after him, too.

But the gingerbread man sang (gesture to entire audience to say this with you): "Run, run, run, just as fast as you can, you can't catch me—I'm the gingerbread man!"

The gingerbread man had run a long way, and he came to a river. The little old man and the little old woman and the cows and the pigs and the chickens were all still chasing him. The gingerbread man couldn't swim over the river, because cookies get soft and spongy when they're dipped in liquids.

At that very moment, a sly fox (put on your fox headband) appeared from behind some nearby bushes and said to the gingerbread man: "I see that you are in a tight place. I can carry you across the river so you will be safe from that little old man and that little old woman, the cows and pigs and the chickens, too! Climb on my tail and I will carry you across."

So the gingerbread man climbed onto the fox's tail (*turn so the audience can see the tail at the back of your headband; place the gingerbread man on the tail and hold him there, then turn to face forward again*), and the fox swam out into the river. The little old man and the little old woman and the cows and the pigs and the chickens all ran up to the riverbank and saw the gingerbread man laughing at them from the fox's tail. "Ha, ha!" he called. "I'm Super-Cookie! I've run away from all of you!"

The little old man and the little old woman, the cows and pigs and chickens all called back (*gesture to entire audience to say this with you*): "You're a COOKIE! Cookies are for eating!"

The gingerbread man and the fox hadn't gone far when the fox said, "The water is growing deeper. Climb up on my back." So the gingerbread man climbed up onto the fox's back (*move the gingerbread man farther forward*). Soon the fox said, "The water is growing deeper still. Climb up on my head." So the gingerbread man climbed up onto the fox's head. (*Move the gingerbread man farther forward, to your forehead.*) When they were right in the middle of the river, the fox said, "The water is growing deeper still. Climb up on my nose." So the gingerbread man climbed up onto the fox's nose (*move the gingerbread man to perch with one foot on your nose*).

The gingerbread man called out, "Ha, ha! I'm Super-Cookie! I can run away from everyone!"

But at that very moment the fox said, "The little old man and the little old woman and the cows and the pigs and the chickens are right. You're a COOKIE! Cookies are for eating! You are safe from them now, but you can't run away from me!" (*Flip your head up and turn the gingerbread man over and around in the air; pretend to catch him then turn away from your audience and pretend to eat him. For younger audiences, tuck the puppet visibly into a pocket or your belt so they will still be able to see him when you turn back toward the front.*)

And the fox gobbled up that gingerbread man right then and there. Snip, snap,

snout—yum, yum, yum! (*Dab at the corners of your mouth with napkin.*) Because cookies really are for eating, not for running away. (*Remove your fox headband.*)

The chickens and the pigs and the cows and the little old woman and the little old man all went back home. The chickens (*gesture toward the chickens*) pecked for grain in the road. The pigs (*gesture toward the pigs*) wallowed in the mud. The cows (*gesture toward the cows*) swished their tails in the meadow. And the little old woman and the little old man mixed up another batch of cookies. But this time they made chocolate chip instead.

(*Bring the gingerbread man back out to bow for the audience; bend his hand to make him blow kisses to everyone.*)

The End

## Additional Resources

**"Cookies"** chapter in *Frog and Toad Together* by Arnold Lobel. HarperCollins, 1971. PK–2. When Toad makes an amazing batch of cookies, he and Frog are unable to summon enough willpower to stop eating them until Frog gives the remaining cookies to the birds.

*Cookies: Bite-Size Life Lessons* by Amy Krouse Rosenthal, illustrated by Jane Dyer. HarperCollins, 2006. Everyone knows cookies taste good, but these cookies also have something good to say. Open this delectable book to any page and you will find out something about life.

**"The Gingerbread Man"** poem by Rowena Bennett in *Sing a Song of Popcorn: Every Child's Book of Poems* edited by Beatrice Schenk de Regniers. Scholastic, 1988. PK–2.

*If You Give A Mouse A Cookie* by Laura Joffe Numeroff. HarperCollins, 1985. PK–2. Giving a mouse a cookie triggers a series of other desires for the enthusiastic mouse. Follow the story with a lively dance to "The Mouse Cookie" song on the sound recording *The Mouse Cookie and Other Songs, Games and Readings* (HarperCollins, 1994). (Available as a BIG Book.)

*Let's Make Cookies* by Mary Hill. Children's Press, 2002. PK–K. Simple text and photographs depict a young boy and his father making chocolate chip cookies.

*Maisy Makes Gingerbread* by Lucy Cousins. Candlewick Press, 1999. Toddler–K. Maisy the mouse makes gingerbread cookies and shares them with her good friends Charley and Tallulah.

*Mr. Cookie Baker* by Monica Wellington. Dutton Children's Books, 1992. Toddler–K. After a day of making and selling cookies, Mr. Baker gets to enjoy one himself. Includes a cookie recipe.

**"Nutty Chocolate Cookies"** by Pauline Watson in *The Poetry Break: An Annotated Anthology with Ideas for Introducing Children to Poetry* by Caroline Feller Bauer, illustrated by Edith Bingham. H. W. Wilson, 1995. Mix this clever recipe as directed to the tune: "She'll Be Comin' Round the Mountain!"
**Extension Idea:** Prepare props and pretend to really mix up the dough as you sing! Hide a tray of plastic cookies ahead of time in your toy oven, and produce them at the end.

**"There Was a Tiny Baker"** in *The Frogs Wore Red Suspenders* by Jack Prelutsky. Greenwillow Books, 2002. PK–2. The tiny baker in this poem bakes a tiny cookie and then eats it.
**Extension Idea:** Make flannel board cutouts or use a finger puppet to accompany the poem.

*Tough Cookie* by David Wisniewski. Lothrop, Lee & Shepard Books, 1999. 2–5. When his friend Chips is snatched and chewed, crime detective Tough Cookie sets out to stop Fingers. Remarkable cut-paper illustrations depict an entire unexpected 1930s era world inside a cookie jar!

*Who Took the Cookie From the Cookie Jar?* by David A. Carter. Scholastic, 2002. Toddler–Grade 2. In this pop-up adaptation of the popular schoolyard clapping game, giant cookie jars open to reveal various animals who may have taken the cookies in question. At the end of the book all of the animals pop up together to provide the solution to the mystery—they all took the cookies!

*Who Took the Cookies from the Cookie Jar?* by Bonnie Lass & Philemon Sturges, illustrated by Ashley Wolff. Little, Brown and Company, 2000. PK–2. A skunk follows a trail of crumbs as he tries to find out which of his animal friends took the cookies from the cookie jar, but they all explain that they prefer other food. Finally the missing cookies are discovered, being consumed by a group of ants on a picnic blanket! An explanation of how to play and sing the original clapping game is included at the front of the book. (Available as a BIG Book.)

**Classic Versions of "The Gingerbread Man"**

- *The Gingerbread Boy* retold by Harriet Ziefert, illustrated by Emily Bolam. Viking, 1995. (Easy-to-read version.)

- *The Gingerbread Man* by Jim Aylesworth. Scholastic, 1998.

- *The Gingerbread Man* by Paul Galdone. Seabury Press, 1975. (Available as a BIG Book.)

- *The Gingerbread Man* retold by Eric A. Kimmel. Holiday House, 1993.

- *The Gingerbread Man* told by Nancy Nolte, illustrated by Richard Scarry. Random House, 2004, 1953.

**Variants of "The Gingerbread Man"**

*Gingerbread Baby* by Jan Brett. Putnam, 1999. A young boy named Matty and his mother bake a gingerbread baby that escapes from their oven and leads a crowd on a chase. Matty eventually captures the gingerbread baby by making him his own little gingerbread house! (Available as a BIG Book.)

*The Gingerbread Boy* by Richard Egielski. HarperCollins, 1997. In this entertaining twist on the old folktale, a gingerbread boy runs away through the streets of New York from the woman and man who baked him as well as from a rat, some construction workers, musicians, and a policeman, until he is at last eaten by a wily fox at the city zoo.

*The Gingerbread Man* by Carol Jones. Houghton Mifflin, 2002. A gingerbread man runs away from a variety of nursery rhyme characters, including Humpty Dumpty, Little Boy Blue, and Little Miss Muffet.

*The Matzo Ball Boy* by Lisa Shulman, illustrated by Rosanne Litzinger. Dutton Children's Books, 2005. In this Jewish version of "The Gingerbread Boy," a matzo ball runs away from an old woman as she prepares her Passover dinner. In a clever nod to the gingerbread story, however, the matzo ball doesn't fall for a fox's tricks, saying, "I'm not made of gingerbread, you know," before swimming across the river by himself!

*The Pancake Boy: An Old Norwegian Folk Tale* retold and illustrated by Lorinda Bryan Cauley. Putnam, 1988. A retelling of the traditional Norwegian tale about the adventures of a runaway pancake boy who is eventually eaten by a pig.

*The Runaway Rice Cake* by Ying Chang Compestine, illustrated by Tungwai Chau. Simon & Schuster, 2001. After chasing the special rice cake Nian-Gao that their mother has made to celebrate the Chinese New Year, three poor brothers share it with an elderly woman and have their generosity richly rewarded. Recipes for baked and steamed Nian-Gao are included.

*The Runaway Tortilla* by Eric A. Kimmel, illustrated by Randy Cecil. Winslow Press, 2000. In this Southwestern version, a tortilla runs away from Tia Lupe and a host of other pursuers until she is finally tricked and eaten by Señor Coyote.

# Story Prop and Craft Directions

Note: Store the runaway cookies and gingerbread kid puppets between layers of wax paper so they don't stick to each other over time.

## "Gingerbread Kids" Stick Puppets

### Tools and Supplies

- scissors
- ballpoint pen
- two large (11½" x 17½") "extra thick" (3 mm) sheets of brown foamies
- four black raisin-like buttons or beads for eyes (or use black felt or foamies)
- six red shank buttons
- three-dimensional "puffy" paint in a variety of colors

- black craft paint
- clear gloss acrylic varnish
- two wooden paint sticks
- hot glue gun and hot glue sticks

### Directions

1. Copy and cut out the Gingerbread Kids/Man pattern from page 208 and trace two copies onto the brown foamies with a ballpoint pen. Cut out the pieces.

2. Draw outlines and clothes onto each gingerbread kid with puffy paints. One gingerbread kid should be a boy and the other a girl to match the words of the action poem. Allow the paint to dry completely.

3. Affix the gingerbread kids' eyes and buttons using hot glue.

4. Paint the wooden sticks black. Allow the paint to dry completely. Varnish and allow to dry.

5. Hot glue a paint stick to the center back of each gingerbread kid so they may be manipulated as stick puppets.

### Gingerbread Kids Stick Puppets Student Craft

Cut out "gingerbread kids" from brown paper or brown card stock. Decorate with stickers, markers, crayons, pompoms, wax wikki sticks, and so forth. Affix each gingerbread kid to a wooden craft stick with glue or double-stick tape. Perform the "Gingerbread Kids" action rhyme with the puppets as a group! Glue or tape a copy of the poem (page 207) to the back of each gingerbread kid for families to act out at home.

## "Runaway Cookie Countdown" Ginger Cookies

### Tools and Supplies

- scissors
- ballpoint pen
- one sheet of brown foamies or brown card stock

- three-dimensional "puffy" paint in a variety of colors (or use wax wikki sticks if making card stock ginger cookies)
- five magnets (magnetic business card backs work well)
- hot glue gun and hot glue sticks
- magnetic cookie sheet

### Directions

1. Copy and cut out the "Runaway Cookie" patterns from page 209. Trace them onto brown foamies or card stock with a ballpoint pen. Cut out the pieces.

2. Draw outlines and other features onto each shape with puffy paints or wikki sticks. Allow the paint to dry completely.

3. Hot glue a magnet to the back of each cookie.

4. Place the cookies onto the magnetic cookie sheet.

### Runaway Cookie Countdown Student Craft

Cover small sheets of cardboard or clean foam trays with aluminum foil to serve as cookie sheets. Cut out "ginger cookies" from brown paper or brown card stock. Decorate the paper cookies with stickers, markers, crayons, pompoms, wax wikki sticks, and so forth. Affix the paper cookies to the foil cookie sheets with glue or double-stick tape as a craft, or keep the pieces separate for playability and perform the "Runaway Cookie Countdown" action poem as a group. Glue or tape a copy of the poem to the tray for families to enjoy at home.

## "Gingerbread Man" Hand Puppet, Dough Outline and Fox Headband

### Tools and Supplies

- scissors
- ballpoint pen
- two large (11½" x 17½") regular thickness (2 mm) sheets of brown foamies
- two black raisin-like buttons or beads for eyes (or use black felt or foamies)
- three red shank buttons
- three-dimensional "puffy" paint in a variety of colors
- sewing machine and brown thread (or hand-sew or use hot glue)
- one large (11½" x 17½") regular thickness (2 mm) sheet of orange foamies
- white craft paint
- craft paintbrush
- hot glue gun and hot glue sticks

### Directions

1. Copy and cut out the Gingerbread Kids/Man pattern from page 208 at 125% (or larger as needed to fit the storyteller's hand) and trace two copies onto the brown foamies with a ballpoint pen. Make sure that one of the gingerbread men is in the very center of its foamies sheet, so that the dough outline can be cut around it. Cut out the foamies gingerbread men, taking care not to cut through the edges of the piece that will also serve as the dough outline.

2. Cut around the edges of the dough outline piece in a wavy design so it looks like the edges of rolled-out dough.

3. Cut the legs off one of your gingerbread men. This will be the hand puppet's back.

4. Machine-stitch or hot glue the gingerbread man puppet's front and back together, leaving the bottom edge open. The seam allowance is ⅜".

5. Outline the gingerbread man puppet with puffy paint along your stitching line, covering it up.

6. Draw hair, a mouth, and clothes onto the gingerbread man with puffy paints. Allow the paint to dry completely.

7. Affix the gingerbread man's eyes and buttons using hot glue.

8. Cut two 1¼" wide strips of foamies from the long edge of the orange foamies sheet. Hot glue the strips together to form a headband that will fit around the storyteller's head.

9. Copy and cut out the fox headband ear and tail patterns from page 210 *at the sizes specified* and trace them onto the orange foamies with a ballpoint pen. Cut out the foamies pieces.

10. Highlight the fox's ears and tail with white paint as shown on the patterns. Allow the paint to dry completely.

11. Hot glue the fox tail and ears onto the headband.

12. Gather the rest of the "Gingerbread Man" story pieces, and you are ready to begin!

## The Gingerbread Man Student Craft(s)

- Make "Running Gingerbread Man" finger puppets with finger holes for running legs! See pattern on page 211. Decorate the puppets with stickers, markers, crayons, wax wikki sticks, and so forth.

- Make cow, pig, and chicken stick puppets from card stock or paper plates for use with "The Gingerbread Man" folktale. Mount the animal figures onto wooden craft sticks with glue or double-stick tape.

# Gingerbread Poem Reproducibles

## Gingerbread Kids

I'm a little gingerbread boy.

I'm a little gingerbread girl.

I can jump,

And I can twirl.

I have raisins for my eyes,

And bright red buttons just this size.

I have a mouth—it looks like this.

I can even blow a kiss!

I'm warm and tasty,

But don't eat me!

Hang me up for all to see!

## Runaway Cookie Countdown

**by Kimberly Faurot**

Five ginger cookies, lying on a tray.

One jumped up and ran away!

Four ginger cookies, lying on a tray.

One jumped up and ran away!

Three ginger cookies, lying on a tray.

One jumped up and ran away!

Two ginger cookies, lying on a tray.

One jumped up and ran away!

One ginger cookie, lying on a tray.

He jumped up and ran away!

No ginger cookies, lying on a tray.

Next time I'll eat them right away!

# Gingerbread Kids/Man Pattern

**Gingerbread Kids/Man Puppet Pattern**

Photocopy at size 125%
(or larger as needed for hand puppet to fit storyteller's hand size).

*Seam allowance ⅜" for hand puppet.*

# "Runaway Cookie Countdown" Patterns

## "The Gingerbread Man" Fox Patterns

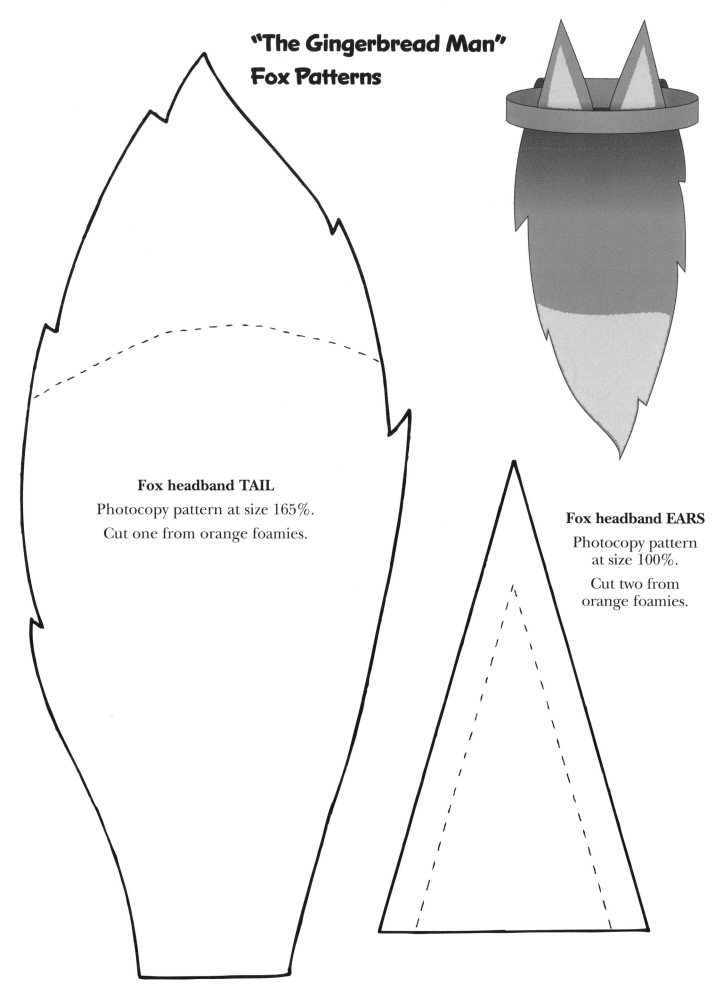

**Fox headband TAIL**

Photocopy pattern at size 165%.

Cut one from orange foamies.

**Fox headband EARS**

Photocopy pattern at size 100%.

Cut two from orange foamies.

# Running Gingerbread Man Pattern

**"Running Gingerbread Man"**

Photocopy pattern at 100% or size desired.
Cut from brown foamies or card stock.

# Resources

## Planning Preschool / Early Elementary / Family Storytime Programs

Baltuck, Naomi. *Crazy Gibberish: And Other Story Hour Stretches from a Storyteller's Bag of Tricks.* Linnet Books, 1993.

Baltuck, Naomi. *Storytime Stretchers: Tongue Twisters, Choruses, Games, and Charades.* August House Publishers, 2007.

Bauer, Caroline Feller. *Caroline Feller Bauer's New Handbook for Storytellers; With Stories, Poems, Magic, and More.* ALA Editions, 1993.

Bauer, Caroline Feller. *Leading Kids to Books Through CRAFTS.* ALA Editions, 2000.

Bauer, Caroline Feller. *Leading Kids to Books Through MAGIC.* ALA Editions, 1996.

Bauer, Caroline Feller. *Leading Kids to Books through PUPPETS.* ALA Editions, 1997.

Bauer, Caroline Feller. *The Poetry Break: An Annotated Anthology with Ideas for Introducing Children to Poetry.* H. W. Wilson, 1995.

Bauer, Caroline Feller. *Read for the Fun of It: Active Programming with Books for Children.* H.W. Wilson, 1991.

Bauer, Caroline Feller. *This Way to Books.* H. W. Wilson, 1983.

Benton, Gail and Trisha Waichulaitis. *Low-Cost, High-Interest Programming: Seasonal Events for Preschoolers* (Book & Multimedia CD). Neal Schuman, 2004.

Benton, Gail and Trisha Waichulaitis. *Ready-To-Go Storytimes: Fingerplays, Scripts, Patterns, Music, and More* (Book & Audio CD). Neal Schuman, 2003.

Briggs, Diane. *101 Fingerplays: Stories and Songs to Use with Finger Puppets.* ALA Editions, 1999.

Briggs, Diane. *Preschool Favorites: 35 Storytimes Kids Love.* ALA Editions, 2007.

Champlin, Connie. *Storytelling With Puppets, 2nd ed.* ALA Editions, 1998.

*Cobb, Jane. *I'm A Little Teapot! Presenting Preschool Storytime, 2nd ed.* Black Sheep Press, 1996.

Cobb, Jane. *What'll I Do with the Baby-oh? Nursery Rhymes and Songs and Stories for Babies.* Black Sheep Press, 2007.

Crepeau, Ingrid M. and M. Ann Richards. *A Show of Hands: Using Puppets with Young Children.* Redleaf Press, 2003.

Cullum, Carolyn N. *The Storytime Sourcebook: A Compendium of Ideas and Resources for Storytellers, 2nd ed.* Neal Schuman, 1999.

Cullum, Carolyn N. *The Storytime Sourcebook II: A Compendium of 3,500+ New Ideas and Resources for Storytellers.* Neal Schuman, 2007.

Dailey, Susan M. *Sing a Song of Storytime* (Book & Multimedia CD). Neal Schuman, 2007.

Dailey, Susan M. *A Storytime Year: A Month-To-Month Kit for Preschool Programming* (Looseleaf binder). Neal Schuman, 2000.

Diamant-Cohen, Betsy. *Mother Goose on the Loose* (Looseleaf Binder & Multimedia CD). Neal Schuman, 2006.

Engler, Larry and Carol Fijan. *Making Puppets Come Alive: A Method of Learning and Teaching Hand Puppetry.* Taplinger, 1973.

Freeman, Judy. *Books Kids Will Sit Still For: The Complete Read-Aloud Guide, 2nd ed.* Bowker, 1990.

Freeman, Judy. *More Books Kids Will Sit Still For: A Read-Aloud Guide.* R. R. Bowker, 1995.

Freeman, Judy. *Books Kids Will Sit Still For 3: A Read-Aloud Guide.* Libraries Unlimited, 2006.

*Ghoting, Saroj Nadkarni and Pamela Martin-Diaz. *Early Literacy Storytimes @ Your Library.* ALA Editions, 2006.

Greene, Ellin. *Storytelling: Art and Technique, 3rd ed.* R. R. Bowker, 1996.

Hicks, Doris Lynn. *Flannelboard Classic Tales.* ALA Editions, 1997.

Huff, Mary Jo. *Storytelling With Puppets, Props, & Playful Tales.* Monday Morning Books, 1998.

Hunt, Tamara and Nancy Renfro. *Pocketful of Puppets: Mother Goose.* Nancy Renfro Studios, 1982.

Hunt, Tamara and Nancy Renfro. *Puppetry in Early Childhood Education.* Nancy Renfro Studios, 1982.

Lincycomb, Kay. *Storytimes ... Plus!* Neal Schuman, 2007.

Lowe, Joy L. *Puppet Magic.* Neal Schuman, 2007.

Lynch-Watson, Janet. *The Shadow Puppet Book.* Sterling Publishing Co., 1980.

MacDonald, Margaret Read. *Bookplay: 101 Creative Themes to Share with Young Children.* Library Professional Pubns., 1995.

MacDonald, Margaret Read. *Booksharing: 101 Programs to Use with Preschoolers.* Library Professional Pubns., 1988.

Macdonald, Margaret Read. *Twenty Tellable Tales: Audience Participation Folktales for the Beginning Storyteller. Rev. ed.* ALA Editions, 2004.

MacDonald, Margaret Read. *Three Minute Tales: Stories From Around the World to Tell or Read When Time Is Short.* August House, 2004.

MacDonald, Margaret Read. *The Storyteller's Start-Up Book: Finding, Learning, Performing, and Using Folktales Including Twelve Tellable Tales.* August House, 1993.

Marino, Jane. *Sing Us a Story: Using Music in Preschool and Family Story Times.* H. W. Wilson, 1994.

Minkel, Walter. *How to Do "The Three Bears" With Two Hands: Performing With Puppets.* ALA Editions, 2000.

Painter, William M. *Story Hours With Puppets and Other Props.* Library Professional Pubns., 1990.

Pellowski, Anne. *The Family Storytelling Handbook: How to Use Stories, Anecdotes, Rhymes, Handkerchiefs, Paper, and Other Objects to Enrich Your Family Traditions.* Macmillan, 1987.

Pellowski, Anne. *The World of Storytelling.* (Expanded and rev. ed.). H. W. Wilson, 1990.

Reid, Rob. *Children's Jukebox; A Subject Guide to Musical Recordings and Programming Ideas for Songsters Ages One to Twelve.* ALA Editions, 1995.

Reid, Rob. *Children's Jukebox, 2nd ed.* ALA Editions, 2007.

*Reid, Rob. *Family Storytime: 24 Creative Programs for All Ages.* ALA Editions, 1999.

Reid, Rob. *Something Funny Happened at the Library: How to Create Humorous Programs for Children and Young Adults.* ALA Editions, 2002.

Reid, Rob. *Something Musical Happened at the Library: Adding Song and Dance to Children's Story Programs.* ALA Editions, 2007.

Reid, Rob. *Storytime Slam: 15 Lesson Plans for Preschool and Primary Story Programs.* UpstartBooks, 2006.

Roney, R. Craig. *The Story Performance Handbook.* Lawrence Erlbaum Associates, 2001.

Sierra, Judy. *Fantastic Theater: Puppets and Plays for Young Performers and Young Audiences.* H. W. Wilson, 1991.

Sierra, Judy. *The Flannel Board Storytelling Book, 2nd ed.* H. W. Wilson, 1997.

Sierra, Judy and Robert Kaminski. *Multicultural Folktales: Stories To Tell Young Children.* Oryx Press, 1991.

Sierra, Judy and Robert Kaminski. *Twice Upon A Time: Stories to Tell, Retell, Act Out, and Write About.* H. W. Wilson, 1989.

Silberg, Jackie, and Pam Schiller, comp. *The Complete Book of Rhymes, Songs, Poems, Fingerplays and Chants.* Gryphon House, 2002.

Stilley, Cynthia and Charles Hansen, eds. *Ring A Ring O' Roses: Fingerplays for Preschool Children, 11th ed.* Flint Public Library, 2002. (See www.flint.lib.mi.us/ringoroses/index.shtml for ordering information.)

VanSchuyver, Jan M. *Storytelling Made Easy With Puppets.* The Oryx Press, 1993.

Wilmes, Liz and Dick. *2's Experience Felt Board Fun*. Building Blocks, 1994.

Wilmes, Liz and Dick. *2's Experience Stories*. Building Blocks, 1999.

Wisniewski, David and Donna Wisniewski. *Worlds Of Shadow: Teaching With Shadow Puppetry*. Teacher Ideas Press, 1997.

## Further Professional Reading

Carlson, Ann D. *The Preschooler and the Library*. Scarecrow Press, 1992.

Cerny, Rosanne, Penny Markey, Amanda Williams, and the Association for Library Service to Children (ALSC). *Outstanding Library Service to Children: Putting the Core Competencies to Work*. ALA Editions, 2006.

De Salvo, Nancy. *Beginning with Books: Library Programming for Infants, Toddlers, and Preschoolers*. Library Professional Pubns., 1993.

Dresang, Eliza T., Melissa Gross, and Leslie Edmonds Holt; foreword by Virginia Walter. *Dynamic Youth Services Through Outcome-Based Planning and Evaluation*. ALA Editions, 2006.

Huck, Charlotte S. et al. *Children's Literature In the Elementary School, 8th ed.* McGraw-Hill, 2004.

Nespeca, Sue McCleaf. *Library Programming for Families with Young Children*. Neal-Schuman, 1994.

Sullivan, Michael. *Fundamentals of Children's Services*. ALA Editions, 2005.

Walter, Virginia A. *Children and Libraries: Getting It Right*. ALA Editions, 2001.

Walter, Virginia A. *Output Measures for Public Library Service to Children: A Manual of Standardized Procedures*. ALA Editions, 1992.

## Early Literacy Web Sites

**America Reads Challenge**
www.ed.gov/inits/americareads/index.html.

**American Library Association: Association of Library Service to Children: Born to Read: How to Raise a Reader**
www.ala.org/ala/mgrps/divs/alsc/initiatives/borntoread/index.cfm

**Children of the Code**
www.childrenofthecode.org

**Early Literacy and Brain Development Resources (Saroj Ghoting)**
www.earlylit.net/earlylit/bibliography.html

**Every Child Ready to Read @ Your Library**
www.ala.org/ala/alsc/ecrr/ecrrhomepage.htm

**Hennepin County Library (MN): Birth to Six**
www.hclib.org/BirthTo6/

**Multnomah County (OR) Public Library: Early Words**
www.multcolib.org/birthtosix/

**National Association for the Education of Young Children**
www.naeyc.org

**Reading Is Fundamental (RIF)**
www.rif.org

**West Bloomfield Township Public Library (MI): Grow Up Reading @ the West Bloomfield Township Public Library**
www.growupreading.org

**Zero to Three's Brain Wonders**
www.zerotothree.org/brainwonders

## Early Literacy Support Materials for Parents and Caregivers

**Multnomah County (OR) Public Library: Early Words**
www.multcolib.org/birthtosix/ecr/products.html

**Every Child Ready to Read @ Your Library**
www.ala.org/ala/alsc/ecrr/resourcesab/resources.cfm

## Finding Out-of-Print or Used Books

**Abe Books**
www.abebooks.com

**Alibris**
www.alibris.com

**Bibliofind**
www.bibliofind.com

**Bookfinder**
www.bookfinder.com

**Half**
www.half.com

## BIG Books

**Childcraft Education Corp.**
www.childcrafteducation.com

**Kaplan Early Learning Company**
www.kaplanco.com

**Lakeshore Learning Materials**
www.lakeshorelearning.com

**Regent Book Company**
www.regentbook.com

**Scholastic**
www.scholastic.com

## BIG Book Stand

**Musician's Friend**
www.musiciansfriend.com
(Manhasset Model 51 Fourscore Stand, 32"
wide)

## Sound Recordings

See *Children's Jukebox, 2nd ed.*, by Rob Reid
(ALA Editions, 2007) for additional children's sound recording vendors as well as a
listing of individual artist Web sites.

**Casablanca Kids**
www.casablancakids.com

**CD Baby**
www.cdbaby.com

**Educational Record Center**
www.erckids.com

**Kiddo Music & Video**
www.kiddomusic.com

**Kimbo Educational**
www.Kimboed.com

**Music for Little People**
www.musicforlittlepeople.com

**Songs for Teaching**
www.songsforteaching.com

## Puppets

**Axtell Expressions, Inc.**
www.axtell.com
(See manipulation tips for the beginning
puppeteer at www.axtell.com/manip.html.)

**Folkmanis, Inc.**
www.folkmanis.com
(See Web site for distributor information.)

**Manhattan Toy**
www.manhattantoy.com

**Puppeteers of America**
www.puppeteers.org

**Puppetry Home Page**
www.puppetry.info

**Sunny & Company Toys, Inc.**
www.sunnypuppets.com
(See Web site for distributor information.)

## Book Character Dolls and Toys

**Crocodile Creek**
www.crocodilecreek.com

**MerryMakers, Inc.**
www.merrymakersinc.com

**Yottoy Productions, Inc.**
www.yottoy.com

## Ready-Made Storytelling Props and Miscellaneous

**Book Props, LLC**
www.bookprops.com

**Childcraft Education Corp.**
www.childcrafteducation.com

**Kaplan Early Learning Company**
www.kaplanco.com

**Lakeshore Learning Materials**
www.lakeshorelearning.com

**Music in Motion**
www.musicmotion.com

## Alphabet Letters

**Childcraft Education Corp.**
www.childcrafteducation.com
(Jumbo 4.7"H Uppercase Letters, item
#358374; Jumbo 4.3"H Lowercase Letters,
item #358382)

**Constructive Playthings**
www.cptoys.com
(Giant 4.75" Magnetic Foam Uppercase
Letters, item #EDL-776; Giant 4.75" Magnetic
Foam Lowercase Letters, item #EDL-617)
(Jumbo 7.5" Foam Uppercase Letters, item
#EDL-170; Jumbo 7.25" Foam Lowercase
Letters, item #EDL-171)

**Lakeshore Learning Materials**
www.lakeshorelearning.com
(Jumbo 5" Magnetic Uppercase Letters, item #RR932; Jumbo 5" Magnetic Lowercase Letters, item #RR933)

## "Letter of the Day" Printables

**First-School Preschool Activities and Crafts**
www.first-school.ws/theme/alphabet.htm

(Note: Remember that there are many different handwriting methods, and they vary in the specific way some letters are taught. Familiarize yourself with the method used by your local school system, and feature handwriting cues from that particular method on any "letter of the day" handouts you provide.)

## Mother Goose Rhyme Time Materials

**UpstartBooks**
www.upstartbooks.com

*Mother Goose Rhyme Time: Animals* Book and Poster/Character Value Kit, Item #94454

*Mother Goose Rhyme Time: Night* Book and Poster/Character Value Kit, Item #25588

*Mother Goose Rhyme Time: People* Book and Poster/Character Value Kit, Item #87959

## "Rhyming Basket"

**Lakeshore Learning Materials**
www.lakeshorelearning.com
(Rhyming Sounds Basket, item #EE236)

## "Magic Change Bag"

Make your own magic bag. See instructions in:

Bauer, Caroline Feller. *Leading Kids to Books Through Magic*. ALA Editions, 1996;

Faurot, Kimberly. "Book! Book! Book! Storytime" in *LibrarySparks Magazine*, Jan. 2005, vol. 2, no. 5, pp. 6–13.
OR

Purchase a magic bag from your local magic shop, online, or from:

**Twin Cities Magic & Costume**
www.twincitiesmagic.com
(Ask for a "Magic Tote Bag.")

## Cheap Novelty Items

(e.g., giant plastic bugs, foil crowns, and miscellaneous other cool stuff)

**Kipp Brothers**
www.kipptoys.com

**U.S. Toy Co., Inc.**
www.ustoy.com

**Oriental Trading Company, Inc.**
www.orientaltrading.com

**Rhode Island Novelty**
www.rinovelty.com

## Rainbow Glasses

(Also sometimes available from the "Cheap Novelty Items" vendors listed above.)

**Rainbow Glasses**
www.rainbowglasses.com

**Rainbow Symphony Store**
www.rainbowsymphonystore.com

**NCAR Science Store**
www.ucar.edu/sciencestore

## Colored Corrugated Storage Boxes

**Brodart**
www.shopbrodart.com

**Highsmith**
www.highsmith.com

## Flannel Boards, Velcro® Boards, Magnet Boards and Easels

**abc school supply**
www.abcschoolsupply.com

**Brodart**
www.shopbrodart.com

**Demco**
www.demco.com

**Gaylord Bros.**
www.gaylord.com

**Highsmith Inc.**
www.highsmith.com

**Kaplan Early Learning Company**
www.kaplanco.com

**Lakeshore Learning Materials**
www.lakeshorelearning.com

**The Library Store, Inc.**
www.thelibrarystore.com

## Craft Supplies

**Ben Franklin Crafts**
www.benfranklinstores.com

The following store provides mail order service:

2020 Weinbach Center Drive
Evansville, IN 47711
812.477.4602

**Crafts Direct**
www.craftsdirect.com

**D & C C (Decorator & Craft Corporation)**
www.dcccrafts.com

**Schrock's International**
(Wholesale prices; no returns)
800.426.4659 phone (orders only)

## Die-Cut Companies

**Ellison Educational Equipment, Inc.**
www.ellison.com

**Accu-Cut Systems**
www.accucut.com